# Dieter Grimm: Advocate of the Constitution

# Dieter Grimm: Advocate of the Constitution

DIETER GRIMM

*In conversation with*

OLIVER LEPSIUS,
CHRISTIAN WALDHOFF,
*and*
MATTHIAS ROSSBACH

*Translated by*
JUSTIN COLLINGS

OXFORD
UNIVERSITY PRESS

OXFORD
UNIVERSITY PRESS

Great Clarendon Street, Oxford, OX2 6DP,
United Kingdom

Oxford University Press is a department of the University of Oxford.
It furthers the University's objective of excellence in research, scholarship,
and education by publishing worldwide. Oxford is a registered trade mark of
Oxford University Press in the UK and in certain other countries

This translation of the book published as
Dieter Grimm, in conversation with Oliver Lepsius, Christian Waldhoff, and Matthias Rossbach,
Ich bin ein Freund der Verfassung,
is published under licence from Mohr Siebeck GmbH & Co. KG, Tübingen



The translation of this work was funded by Geisteswissenschaften International—Translation Funding for Work in the Humanities and Social Sciences from Germany, a joint initiative of the Fritz Thyssen Foundation, the German Federal Foreign Office, the collecting society VG WORT and the Börsenverein des Deutschen Buchhandels (German Publishers & Booksellers Association)



First Edition published in 2020

Impression: 1



Published in the United States of America by Oxford University Press
198 Madison Avenue, New York, NY 10016, United States of America

British Library Cataloguing in Publication Data

Data available

Library of Congress Control Number: 2020937903

ISBN 978–0–19–884527–0

Printed and bound by
CPI Group (UK) Ltd, Croydon, CR0 4YY

# My Friend Dieter

I first met Dieter at a triumphant moment. The year was 1989, and a democratic revolution was sweeping Eastern Europe. It was also precisely 200 years since the storming of the Bastille had initiated the French Revolution. Perhaps the time had finally come to redeem the Revolution's democratic promise?

The government of Francois Mitterand convened a special conference to take this question seriously. Dieter's central position in the scholarly community, and his recent appointment to the Constitutional Court, made him the obvious choice as Germany's representative. For less obvious reasons, I was asked to address the potential contributions of the United States.

The public discussions were intense, but a gap in the schedule gave Dieter and me a chance to arrange a private dinner at a restaurant. We found that we had lots to talk about, but neither of us could predict the great challenges Dieter would confront as the Berlin Wall fell and a reunited Germany confronted an uncertain future in new European (dis)order.

During his term on the bench, ending in 1999, Dieter played a leading role in the Court's struggle to redefine Germany's constitutional identity. In contrast to American practice, each German justice is given special responsibilities to guide doctrinal development in a particular area throughout the course of his or her twelve-year tenure.

Dieter was assigned the fateful task of responding to the pressing problems confronting a reunited Germany in areas Americans associate with the First Amendment—including freedom of speech, as well as freedom of the media and of assembly. Given the framework of the Basic Law, these questions are inextricably linked to fundamental issues surrounding the right to privacy and each individual's inalienable right to personal self-determination.

As a consequence, Dieter was repeatedly required to deal with concrete constitutional dilemmas that had explosive political consequences—some of which challenged the very legitimacy of judicial review in the eyes of the general public. Despite the recurrent uproar generated by particular decisions, Grimm gained broad-ranging respect for the thoughtful and balanced way he led his colleagues to consider the hot-button issues at stake, as well as his courage in defining the limits imposed by foundational principles.

As a young man, Dieter survived the terrors of Nazi Germany and the terrible destruction of the early post-war period. How did he manage to emerge as such a remarkable leader of Western constitutional theory and practice during the present era?

This is the question that makes this book such a worthwhile experience. Yet, so far as I am concerned, it also leads me to reflect more deeply on the way in which my friendship with Dieter has thrived since our brief encounter in the Paris of 1989.

The crucial turning point came during 1991–1992 when I was invited to Berlin as a Fellow at the Institute for Advanced Study. Dieter was spending most of his time in Karlsruhe with his colleagues on the Court. Nevertheless, when he did come to Berlin, we managed to arrange quite a large number of private dinners that allowed free-wheeling discussions of the dramatic constitutional transformations in Eastern Europe and the Soviet Union (as it was then still called).

In retrospect, my wife, Susan Rose-Ackerman, was principally responsible for our ongoing conversations. She had also taken a leave from her Yale professorship to serve as a Fulbright and Guggenheim scholar at the Free University. Her high intelligence, and personal insight, made our dinner-triangles especially rewarding.

My year long stay in Berlin set the stage for Dieter's decades of engagement at Yale Law School—both as a visiting professor and a participant at the Seminar on Global Constitutionalism, where leading jurists throughout the world traveled to New Haven to consider pressing problems.

Our friendship deepened further when my wife and I returned to Berlin in 2014–2015. This time it was Susan who served as a Fellow at the Institute for Advanced Study while I held a similar position at the American Academy.

Over the course of forty years of comparative study, I have had the good fortune of developing many rewarding personal relationships in Europe.

But Dieter, my friend, you are special.

The stories Dieter tells in this volume have led me to reflect on the larger paradoxes surrounding our friendship.

Begin from the beginning. Immediately after the war, Dieter vividly describes how he made his way through bombed out cities as his mother desperately tried to find enough food for them to survive. Within this setting, it is entirely understandable that he was entirely unaware of any of the events surrounding the constitutional construction of the Federal Republic.

My own experience was completely different. While Dieter was twelve years old when the Federal Republic was established in 1949, I was only six. Yet as a young child attending public school in New York City, my teachers were already explaining why the American Constitution should serve as a model for the Free World after the defeat of Nazism. As my classmates and I entered school each day, we proudly burst into song: "This is *my* country, grandest on earth."

*My* country? As a child, I did not consider the fateful accidents that led to my birth in the United States rather than Europe. My mother was a Polish Jew who arrived in America shortly after the First World War at the age of twelve when her family successfully escaped anti-Semitic death squads ravaging her homeland. My father's family was also Jewish and had lived in Austria for centuries. They fled to America in response to a wave of anti-Semitic violence in the 1880s. If they had not done so, my father, born in the United States, would have been exterminated in a Nazi death camp along with my mother.

Yet here I was, proudly affirming my identity as a young American devoted to its Constitution, while young Grimm was oblivious to the Founding of the Federal Republic as he made his way through the rubble.

Despite the profound differences in our situation, Dieter and I had one thing in common. We were not intimidated by the demands of our schoolteachers—even though our parents couldn't provide us with role models, because they hadn't obtained university educations themselves. Nevertheless, we were determined to rise to the occasion and demonstrate that we were equal to our scholarly challenges.

We were also alike in finding that our math skills were relatively modest and that it was wiser to focus on social and political studies. Once we figured this out, without much help from others, our test-taking abilities propelled us to the top of the academic hierarchy in our two countries.

In Dieter's case, his educational career reached its high point during his year at Harvard in 1964–1965. As he explains, he almost chose Yale over Harvard as the place to gain an insight into American legal culture. If he had done so, he would have met a very talkative student named Bruce Ackerman confronting a remarkable group of Yale professors including Guido Calabresi, Ronald Dworkin, and Harry Wellington. Wellington was a leading member of the Legal Process School that made such a powerful impact on Dieter during his time in Cambridge—and he influenced me as well.

Calabresi and Dworkin were even more important. They were in their thirties at that time, and their brilliant classroom discussions redefined the relationship between law, economics and philosophy in ways that have profoundly shaped my own work ever since. If Dieter had been around, he might well have helped me appreciate the importance of the Continental tradition at this early stage of my career. Yet given his choice of Harvard, I graduated in 1967 without an adequate appreciation of its significance.

Nevertheless, with his great assistance, I have tried to make up for this deficiency over time. As I mentioned, my stay at Berlin's Institute for Advanced Study in 1991–1992 was especially important. During that year, the Institute had invited a host of leading jurists from Eastern Europe and the Soviet Union to define alternative futures for the Continent. Without participating in these extraordinary conversations, I would never have tried to make a serious contribution to the public debate in *The Future of Liberal Revolution* (1994).

For the next quarter century, Dieter and I have disagreed on the nature of the legitimacy-deficits confronting the European Union, and the best way of resolving them over time—as have, of course, many other thoughtful contributors to this essential debate. The rise of Donald Trump to the presidency, however, has challenged this debate's basic premise—which is that the United States and the European Union are both committed to the fundamental ideals of constitutional democracy, and that the only hard issues involve the best way to realize these principles in practice.

Trump has instead publicly supported would-be dictators throughout the world, and he has demonstrated his hostility to the trans-Atlantic vision of democracy that, despite its disappointments, has provided the framework for Euro-American relations since the Second World War. If Trump wins a second term as president, he will claim that his victory is a mandate from the people for his racist and anti-democratic principles. He will then deploy the country's military and economic power to pursue his short-term nationalistic objectives.

This prospect opens a final chapter in my relationship with Dieter. I began my account by contrasting my youthful pride in America's constitutional tradition with Dieter's struggle amidst the ruins of Nazi Germany. But a second victory by Trump would inaugurate a terrible reversal of fortune. America will be governed by an autocrat whose erratic policies could readily provoke nuclear war abroad and racist and religious persecutions at home.

In the meantime, my friend Grimm is living in a country that remains, for now at least, profoundly committed to the constitutional tradition that his friend Bruce was once proud to represent.

I am writing these lines in March of 2020. I do not know whether Americans will go to the polls on Election Day to repudiate Trump or to renew his mandate.

This much is clear: the scene has been set for tragedy, in the classical Greek sense.

Bruce Ackerman

# Preface

In May 2017, Dieter Grimm, one of the most influential constitutional scholars and theorists in Germany, celebrated his eightieth birthday. We took that occasion as an opportunity to talk to Grimm about his life and his numerous involvements in the development of the law—as a teacher and academic on both sides of the Atlantic, as a justice, as a public intellectual. Among the things that stand out is his tenure in the German Federal Constitutional Court from 1987 to 1999 as one of the most influential and most distinguished justices in Germany. Since Grimm is among the most eminent witnesses of the history of the Federal Republic of Germany, we also talked to him about his perspective on the key moments and developments of the second half of the twentieth century—such as the end of the Second World War, the Protests of 1968, Reunification, and European integration. Our conversation originally appeared as a book published by Mohr Siebeck in Tübingen.

The book gained quite a deal of attention and was favorably reviewed. Oxford University Press suggested this English translation. For translating the book, we are very grateful to Justin Collings, Professor of Law at Brigham Young University. Collings has known Grimm for years: Grimm was his teacher at the Yale Law School and a member of his dissertation committee in the Yale History Department. Today, Collings ranks among the leading experts on the German Federal Constitutional Court. His books on the subject are also published with Oxford University Press. Nobody could have done a better job, being so well acquainted with the intricacies of legal German.

May the English edition attract, instruct, and entertain many readers!
Münster and Berlin, June 2020
Oliver Lepsius Christian Waldhoff Matthias Rossbach

# Table of Contents

# Biographical Note

**Oliver Lepsius** is a Professor of Public Law and Constitutional Theory at the University of Münster. He is co-author of *The German Federal Constitutional Court: The Court without Limits*, also published by Oxford University Press.

**Matthias Rossbach** is Head of Coordination of Federal and European Policy and International Affairs at the State Chancellery of North Rhine-Westphalia, Berlin Office. He received his LLM from Yale Law School and his PhD from the Humboldt University Berlin Faculty of Law, where he regularly attended Dieter Grimm's seminars.

**Christian Waldhoff** is a Professor of Public Law at Humboldt University Berlin. He was Dean of the Faculty of Law at Humboldt University from 2014 to 2017 and was a Member of the Board of the Association of Constitutional Law Professors in 2018 and 2019.

# I.

# Biographical Imprints—Childhood Home, War, School, Career Hopes

OLIVER LEPSIUS: Tell us about your family background. What did your parents do? Did they have an academic background?

DIETER GRIMM: In my family no one before me had ever seen a university from the inside. My father was a civil servant in the railroad administration, like his father before him—my paternal grandfather. I knew my father only in plainclothes, but there were some lovely photos that showed him in his railroad uniform. I would have liked it better if he had still worked in the field service with an apartment at the train station, as he had at the time of my parents' wedding in 1934. As a child I was fascinated by the railroad and couldn't get enough of trains and rail facilities.

My parents would never have met at all if my father hadn't moved, for the sake of better odds of advancement, from his native Württemberg "to Prussia." He thus came into the service of the State Railway regional headquarters in Kassel, which at the time stretched deep into Westphalia—to Bestwig, to be precise. I mention this on purpose, because my mother came from Bestwig in the Sauerland. They didn't meet there, however, but in Paderborn. My father was a lodger in a house where my mother cared for the children of the widowed homeowner. My mother shared the fate of many women of her generation who attended primary school and learned how to cook, then waited around for a husband. But my mother had also learned French in private lessons and was happy to have a position in Paderborn.

Her father, my maternal grandfather, came from Münsterland. He learned watchmaking and, after a time of wandering, settled in Bestwig and opened a store: "Ferdinand Fröndhoff: Watches, Gold- and Silverware." My grandmother came from a farming family in nearby Nuttlar. My paternal grandfather, an official of the Royal Württemberg State Railroad, had married an innkeeper's daughter from Baden. Both sets of grandparents had numerous children. When I was born in May 1937, my father had recently

*Dieter Grimm: Advocate of the Constitution.* Dieter Grimm, Oxford University Press (2020). © in the original German edition, Mohr Siebeck GmbH & Co. KG, Tübingen 2017, © this translation, Justin Collings 2020.
DOI: 10.1093/oso/9780198845270.001.0001

been transferred from Bad Hersfeld to Kassel. I grew up in Kassel. It is my hometown.

When my parents were married they received at the registry office, as did thousands of others, a gift copy of Hitler's *Mein Kampf*. Their families, however, as near as I can judge, were not sympathetic to National Socialism. About my father's side of the family, I have no evidence at all. A younger brother of my mother was in the Sturmabteilung (SA) and was much criticized for it. Another brother, the eldest, who had lost a leg in the First World War, listened to "enemy broadcasts" by night and was told more than once by a family member, "Ferdinand, you're going to get us all jailed!" He was a critical spirit and after the War became a reader of *Der Spiegel*. Uncle Ferdinand always knew more. I liked chatting with him.

My father joined the Nationalsozialistische Deutsche Arbeiterpartei (NSDAP) late. When I reproached him for this years later, he said that he had done it for me and my mother. He risked being sacked otherwise. It must have been around 1942 that he was conscripted and sent to Russia.

OL: You lived through the War quite conscious of it, then?

DG: Yes. I even claim to remember the outbreak of the War precisely, though I'm told that, at the age of two years and four months, that's improbable. Our home in Kassel was near some military barracks, and I have vivid memories of going to the barracks' main gate and, with many other curious onlookers, watching the soldiers depart. Some threw flowers. One could also get pea soup from the field kitchen. I developed at the time a considerable enthusiasm for soldiers. Troops often marched through our street to a nearby drilling ground. As soon as the marching music or the soldier songs rang out, I couldn't be refrained. My surviving drawings from this period are all of soldiers. And when I was asked, as children always are, what I wanted to be when I grew up, I'm told that I answered, "A general—but only in peacetime."

The luster of the military soon faded, however, as the march music was replaced by the howling of sirens, the roaring of airplane squadrons, and the boom of detonating bombs. Bunkers and bomb shelters were soon part of daily life. One time, in a bomb shelter, I asked, "How do you know when you are dead?" Someone answered, "As long as you hear the bombs whistling, you're still alive." All of this came vividly back to me a few years ago when I had the opportunity to visit the air-raid bunker beneath Kassel's Weinberg. The bunker had been carefully carved from the rocks long before the War began. I then saw the Central Command, where status reports arrived and where the city commander gave orders. And I saw a room in which—as the guide related—Dr. Sommerfeld worked himself into exhaustion after air raids. After the War, Dr. Sommerfeld was my pediatrician. He ran his practice near the Weinberg.

OL: Were you also bombed out?

DG: Our house in Kassel was damaged but not destroyed. Other houses in our street were totally demolished. As the bomb raids on Kassel intensified—my father was already in Russia by this time—my mother took me back to her parents' home in Bestwig, where I started school in 1943. The schoolhouse, which consisted of three classrooms and a teacher's apartment, was right next to our home. I could just get there on time if I started running when the bell rang.

In many ways, Bestwig was a contrast to Kassel—beginning with the train tracks, which I now saw daily. They were right in front of our house. At the time, Bestwig was a station on the express train line Leipzig-Kassel-Cologne. The steam engines had to refuel there. I was especially struck by a streamline-cased locomotive that stopped twice a day in Bestwig and that I called the "Bumbas Machine." Even more formative, however, was that I had gone from being a city kid to being a country kid—and from being an only child to being part of an extended family. Nearly all my mother's siblings lived in the neighborhood. I was no longer "Dieter Grimm," but "Fröndhoff's Dieter." I found myself surrounded by numerous cousins. And above all, I found myself in a thoroughly Catholic environment. In Kassel, religious life was limited to attending Sunday Mass and saying daily prayers. In Bestwig religion permeated everything. "Do all that you do," my grandmother constantly admonished, "for the greater glory of God." I didn't draw soldiers anymore. Only priests.

Becoming a priest was now my vocational aim as well. My grandmother—who did everything she could to further this ambition—arranged for me in the attic of our house a small storage room furnished as a chapel, complete with altar and tabernacle. The women sewed chasubles. A biretta was ordered from the nuns in nearby Velmede. The local vicar still possessed from his own youth some small tin mass instruments, which he gave to me. I cajoled my cousin, Willy, who was already a senior altar boy, into siphoning off for me a couple of censors. Thus, I imitated what I saw and heard at church, while my aunts chuckled behind a crack in the door.

Toward the end of the War Bestwig, as a railroad hub, was also bombed, and we moved again—this time to Madfeld, an abandoned borough without transport connections reachable only after a long march on foot from the Bredelar train station. Once we had to hide in a ditch from low-flying aircraft fire. One of my mother's older sisters had married the local teacher in Madfeld, but he too was away at War. We lived in the schoolhouse, where we were educated by nuns who had fled from Silesia. Whenever we heard the sound of airplanes, we were to drop to the floor and cry: "Thrice-holy Mother of God of Schönstatt, save us!" In Madfeld, I experienced the end of the War just days before my eighth birthday. For one day our schoolyard became the center of events, as Field Marshal Model established his headquarters there. Soon we were to see the Jeeps of American soldiers on those same school grounds.

One Sunday, shortly thereafter, my father arrived in Madfeld with two of his colleagues—unshaven, bone weary, and donning an oversized suit. He had been sent from Russia to the Westwall in 1944, avoided imprisonment, and scraped his way back to us. By day the three had hid themselves; by night they walked. Soon my father returned to Kassel to report at his prior place of work. We first went back to Bestwig, where we remained until the end of the school year in 1946. Then the family was reunited in Kassel. On New Year's Eve, my sister Gisela was born.

OL: Did the occupation period—from 1945 to 1949—affect you?

DG: Bestwig was in the English Occupation Zone, Kassel in the American. I learned the hard way what that meant. In the summer of 1945, I went to First Communion. It was an exceptional First Communion. On Divine Mercy Sunday, we were still in Madfeld. But the Priest wanted me at all costs to take First Communion in Westphalia. So there was an extra First Communion for me and three girls. We rode in a carriage to Velmede. (At the time, Bestwig had no church of its own.) But my father wasn't there. As we later learned, he and other men had been pulled from their train at the zonal border and forced to shovel coal or potatoes—he in his black holiday suit. Otherwise, we little noticed the occupation—not in the country, at least, and not in Kassel either. I was aware of the Americans' presence largely through the Quaker foods we were given at school. We were still hungry. I remember asking my father once how long we would be occupied. He answered, "Fifty years?" That was beyond my powers of imagination.

What affected me more directly was that I grew up in ruins. Kassel was one of the most devastated cities in Germany. How lovely it must once have been I can tell only from pictures. For a long time heaps of rubble lay along the streets—including our street. The ruins were not sealed off, and you could have a glorious time playing in them. We never thought of the danger. Home life suffered from the fact that we, like countless others, had to share our home with refugees or bombed-out persons. For the children this meant consideration, consideration, consideration. I can no longer say how long it was before we had our home to ourselves again.

CHRISTIAN WALDHOFF: You then went to *Gymnasium*,[1] which at the time was not an obvious thing to do, given that your parents were not university-educated and that it probably entailed tuition fees.

DG: Both of my parents had a pronounced desire for upward mobility. They were determined that their son should accomplish more than they had. My father finished his career as a middle-ranked official for the National Railway. Further promotion required a university degree. My mother lamented all her life that the circumstances of the time foreclosed opportunities that she would gladly have embraced. Accordingly, it was agreed on all sides that I would attend *Gymnasium* and then university. My parents would have been deeply hurt if I had told them I wanted to pursue vocational training. But my parents' attitude was not unique. Many in their generation thought similarly. Of the seventeen students in my graduating class, only two had university-educated fathers, and one had a mother who was an elementary school teacher.

It was very clear to me which *Gymnasium* I wanted to attend: the Wilhelm *Gymnasium*. In the apartment above us in Kassel lived a divorced woman, Mrs. Keil, together with her son, Max. Max was a student at the Wilhelm *Gymnasium*, and I liked him a lot. I listened raptly as Max talked about the school. During the War, Max was plucked away from the *Gymnasium* in uniform and sent to Russia. He never returned. But I knew which *Gymnasium* I wanted to attend. My parents had no objection, and they signed me up. I went with joyful anticipation to the days-long entrance exam. After I passed it, some of my elementary school classmates told me: "From now on things will be different for you. In the *Gymnasium* you won't be the best anymore." I hadn't known that I had been the best in elementary school.

The school building still lay in ruins. We were taught in what was formerly the principal's house and in one of the two nearby guard buildings—formerly the home of the Brothers Grimm. The big kids were taught in the morning, the small ones in the afternoon. In 1950, we moved to a former barracks that, unlike the schoolhouse, had been left standing.

[1] The German school system is divided up into different types of schools which lead to different qualifications. The *Gymnasium* has traditionally been the only type of school which directly qualifies for attending university afterwards.

OL: Do you remember any specific intellectual influences from your childhood home? Some homes have certain "household gods" such as Beethoven, Bach, and Bismarck, or fictional heroes that are held up to children as models.

DG: I can't recall any "household gods." There was occasional talk of monarchs—the king of Württemberg, whom my father had seen in the streets of Stuttgart, or Kaiser Wilhelm, whose train had once stopped in Bestwig. But such talk was not fueled by any nostalgic longing for the monarchy. At most there was some regret that there were no longer such figures with whom one could identify. Music was absent. My father was entirely non-musical. My mother liked to sing, but there was no piano and no record player in the house—only a radio. In the living room there was a handsome and handsomely equipped bookshelf, of which I was initially proud. Later I realized that it didn't contain much of importance, though it did have a three-volume edition of Kant, the Divine Comedy, and the works of Scheffel and Storm. But there was no Goethe and no Schiller—to say nothing of Shakespeare. Were there any pictures? One day my father brought home a landscape painting that he hung above the sofa. He himself liked to draw and always observed with pleasure when I had to do fretsaw work or linocuts for my art class. The pious pictures that I was familiar with from my grandparents' home were absent in Kassel. But I do remember fondly that from an early date my mother often read to me, so that it was completely natural later on that I became I reader myself. But the stimulus for what I actually read came more from school than from home.

CW: As you already mentioned, your childhood home was Catholic.

DG: My childhood home was Catholic. Attending Mass on Sunday was a given. We prayed before and after meals—something my mother insisted upon even when we had guests of other faiths. But my father had a Lutheran mother, whose maiden name was Gillardon. She came from Bretten in Baden, the birthplace of Melanchthon. It was long believed that the Gillardons were Huguenots, until my uncle's research uncovered that they had been expelled from Sondrio in Veltlin in the seventeenth century. The fact that my father's mother, who died young, had been a Protestant may have contributed to his being broader-minded in religious matters than my mother, who had been raised in a narrow, Sauerland Catholicism that was forever threatening with the fires of hell.

CW: Kassel is a decidedly Protestant city in a decidedly Protestant region (Kurhessen). Does that mean yours was a decidedly diaspora situation?

DG: The War refugees from the East softened that a bit. But Catholicism remained a foreign force in Kassel. That was also evident at school. In the Catholic religion class there was just a small group of students from different grades.

CW: Such a situation actually sharpens one's self-awareness.

OL: Which is not without interest for lawyers—experiencing, and being able to abstract from, a minority position. Or is that not how you experienced it?

DG: I was very aware of it, not least from the contrast with Bestwig. But it was not a painful experience. I faced neither animosity nor teasing nor intolerance. Indeed, even though I was firmly convinced that mine was the true religion, I rather envied the Protestants because they had it easier than I did. They didn't have to go to church every Sunday. They didn't have to fast. And they never had to go to confession.

CW: Were you shaped by the Catholic associations, or were you part of church youth groups, or an altar boy?

DG: In Bestwig I was an altar boy and a very devoted one. But I didn't do anything to pursue that in Kassel. I went to Catholic scout activities a few times, but then my sports association, KSV Hessen, became more important to me. Unfortunately, I only played handball. Soccer was the most important pastime, but I wasn't good enough to make the soccer team. From the Catholic associations[2] I kept completely aloof. My parents didn't have any such ties either. The only institutional tie came later on—with the *Cusanuswerk*[3] during my university years. In Frankfurt, I often attended events of the Catholic Students Association, which was led by an impressive cleric, Ottmar Dessauer.[4] He recommended me for a scholarship, and my joy upon receiving it was especially great because it took some financial pressure off my parents. They had to sacrifice for their drive for upward mobility.

CW: Let's go back to your time at the *Gymnasium*. You were student body president and editor-in-chief of the student newspaper. You must have been somewhat exposed.

[2] There are several associations which are legally independent of the Catholic Church but which share and promote the Catholic faith in different segments of society, such as the Catholic Rural Youth Movement of Germany (KLJB).

[3] The *Cusanuswerk* awards scholarships to particularly gifted Catholic students of all disciplines. It was founded by the German Bishops' Conference in 1956.

[4] Ottmar Dessauer (1914–97), a priest for students in the 1960s; son of Friedrich Dessauer, a physicist and member of the Reichstag.

DG: That must have been so, but I wasn't aware of it. I hadn't pushed for those positions either. Up through eighth grade[5] we had a very popular class president who was a great guy and the best athlete in the class. But he left school to learn beer brewing, and I became his successor. I kept the job until graduation, excepting the year when I was student body president. That, too, came about as if of its own accord. Something similar happened with the student paper. The school had already had an alumni magazine, which was now to be converted into a student-run newspaper. There was a planning meeting, and by the end of the meeting, I was the editor-in-chief. At the time there was already an association of student newspapers, the *Junge Presse*.[6] When we joined with our paper, I was thinking only of the press badges we could receive. But almost immediately, I became a member of the state board, and soon after that a member of the national board. In this role I not infrequently came in contact with politics and politicians. This was still the era of "re-education," and politicians ascribed some importance to student newspapers in that effort. The money for the one-man office and the meetings of student newspaper editors came mostly from the state treasury. Dealing with politicians and ministries was something that I became familiar with even in my school days.

I must also have enjoyed a certain authority even beyond my peer group. At the end of eleventh grade, two of our classmates were held back—one of them rightly, in my view, the other one not. In the latter case, I succeeded in persuading the faculty to reverse the decision. Shortly thereafter, the other classmate's father, a respected lawyer in Kassel, invited me to dinner. It quickly became clear that his sole purpose was to get me to intervene in behalf of his son as well. I declined, however, because in his case I had no convincing reasons. He advanced to the next grade anyway, but in a different school. I mention these details because in hindsight they seem symptomatic. In completely different settings and in completely different phases of life, I quickly found myself in formal or informal leadership roles without having sought them. And each time, if I became aware of it, I was astonished.

CW: Would you say that your essential educational experiences came at school?

DG: I ascribe to school the utmost importance. Without ever being held back, I attended school not for thirteen years, but for fourteen. In Westphalia,

[5] Primary and secondary school education together have traditionally taken thirteen years. The grades at a *Gymnasium* were given the names of Latin numbers, counting down toward graduation. This was abolished in the 1960s and 1970s.

[6] "Young Press."

the school year began at Easter; in Hesse, it began in the fall. As a result, my elementary school days were lengthened by half a year. Then Hesse switched from fall to Easter, and the current school year was lengthened rather than shortened. I was more annoyed by the first extension because to me it felt like a demotion back to third grade, which I had already finished in Bestwig. My parents were even more annoyed. But I soon saw the delay as a blessing. I'm not sure that I would speak as fondly of my school days if things had played out differently.

Let me explain. In those days, Hesse launched a school experiment. Politics (later "social studies") was to become a main field of study, with French as a second language and Latin as a third. Our school was one of six Hessian schools that took part in the experiment. The best students were then taken from each of the sixth-grade classes to form a special "S"-class ("S" for social studies) going forward. I can hardly imagine a better class than this one. We were not only well read, but the different curriculum meant that no one who had been held back from older classes could join ours. We were thus relatively homogeneous, got along well, and were generally eager to learn, though without being overachievers.

We were socially homogeneous as well. I mentioned earlier that of the seventeen of us who graduated with the *Abitur* only a few had university-educated parents. Most were middle class, two were working class, one was the child of refugees, one had lost a father in the War, one was the child of divorced parents and lived with his father, and one, who hadn't been baptized, was labeled merely "religious" in the class register. The differences in parental income were insignificant. When we graduated in 1957, only two of the families had cars. We spent most of our free time with our classmates. That was the early Federal Republic. As one proof that I regarded this class as a blessing, I might mention that we have gotten together every year since graduation—obviously in varying numbers, and I myself haven't always been there, but I've gone whenever I could. When the school celebrated its 125th anniversary in 2012, I was asked to give the ceremonial address. I have rarely been as pleased by a speaking invitation as I was by this one.[7]

But now back to the lessons, which is what your question was really about. On the whole, I was well taught, and I had a few impressive teachers. One of them, a Catholic priest who instructed us in Latin and religion,[8] had

[7] Dieter Grimm, "Festrede aus Anlass des 125-jährigen Jubiläums des Wilhelmsgymnasiums Kassel," 2011.

[8] Religious instruction in German public schools is guaranteed by Article 7 of the Basic Law. The state has a right of supervision, but the content of religious instruction shall be in accordance with the

returned from Russian imprisonment in 1950. He could have been released earlier, but he stayed voluntarily until every man in his prison camp was able to return to Germany. As in every school class, ours had its share of rebellion and pranks, but no one was as little exposed to them as Franz Vogt.

I can't say whether I brought my political interest *to* my lessons or whether I picked it up *from* my lessons. In any event, the lessons on politics were of great importance for me. At the time, there was still no curriculum for the subject. Our home room teacher, Dr. Berthold Wiegand, proposed one and thereby gained great influence over teaching plans in Hesse. His curriculum focused on democracy and dictatorship, state institutions, elections, and parties. But it focused even more on socialism and capitalism, social classes, working life, urban and rural. For our penultimate field trip we went—unconventionally, but tellingly—to the Ruhr region.[9]

The same teacher also taught German and history. History was not only political history. I remember best the great synopses that he developed on long blackboards: political history, cultural history, economic and technological history. History lessons also didn't end, as with many other teachers, with the German Empire or the Weimar Republic. We covered National Socialism as well.

To my German lessons I owe my basic familiarity with the classical literary canon. But we also read Thomas Mann and post-War literature. The German, music, and drawing teachers hosted evening events (to which parents were also invited) that focused on the poetry, music, and visual arts of a given period. We also went frequently to the theatre—not formally as a class, but nonetheless motivated by our lessons. I owe my first and most enduring dramatic experiences to what was later derisively dubbed "city theater." I can still name several actors from the period, some of whom later appeared on larger stages. I recently read of the death of Hans Korte, who for a long time played the villains in Kassel. One particularly ambitious classmate took private lessons from him when we performed Goethe and Schiller, first in our school and later in other schools in Kassel. We also studied literature, of course, in the foreign language classes. I had no talent, by contrast, for mathematics and the natural sciences, but some of my schoolmates were inspired to study math and physics by a teacher who was

teachings of the religious community concerned. Parents have the right to decide whether children receive religious instruction. From the age of fourteen, students can make this decision themselves.

[9] The Ruhr region has been the industrial heart of Germany. It was the home of black coal and steel industry and is identified with the German *Wirtschaftswunder* after the Second World War.

pedagogically incompetent but brilliant in his field and who during the War had been part of the Peenemünde team of Wernher von Braun.

CW: What did you read back then?

DG: In the early years I read adventure tales and seafaring tales, and I read Karl May again and again.[10] Just as priests had previously displaced soldiers in my artwork, so priests now yielded to Indians. Then, with great pleasure, I read Erich Kästner.[11] That might have been the basis of my early affinity for Berlin. I also read a lot of historical fiction. A favorite novel from my parents' aforementioned bookshelf comes to mind: Kurt Müno's, *Two Guys in the Hay*, a heartrending story set during the Battle of Kunersdorf in the Seven Years War; after that Annemarie Selinko's *Desirée*, mistress of Napoleon, wife of Marshall Bernadotte, later queen of Sweden, plus the entire Napoleonic staff; also a doorstopper like Henryk Sienkiewicz's *Quo Vadis?* In my later school years my reading was heavily influenced by school and by my visits to the theater. In many instances, lesser prose aroused my interest in greater works, as with Döblin and Dostoevsky. The theater led me to contemporary American dramatists, especially Tennessee Williams. It caused me to reflect, however, when, toward the end of my school days, as politics absorbed more and more of my interest, one of my teachers told me, "You could be even better. You should read more."

OL: The Federal Republic was founded in 1949 when you were twelve—an age when one begins to be aware of such things.

DG: As important as the Basic Law[12] would later become for me, I remember little of the origins and founding of the Federal Republic. I can recall only one local aspect. Kassel was in the running, along with four or five other cities, to become the new federal capital. So I knew that there was to be a new state. As an event, though, the founding left no impression on me. By contrast, I remember well the day of the currency reform. My father took me by the hand and said, "Come with me. There's new money now, and a lot of things are now going to change." We then went to the issuing office where he received our allotment of Deutschmarks. I remember saying, "Now all Germans are equally rich." "Yes," he answered, "for one day."

[10] Karl May (1842–1912) was a German writer who is well known for his adventure novels which are set in America's "Wild West." His books were hugely popular especially among German children in the early years of the Federal Republic.

[11] Erich Kästner (1899–1974) was a German writer who was one of the most prominent intellectual opponents of National Socialism. His most famous book for children "Emil und die Detektive" (Emil and the Detectives) is set in Berlin-Schöneberg.

[12] The German constitution was given the name "Basic Law" because it was originally planned to be only a provisional constitution which should be replaced by a new constitution after reunification. In 1990, however, the Basic Law became the constitution for the unified Germany.

My interest in politics came later—when exactly, I can't say. But by the second Bundestag elections in 1953 it was already pronounced. I listened eagerly to parliamentary debates on the radio and went to the parties' election rallies. At one such rally, I was temporarily detained by the authorities. It must have been in connection with a state election. Adenauer[13] was to speak in a Henschel[14] factory hall. The local candidate preceded him at the podium. During the local candidate's speech, Adenauer sat in the front row leafing through some papers. I was running the student paper and thought this a wonderful chance for an interview. I was well positioned and accosted him with pad and pen. A few meters shy of my goal, however, I was seized and pulled away. It was his bodyguards, of whose existence I had thitherto had no clue. After some back and forth—perhaps we should call it an interrogation—they believed me that it was all about the student paper and let me go.

CW: Were you shaped politically earlier on at home?

DG: My parents were rock-ribbed conservatives. But how one voted was never discussed. Perhaps my parents never even discussed it with each other. I have no doubt, however, that they voted CDU. My mother related that during the Weimar Republic her father used to close his letters with, "And vote Center!"[15]

During my school years and early on at university, I too was entirely in the CDU camp—without any thought, however, of joining the Young Union. At the time of the second Bundestag election my class, along with one other class, was on a field trip to Borkum, an island in the North Sea. Each class in the school got to enjoy one four-week stay there. Lessons continued, but they were oriented toward the locale—we studied sea literature in German, sea animals in biology, and so forth. In the Borkum Newspaper—a little hectographed leaflet that we put together—I wrote a glowing, pro-Adenauer post-election commentary that brought upon me the reproach that such partisanship was out of place in a student newspaper.

[13] Konrad Adenauer (1876–1967) was a politician—mayor of Cologne from 1917 to 1933, president of the Parliamentary Council, and chancellor of the Federal Republic of Germany from 1949 to 1963, party leader of the CDU.

[14] Henschel, a locomotive and truck manufacturer, was Kassel's largest and most important business.

[15] The CDU is the major center-right party of the Federal Republic of Germany. It has Christian-social, liberal, and conservative elements. Most German chancellors of the Federal Republic were members of the CDU. The CDU was founded in 1945 as an interdenominational Christian party, thereby effectively replacing the party "Zentrum" (center) of the Weimar Republic which was a Catholic party. It is the model for the *Volksparteien*, a party-type for the whole population in contrast to class- or interest-parties.

I was first put off when Adenauer decided (in 1959, when I was already at university) to become federal president, only to realize that this post wouldn't offer him the influence he hoped for. As I recall, Adenauer justified his retreat on the ground that Dulles's[16] sudden death made it necessary for him to remain chancellor. The process of my estrangement was slow. Conversations in the *Cusanus* circle, the Frankfurt group, and the Ferien Academy—together with my reading of *Die Zeit*, which I took alongside the *Frankfurter Allgemeine Zeitung*—might have played a role. When I returned from the United States in 1965, I had distanced myself from the CDU. That doesn't mean, however, that I changed parties. I did not join the SPD. Indeed, in Hessian state elections I continued to vote CDU because I thought it was bad for a state to be always ruled by the same party. Nineteen sixty-eight also played a role.[17] I was too old for the barricades and too deeply inoculated against communism for "Ho Ho Ho Chi Minh." But the Brandt government[18] had my complete sympathy.

CW: When people look back on the 1950s today, there is this narrative of a stuffy, dusty, narrow decade. But you can also find people who didn't experience it that way and who view such descriptions as retrospective assessments.

DG: I wouldn't appraise the fifties with quite those adjectives. To me it seems much more meaningful to say that in many respects the early Federal Republic still closely resembled pre-War society. It was not cosmopolitan, not multi-cultural, not generous in the sense of allowing everyone to make their own life choices. The traditional values of punctuality, courtesy, duty, and the need to preserve an appearance of respectability were upheld. The different milieus were still largely intact. The family, the churches, the trade unions, and the numerous voluntary associations provided living spaces, not just functional units. The entertainment options were limited and harmless. Drugs were totally unavailable. Television was new with respect to pre-War society, but it provided a powerful force for integration in those early days of public monopoly in broadcasting. It kept individuals in conversation regardless of vocation, prestige, or income. Everyone had watched the same thing the night before.

Sexuality was publicly taboo. Children had to be shielded from it as long as possible. My parents in those years subscribed to an illustrated

[16] John Foster Dulles (1888–1959), politician, US Secretary of State (1953–1959), took an uncompromising stance toward the Soviet Union.

[17] This refers to the student revolts in 1968; cf. below Chapter IV.

[18] Willy Brandt (1913–1992) was the first German chancellor from the Social Democratic Party (SPD) 1969 until 1974; party leader of the SPD (1964–1987); recipient of the Nobel Peace Prize 1971.

magazine—I think it was *Die Bunte*. When it happened that there was a picture of a scantily clad woman, my parents tore the page out before I could get my hands on it. At such times I realized that I desperately needed a haircut. At the barber the magazines were uncensored.

Sex education was embarrassing for parents and children. When I reached an age in which some things began to change, my father, after delivering a short preliminary address, placed in my hands a pamphlet that didn't really say anything. Under such circumstances one learned about sex from the boys in the street.

Relations between the sexes were awkward. All the middle schools and high schools in Kassel were divided by sex. The dance lessons helped a little. When I advocated coeducation in the student newspaper, I was praised by a teacher who later founded the first coed *Gymnasium* in Kassel. But others thought the article inappropriate.

Sexuality was obviously present beneath the surface, but it was attended by a well-cultivated consciousness of sinfulness. The antithesis of respectfulness, at once repellent and alluring, carried in those days the name of *Nitribitt*.[19] After I graduated from *Gymnasium* and decided to attend university in Frankfurt, acquaintances told my parents: "Oh, you're allowing the boy to move to that cesspool of sin!"

CW: And how did you experience of the fifties politically?

DG: Above all I was shaped by the opposition between East and West. The division of Germany hadn't yet been accepted. Although without exception my family members lived in West Germany, I still suffered under German division. I regarded overcoming this division as the most important political aim, and I worked toward that end with the modest means of a schoolboy. Together with the other schools in Kassel, we organized an exchange with students from Erfurt.[20] It took place at a time when many GDR citizens still believed in the superiority of socialism. (That, at least, was my experience with the family who hosted me.) We took part in lessons at school and were allowed to attend a workers' meeting. A field trip was organized to Leipzig, where I saw the *Reichsgericht* for the first time.[21] But none of the Kassel participants converted to socialism. Things were different six months later

[19] Rosemarie Nitribitt (1933–1957) was a famous call girl with high society customers. Her murder in Frankfurt in 1957 caused a scandal in the early Federal Republic.

[20] Erfurt is a city of about Kassel's size, but located a hundred kilometers to the East and then part of East Germany.

[21] The Reichsgericht was the supreme civil and criminal court of the German Reich from 1879 until 1945, predecessor of the Bundesgerichtshof.

when the Erfurt students came to Kassel. The propaganda images of the West were refuted by the reality, and they returned home with doubts. In any case, the Erfurt NO canceled the already-planned third visit. Years later, the Erfurt party secretary who had organized things on the GDR side appeared at our door in Kassel. He said that he had fled from the GDR and asked if we could help him professionally. With great effort, I put out a special issue of the student newspaper that dealt with the division of Germany, the GDR, and socialism.

CW: Perhaps your interest had something to do with the fact that Kassel had a *Zonenrandlage*?[22]

DG: Yes, but at the time that was not unusual. There were precedents for such a special issue. The previously mentioned *Junge Presse* had a board member, Manfred Rexin,[23] who was responsible for pan-German questions. As I recall, he belonged to the SDS[24] but distanced himself sharply from communism. There was public funding available for conferences or student papers dealing with pan-German questions or with the rearmament of the Federal Republic. We always organized the conference schedule so that there was also room for questions about journalism—questions, for instance, about the rights of school principals vis-à-vis student papers. I was dissatisfied by the thematic one-sidedness. So I tried one time to organize a conference on the role of culture in student newspapers and another on National Socialism. The money didn't flow quite so readily for these. And for the National Socialism conference there was an additional problem. After the funds were secured, we had a hard time finding speakers. Many of those I asked replied, "It's still too soon to talk about that."

OL: A "culture of silence," it was then called.

DG: The conference took place after all and, as I remember, it wasn't at all bad. But it was a bit of a struggle to find money and speakers who were willing to talk about it.

OL: The first Bundestag election was then . . .

DG: The first Bundestag election that I consciously experienced was that of 1953.

[22] Kassel was located not too far from the border to the GDR. The word "Zonenrandlage" refers to its proximity to the former Soviet Occupation Zone.

[23] Manfred Rexin (1935–2017) was a journalist and contemporary historian inter alia at the Berlin office of the Second Germany Television channel (ZDF) and the RIAS Berlin (Radio in the American Sector Berlin).

[24] The Social German Student Union was founded in 1946 and is close to the SPD.

OL: But the first time you could vote was 1961. By then the Federal Republic was well established. So you are really a child of the Federal Republic?

DG: Yes, I am surely a child of the Federal Republic, but I was always aware that it was only half of Germany. It needed to make itself superfluous.

OL: You were born in 1937, so you have memories of the War and of the Nazis. But if I understand you correctly, your personality was really shaped in the swiftly established and well-functioning political and economic order of the Federal Republic.

DG: I was not drawn into the events of the War, as were members of the so-called *Flakhelfer* generation,[25] such as Ernst-Wolfgang Böckenförde,[26] who also completed his *Abitur* at the Wilhelm *Gymnasium*, but whom, because of our age difference, I never knew there. But it's true: after the confusion of the earliest post-War period, you might say that I grew up alongside the Federal Republic. It was my present reality. What had gone before served as antithesis.

OL: Are there any exact contemporaries among your fellow public law scholars with whom you feel a generational affinity? Isensee[27] and Scholz[28] were also born in 1937.

DG: I've never thought about it. *Herr* Schulze-Fielitz surely knows better than I.[29]

OL: There are social cohorts[30] that define themselves by common socialization experiences. Would you say that those born in 1937 form such a cohort?

DG: I wouldn't rule it out, but I wouldn't want to limit it to 1937.

CW: You mentioned Böckenförde. That's interesting that you attended the same *Gymnasium* in Kassel. But you also said that you didn't know him personally. Was that true of your families as well or was there some contact, perhaps through the parish?

[25] *Flakhelfergeneration* refers to the generation of young underaged people who were drawn into military service toward the end of the Second World War as auxiliary personnel of the German air force.

[26] Ernst-Wolfgang Böckenförde (1930–2019), professor of public law at the universities of Heidelberg, Bielefeld, and Freiburg im Breisgau; justice on the Second Senate of the Federal Constitutional Court from 1983 to 1996.

[27] Josef Isensee (1937–present), professor of public law at the universities of Saarbrücken and Bonn.

[28] Rupert Scholz (1937–present), professor of public law at the Free University of Berlin and the University of Munich; politician (CDU); senator for justice in Berlin (1981–1983); senator for federal affairs in Berlin (1982–1988); member of the Berlin Chamber of Deputies (1985–1988); federal minister of defense (1988–1989); member of the German Bundestag (1990–2002).

[29] Reference to Helmuth Schulze-Fielitz, *Staatsrechtslehre als Mikrokosmos: Bausteine zu einer Soziologie der Wissenschaft des öffentlichen Rechts* (2013). Helmuth Schulze-Fielitz (1947–present), professor of public law at the University of the Bundeswehr in Munich and the University of Würzburg.

[30] A cohort is a collection of people who share an experience or characteristic over time. The concept of a cohort is a research tool in sociology.

DG: No. Because his father was a forestry commissioner, I suspect that the family lived in Wilhelmshöhe. But even if we had gone to the same church, that wouldn't have changed things. The circle of my parents' acquaintance was determined more by the neighborhood than the parish. But when Böckenförde and I consciously met for the first time—as I recall it was at a conference of the Center for Interdisciplinary Research[31] in Rheda Castle—and realized that we had both gone to the same school, we exchanged a lot of memories. To a considerable extent, we had the same teachers.

CW: Kassel seems to be something of a factory for jurists. An astonishing number of good jurists come from there.

OL: But Duisburg beats Kassel in terms of the number of prominent public law professors.

DG: But not in terms of the number of Federal Constitutional Court justices stemming from the same *Gymnasium*. The first was Hermann Heußner,[32] who graduated during the War and was then drafted immediately, and who spoke in an indelible Kassel dialect. Böckenförde was the second, and I was the third. For a couple years we were all together on the Court. There is a photo of the three of us from this period that is said to have hung for a time in our school. In my speech at the school's anniversary celebration, I noted that perhaps all three of us were necessary to compensate for a truly terrible jurist who also graduated from the Wilhelm *Gymnasium*: Roland Freisler.[33]

CW: Already in the 1950s Kassel was associated with the *Documenta*.[34] Were you aware of this as a schoolboy?

DG: I had a season pass to the first *Documenta*. I can still recount today what hung in the individual rooms of the *Fridericianum*.[35] Unfortunately, I never thought at the time to buy a catalog. I do own a reprint.[36] I haven't seen all of the *Documenta*, but I have seen most of them. None left as large an impression as the first. For our elders, of course, it was a means of catching up.

[31] The Center for Interdisciplinary Research (ZiF) is an Institute for Advanced Study at the University of Bielefeld. It was founded in 1968 and has a special focus on interdisciplinary and international work.

[32] Hermann Heußner (1926–1996), judge on the Federal Social Court (1964–1979); justice on the Federal Constitutional Court (1979–1989).

[33] Roland Freisler (1893–1945), lawyer in Kassel; state secretary in the Reich Justice Ministry; president of the *Volksgerichtshof*. The *Volksgerichtshof* was a special court that was established by the Nazi regime primarily in order to deal with so-called political offenses. The *Volksgerichtshof* issued thousands of death penalties. Its procedure lacked basic rule of law standards. It was more an instrument of terror than a court.

[34] The *Documenta* is an exhibition of contemporary art which takes place in Kassel every five years. It first took place in 1955.

[35] A classical building on Friedrich's Square in Kassel; one of the first public museums in Europe (1779); centerpiece of the *Documenta*; now the Museum of Modern Art.

[36] *Documenta Catalog* (1955). Reprinted by the Prestel-Verlag in 1995.

They saw for the first time in broad overview what had happened abroad between 1933 and 1945 and what had been suppressed in German art. For me, it was a first encounter with modern art.

CW: In the realm of art and music, which aroused your interest more: the visual arts or music?

DG: By far the literary, performing, and visual arts. That isn't to say, however, that I didn't care for music. My *Gymnasium* maintained a proud musical tradition. There was a big school orchestra—which I didn't join because I didn't play an instrument—and a school choir in which I sang. I do listen to a lot of music—at home, in the concert hall, at the opera—but I have always been one who enjoys music rather than one who truly understands it. I couldn't say, for instance, why one performance of a Beethoven symphony is a particularly successful and another not, nor where exactly the differences of interpretation lie.

OL: After graduating from *Gymnasium* and entering university, you eventually had to choose a field of study.

DG: On that score I had no difficulties. In terms of my interests there were a lot of fields in play, but in terms of my professional aspirations there was only one: law. I was at the time resolved to go into politics, and law seemed to me the best preparation for that.

OL: But wouldn't you then have had to join a party?

DG: Yes, I would have had to join a party, but I didn't take that step. I thought at the time that I could join one later on. Later I no longer identified with any party to such a degree that joining would have been a natural consequence. My desire to become a politician also didn't last that long. I didn't develop a purely instrumental approach to the study of law. The subject soon exerted its own attraction.

OL: Did you have an idealistic conception of politics?

DG: I certainly had an inadequate understanding of politics. But an idealistic one? Yes, politics was important to me because in political office you could accomplish things. And for me, Reunification was something that deserved the utmost effort. The lofty perspective, then, of student newspaper editor and a student body president? So, in retrospect, it sometimes seems.

OL: A sense of responsibility for the community?

DG: That I undoubtedly had. "Leave it to others" was never my approach. But there was also a certain zest for the political game—the exchange of blows, the tactics that led to one's goal. In the *Junge Presse* practice that.

OL: Interested in politics, perhaps wants to become a politician, but doesn't join a party. That's a rather idealistic approach to the common good, isn't it?

DG: I think that I was enough of a democrat not to think of the common good as something predetermined or settling independently amidst the parallelogram of forces. As my drive to enter politics waned, an entrance by way of the ministerial bureaucracy was also possible. Under favorable circumstances, a state secretary can become a minister without owing his authority exclusively to politics and without having to undertake certain tiresome but necessary tasks at the local level—tasks for which I didn't feel especially suited. For a long time, diplomatic service also seemed like an option.

CW: You told us about the experiment in political education in Hesse. They obviously didn't teach about the life of a party democracy?

DG: That's how I remember it. There was a lot of societal policy and social policy. We were also, of course, taught about government systems, which in those days meant describing institutions and procedures. And the general feeling—not just at home—ran in another direction. Many had been members of the NSDAP, and their reflex reaction was: parties—never again.

OL: Which is not a compelling conclusion.

DG: Parties came up, of course. We observed election campaigns and analyzed party platforms. But we didn't go beyond that. Later, when I studied law and took the exam in constitutional law with Konrad Hesse,[37] he gave us a homework assignment on whether parties must be oriented toward the public good. I said yes, not of course thinking of a prescribed material public good, but as a demarcation from mere interest-group or one-issue parties. When he gave the assignment back, Hesse said, "My predecessor would surely have given you 'Good.' But for me it is only 'Satisfactory.' "

CW: He, of course, was one of the great theorists of parties.

DG: I have long been of his view. It must be possible to found a party for any purpose. Voters make the decision, not some Party Permit Authority.

[37] Konrad Hesse (1919–2005), professor of public and church law at the University of Freiburg im Breisgau; justice on the First Senate of the Federal Constitutional Court (1975–1987), predecessor of Dieter Grimm.

# II.
# University

OL: So you began your study of law with great self-assurance. That wasn't an existential decision, but one that began without doubt or need for orientation. You then went to Frankfurt—in what year was that? 1957?

DG: I began my studies in Frankfurt in the summer semester of 1957.

OL: The law faculty in Frankfurt, for its part, was rather oriented toward the economy—at least that's my impression. Its basic orientation was ordo-liberal.[1] It wasn't a faculty of the Left . . .

DG: Certainly not. That changed later on with the appointment of Rudolf Wiethölter.[2] The Leftists of the day were in other departments. But I hadn't chosen Frankfurt for the richness of its law faculty. I had no opinion on that matter. Kids from Kassel usually went to study in Marburg. That was the old Hessian-Kasselian State University and was still regarded as such. Students especially interested in mathematics might go to Göttingen, thirty miles north of Kassel. But as much as I loved my high school days, I didn't want to go to university in the same setting. On the other hand, I did want to remain in Hesse because in-state students didn't have to pay tuition. Paying for my studies was no small matter for my parents. So there was only Frankfurt. Gießen didn't have a full university at the time, but even if it had, I wouldn't have considered it. When I decided to go to Frankfurt, one of my *Gymnasium* teachers told me that he wanted to draw my attention to two "subversive" teachers there whom I had better avoid.

"Oh," I asked, my curiosity piqued, "what are their names?"

"Horkheimer,"[3] he answered, "and Adorno."[4]

[1] Ordo-liberalism promotes a vision of a social market economy with a strong role of the state to provide a framework for economic activities. It was mainly founded by the Freiburg School which was dominated by Walter Eucken.

[2] Rudolf Wiethölter (1929–present), professor of civil law, commercial law, corporate law, and international private law at the University of Frankfurt am Main.

[3] Max Horkheimer (1895–1973), philosopher and sociologist; leader of the Institute for Social Research at the University of Frankfurt am Main (1930–1933); emigration to Switzerland (1933) and the USA (1934); 1949 professor again at Frankfurt; *Rektor* (head) of the university (1951–1953).

[4] Theodor W. Adorno (1903–1969), philosopher, sociologist, and music theorist; 1931–1933 *Privatdozent* University of Frankfurt; emigration to England (1934) and the USA (1938); after returning from emigration in 1949 professor at the University of Frankfurt.

*Dieter Grimm: Advocate of the Constitution.* Dieter Grimm, Oxford University Press (2020). © in the original German edition, Mohr Siebeck GmbH & Co. KG, Tübingen 2017, © this translation, Justin Collings 2020.
DOI: 10.1093/oso/9780198845270.001.0001

OL: But they weren't on the law faculty. There you had Kronstein[5] and Böhm.

DG: The most prominent member of the group was actually Hallstein.[6] But he was Adenauer's state secretary and never around on campus. Böhm was a member of the Bundestag and often away on official business. Kronstein moved back and forth between Frankfurt and Georgetown. It made a big impression on me that one could teach simultaneously in Germany and the United States. But I never took a class from him. Friends who heard him lecture really liked him. The most famous member of the faculty was Coing.[7] He taught Roman law, private law, and legal philosophy. The public law teachers were Schlochauer[8] (international law), Mallmann[9] (constitutional law), and Jaenicke[10] (administrative law). Schlochauer became terribly agitated at times, such as when a student arrived late or left early. He would pace around muttering maledictions and turning beet-red beneath his frizzled still blond or already whitening hair. He was passed over twice for the rectorship of the university.[11] Mallmann, as far as I can tell, had not finished his *Habilitation*.[12] Before his appointment in Frankfurt, where he succeeded Ridder, he had been editor in chief of the *JuristenZeitung*.[13] He thought highly of Ridder,[14] especially his essay on Article 5 GG[15] in

[5] Heinrich Kronstein (1897–1972), 1935 emigration to the USA; 1941 Special Attorney US Justice Department (Claims Division, Antitrust Division); 1946 professor of corporate and antitrust law at Georgetown and after 1956 simultaneously at the University of Frankfurt am Main.

[6] Walter Hallstein (1901–1982), professor of private and corporate law at the universities of Rostock and Frankfurt am Main; state secretary in the office of the federal chancellor, especially in the Foreign Office (1950–1958); first president of the European Commission (1958–1967); member of the German Bundestag after 1969.

[7] Helmut Coing (1912–2000), professor of Roman law and private law at the University of Frankfurt am Main; founding director of the Max Planck Institute for European Legal History in Frankfurt am Main (1964–1980); chair of the West German Conference of Rectors (1956–1957); chair of the German Research Council, member, and chancellor of the Order "Pour le Mérite" (1958–1960).

[8] Hans-Jürgen Schlochauer (1906–1990), professor of international law, and foreign and international business law at the University of Frankfurt am Main.

[9] Walter Mallmann (1908–1982), professor of public law at the universities of Frankfurt am Main and Gießen; co-editor of the *Archiv des öffentlichen Rechts*.

[10] Günther Jaenicke (1914–2008), professor of public law—including international and European law—at the University of Frankfurt am Main.

[11] Dependent on the respective state, the head of a university is called either "Rektor" or "Präsident."

[12] The *Habilitation* is the qualification which has traditionally been necessary to become full professor at a German university. It typically consists of a *Habilitation* thesis and a presentation in front of the whole faculty. A candidate who completes the *Habilitation* is conferred a "venia legendi" which allows him or her to teach specific subjects at a university.

[13] The *JuristenZeitung* is one of the most important German law journals. It is published by the academic publisher Mohr Siebeck and encompasses all fields of law. Its audience is predominantly academic.

[14] Helmut Ridder (1919–2007), professor of public law at the universities of Frankfurt am Main, Bonn, and Gießen.

[15] Here, and throughout, "GG" stands for *Grundgesetz* or Basic Law. "Article 5 GG" is the standard German notation for Article 5 of the post-War constitution comprising freedom of speech and of the press, freedom of information and of broadcasting.

the *Handbook of Fundamental Rights* edited by Neumann, Nipperdey, and Scheuner.[16] Jaenicke was really a scholar of international law. He came from the Max Planck Institute in Heidelberg and was *the* expert on continental shelves. In Frankfurt, however, he wasn't allowed to teach international law but was appointed for administrative law instead.

Because my original motive for studying law was my aspiration for a political career, I used to listen to other lectures as well. I was always studying political science on the side. The offerings were admittedly slim. The field was chaired in Frankfurt by Carlo Schmid,[17] but he saw his main responsibility as being in Bonn. He would arrive from Bonn on Friday afternoons and lecture from 4 to 6 p.m. and again on Saturday from 10 a.m. to noon. He always filled the biggest lecture halls. In my first three semesters at Frankfurt, I also listened to lectures by Oswald von Nell-Breunig,[18] Horkheimer, and Leopold von Wiese.[19]

CW: After three semesters in Frankfurt you transferred to Freiburg. You once said that you were distantly related to Joseph H. Kaiser,[20] who taught there.

DG: A brother of my mother was married to Joseph Kaiser's cousin. When I announced my intention to transfer to Freiburg, she told me that I must at all costs go visit Joseph and convey her regards. I first met him before the semester began as I was looking for an apartment. He immediately invited me to his home for dinner, where he interrogated me about all sorts of books, especially Theodor Eschenburg's *State and Society in Germany*, which I hadn't read.[21] I then took his class on international law and in the following semester felt obligated to take his seminar on theories of the state as well, though I would have preferred to take Hesse's seminar. When I signed up for the seminar, Kaiser asked me what topic I wanted to address in my presentation. I mentioned my interest in political science and asked whether I could make a topic out of it. He then summoned his assistant,

[16] Helmut Ridder, "Meinungsfreiheit" in Franz L Neumann, Hans Carl Nipperdey, and Ulrich Scheuner (eds), *Die Grundrechte: Handbuch der Theorie und Praxis der Grundrechte* (2 vols) (1st ed. 1954, 2d ed. 1968) 243.

[17] Carlo Schmid (1896–1979), professor of public law at the University of Tübingen and of political science at the University of Frankfurt am Main; member of the Parliamentary Council; politician (SPD); member of the German Bundestag (1949–1972); repeatedly vice president of the Bundestag; federal minister for federal-state relations (1966–1969).

[18] Oswald von Nell-Breuning (1890–1991), Jesuit, economist, and social philosopher; doyen of Catholic social teaching; professor at the Jesuit College of St. Georgen in Frankfurt am Main; honorary professor at the University of Frankfurt.

[19] Leopold von Wiese (1876–1969), sociologist at the University of Cologne, presumably at the time a visiting professor in Frankfurt.

[20] Joseph H. Kaiser (1921–1998), professor of public law and international law at the University of Freiburg am Breisgau.

[21] Theodor Eschenburg, *Staat und Gesellschaft in Deutschland* (1956).

Hartmut Jäckel,[22] who later taught political science at the Free University of Berlin, and said in his indelibly sardonic way, "*Herr* Grimm has great merits in political science. We should give him a topic that will allow him to display them. What would you think of, 'The Method of Political Science'?" I have no desire to see today what I presented back then.

Toward the end of the semester, Kaiser invited the seminar participants to his home. The atmosphere was so rigid and stifling that when he gave the welcome toast we all retreated further and further toward the wall. Unfortunately, on the bit of wall toward which I was inching backward there sat a Chinese vase. I knocked it over. Kaiser acted as though nothing had happened—*pas d'histoire*—but I must suspect that the vase was worth something.

Political science was chaired in Freiburg by Arnold Bergstraesser,[23] an influential figure—today we would call him well networked—who had returned from America in the early 1950s. The atmosphere wasn't as stiff as it was with Kaiser, but it too was idiosyncratic in its way. Bergstraesser had many students who later formed a major part of the second generation of political science in the Federal Republic (the names Hans Maier,[24] Schwan,[25] Schwarz,[26] Sontheimer,[27] Oberndörfer,[28] Kindermann,[29] and Häettich[30] immediately come to mind). They took part in the seminar but had developed a curious way of hiding their views behind some authority ("As Tocqueville once said . . ."). One of them always had to carry Bergstraesser's briefcase. We were still a long way from the anti-authoritarian movement.

CW: How did studying in Freiburg compare with studying in Frankfurt?

[22] Hartmut Jäckel (1930–present), professor of political science at the Free University of Berlin; vice president of the Free University (1974–1977); High Officer in the Berlin Executive Department for Science and Research (1977–1981).

[23] Arnold Bergstraesser (1896–1964), political scientist; professor at the University of Heidelberg (1929–1935); during his emigration a professor at the University of Chicago; professor of sociology and political science at the University of Freiburg im Breisgau from 1954 until his death.

[24] Hans Maier (1931–present), professor of political science, later of Christian Philosophy at the University of Munich; politician (CSU); Bavarian minister of education (1970–1986); member of the Bavarian Parliament (1978–1987).

[25] Alexander Schwan (1931–1989), professor of the history of political ideas at the Free University of Berlin.

[26] Hans-Peter Schwarz (1934–2017), professor of political science at the universities of Hamburg, Cologne, and Bonn.

[27] Kurt Sontheimer (1928–2005), professor of political science at the Free University of Berlin, the University of Munich, and in Paris.

[28] Dieter Oberndörfer (1929–present), professor of political science at the University of Freiburg im Breisgau.

[29] Gottfried-Karl Kindermann (1926–present), professor of international politics at the University of Munich.

[30] Manfred Hättich (1925–2003), professor of political science at the universities of Mainz and Munich; director of the Tutzing Academy for Political Education (1970–1993).

DG: On the whole, I'd have to say that in Freiburg much more than in Frankfurt I got a sense of what university life is. I found the lectures more demanding. Erik Wolf[31] has an enduring place in my memory, as does the bizarre but brilliant Gustav Böhmer,[32] from whom I took inheritance law. He always descended on Freiburg, chauffeured by his wife, from the heights of the Schwarzwald; he liked to parade his vitality; and he lamented his emeritus status. ("*Relieved of duties*, they call it. I've been relieved of rights—*of rights*!") When it was very hot, he could be seen on campus in shorts. But I never had the privilege of seeing his showpiece: a handstand in the lecture hall. His lectures were pedagogically superb. They clarified the framework of inheritance law in such a way that it was always easy for me, later on, to connect specific problems to the overall framework and to draw the necessary conclusions.

But even apart from the lectures, university life was richer in Freiburg. I attended guest lectures by foreign scholars, and once I was even taken along for the post-lecture drinks. Bergstraesser invited me to a weekend seminar in the Schauinsland.[33] During my second semester in Freiburg, I lived in a small dormitory at Maximilianstraße 15, which, if I remember right, had previously been a forestry institute. That was a true joy—about thirty tenants who organized common events and were eager for discussion. My favorite conversation partner was Friedrich Müller,[34] with whom I talked a lot but who also scared me a little. He was exceptionally serious and loved to discuss legal problems and literary opinions of which I had never even heard, even though he was not ahead of me, but a year younger than I. We stayed in touch for a while. His book on the *Structure of Norms and Normativity*[35] was very important for my later understanding of constitutional interpretation.

OL: Frankfurt, Freiburg, and finally the Free University of Berlin . . .

DG: Berlin was only one semester—a patriotic semester, so to speak—that one owed to the constricted city. It was the winter semester of 1959–1960—still before the Wall. As far as my studies were concerned, I didn't find it

[31] Erik Wolf (1902–1977), professor of legal philosophy, criminal law, and ecclesiastical law at the universities of Kiel, Rostock, and Freiburg im Breisgau.

[32] Gustav Böhmer (1881–1969), professor of private law at the universities of Halle, Frankfurt am Main, Marburg, and Freiburg im Breisgau, where he still gave regular lectures after his retirement in 1949.

[33] The Schauinsland is a mountain in the Black Forest close to Freiburg im Breisgau, 1284m.

[34] Friedrich Müller (1938–present), professor of public law and legal philosophy at the University of Heidelberg.

[35] Friedrich Müller, *Normstruktur und Normativität: Zum Verhältnis von Recht und Wirklichkeit in der juristischen Hermeneutik, entwickelt an Fragen der Verfassungsinterpretation* (1966).

all that fruitful. I took my exam in administrative law with Bettermann.[36] I listened to a lot of lectures from the politics professors. At the time, the Free University was the only university with multiple chairs in political science. I remember von der Gablentz[37] and Fraenkel.[38] I also attended a course from the journalism scholar, Dovifat.[39] Essentially, though, it was a semester of theater-going and bargain book buying in East Berlin. But Berlin as a city had captured me again. Perhaps it was no accident that when the semester ended, I missed my train for Kassel and stayed a day longer than planned in Berlin.

Then came my second period of study in Frankfurt. By this time, I was much further along in my studies and my scholarly interests were much more pronounced. I again attended Schmid's lectures, including now a Friday-evening seminar from 8 to 10 in the *Kettenhofweg*.[40] I also attended the seminars of Coing, Mallmann, and Jaenicke.

CW: You already mentioned that you had a scholarship from the *Cusanuswerk*.[41]

DG: Yes, after my return to Frankfurt I was recommended for the *Cusanuswerk* and accepted. My interview was conducted by Hans Tietmeyer,[42] the managing director of the *Cusanuswerk*. As I recall, we talked about whether parents should avoid imposing a religion on their children, so that when they reach maturity they can make an informed and independent decision about their religious affiliation. If I remember right, the Frankfurt *Cusanus* group—scholarship students from all disciplines—met every two weeks to discuss actual or theoretical issues. Those were discussions unlike anything I had experienced in seminars—fired by engagement, informed, critical, horizon-expanding, with great zest for intellectual exchange. Two members of the group surpassed all others for their incisive

[36] Karl August Bettermann (1913–2005), judge on the ordinary and administrative courts, concluding with the Federal Administrative Court (1956–1970); professor of public and administrative law at the Free University of Berlin; professor of civil procedure and general procedure at the University of Hamburg (1970–1978).

[37] Otto Heinrich von der Gablentz (1898–1972), professor of political science at the Free University of Berlin.

[38] Ernst Fraenkel (1898–1975), attorney; 1938 emigration via England to the USA; 1945–1950 counselor for the US Justice Department in Korea, 1951 return to Germany, professor for political science at the Free University of Berlin (1953–1967).

[39] Emil Dovifat (1890–1969), professor of newspapers and media at Berlin University, later at the Free University of Berlin.

[40] Kettenhofweg is an elegant street in the Westend of Frankfurt am Main.

[41] Cf. Chapter I, fn. 3.

[42] Hans Tietmeyer (1931–2016), economist; state secretary in the Federal Finance Ministry (1982–1989); member of the directorate of the German Bundesbank (1990–1993); president of the German Bundesbank (1993–1999).

intelligence: Heinz Riesenhuber[43] and Otwin Massing.[44] But there are many others I could name.

This was supplemented by the *Cusanuswerk*'s holiday academies, in which we were required to take part once a year. But for me they were not a duty but a joy. I became a scholarship student comparatively late and so took part in only two holiday academies. The first week was always devoted to theology, the second to philosophy, and the third to other topics—literature, politics, sociology. I attribute tremendous importance in my life to the *Cusanuswerk*. It set standards and led me to redefine my expectations for myself. I've always maintained ties with the *Cusanuswerk*. Perhaps we'll have other occasion to talk about that.

OL: Which teachers impressed you?

DG: That's not easy to answer. Obviously, I was in Frankfurt with Horkheimer and Adorno. I learned a lot from Horkheimer's lecture on the idea of freedom. Adorno I couldn't understand. Now and then I tested whether he brought his convoluted, periodic sentences correctly to a close. He did. Carlo Schmid was an impressive speaker. But he had no time for scholarly research. He drew upon his extraordinary culture and reading and, when it came to the political system of the Federal Republic, his knowledge of Bonn's inner workings. Other names have already come up.

CW: As you mentioned, you constantly attended seminars. With whom did you have the closest contact?

DG: Beginning in the fourth semester, I always attended multiple seminars, including some in political science. I was probably closest to Mallmann. He wasn't exciting, but he had a stronger democratic streak than the others. I also found him to be especially upright. I was all the more dismayed, then, when I read the foreword to his dissertation on Laband's concept of law.[45] That Laband was wrong, he said, followed from the fact that he was a Jew. In the book itself there was no hint of antisemitism. Laband's concept of law was explained on the basis of the dualist constitutionalism of the German empire. Perhaps the foreword was a concession he had to make to get his book published at all.

[43] Heinz Riesenhuber (1935–present), chemist and economist; politician (CDU); member of the German Bundestag (1976–2017); federal minister for research and technology (1982–1993).

[44] Otwin Massing (1934–2019), professor of political science at the University of Hannover; rector (1977–1978) and vice president (1978–1979) of the university and later (1997–1998) dean of its law faculty.

[45] Walter Mallmann, *Die Sanktion im Gesetzgebungsverfahren* (1938).

Mallmann was also one of my examiners for the state examination.[46] I had asked that my take-home portion of the exam be related to constitutional law, which was rare. The oral exam I could master without stress. The only difficulty was that the head of the committee had a lazy eye, so you could never be sure to whom he was speaking. One of the practitioners only addressed my fellow candidates. I expected that he had some special subtlety in store for me. But no. He never asked me anything. And then (according to Mallmann) in the deliberations of the exam committee the chairman asked this examiner, "How would you evaluate *Herr* Grimm's performance during your exam discussion?"

"He didn't say anything," he answered, "so he's probably like all the others: about average."

"You never asked him anything," Mallmann retorted, "so you must assume that he would have been just as good for you as he was for us."

I think Mallmann was sad that I wanted to do my dissertation under Coing instead of under him. I could see it in his face when I told him. And in fact, a dissertation under Mallmann would have made a lot of sense. But I had plans to go abroad and for that I needed scholarships. I figured that Coing's greater prominence outside Germany would be more helpful in that regard.

CW: Did you have a topic in mind for Mallmann?

DG: It would have mostly likely dealt with broadcasting law. That was Mallmann's strength, and several of his graduate students ended up working for the legal division of the Hessian Broadcasting service. When I returned to Frankfurt from Harvard in 1966, Mallmann was no longer there. Like Ridder, he had gone to join the newly founded faculty in Gießen. He was replaced by Erhard Denninger,[47] who was later the second reader of my dissertation.

CW: Wasn't Martin Drath[48] an interesting figure in Berlin?

[46] German legal education is completed by taking two state examinations: The First State Examination is taken after law studies at a German university. The Second State Examination is taken after a two-year legal traineeship (*Referendariat*). Both state examinations consist of several written exams, which are graded blindly by law professors, judges, or senior civil servants, and by one oral exam, which takes several hours. In previous decades, the state examinations also included a take-home portion. The First and Second State Examinations are both administered by the courts and/or the Ministry of Justice of the respective state.

[47] Erhard Denninger (1932–present), professor of public law and legal philosophy at the University of Frankfurt am Main.

[48] Martin Drath (1902–1976), professor of public law at the University of Jena, the Free University of Berlin, and the Technical University of Darmstadt; justice on the Federal Constitutional Court (1951–1963).

DG: When I said goodbye to Kaiser before leaving Freiburg for Berlin, he said to me, "Then you'll be going to our colleague Drath." He said it in a tone that suggested he didn't think much of Drath. I never met Drath at the Free University. I would have to check to see if he was even teaching there at the time.

CW: Were Lerche[49] and Stern[50] not in Berlin yet?

DG: No. Neither was there yet. I once heard Lerche lecture in Munich. I could get cheap train tickets thanks to my father, so I liked to travel to other university cities, such as Munich. I had taken a look at the Munich course directory beforehand. I had heard from friends that Lerche was a young, rising scholar and worth listening to. I did the same thing in Tübingen. At the time the faculties in Munich and Tübingen were excellent.

CW: Tübingen, yes—but Munich?

DG: From the perspective of the students of the time, I would say the same for Munich. The textbook offerings were still slim, and several authors of standard treatises taught in Munich: Larenz,[51] Mezger,[52] Maunz,[53] Hueck,[54] and Rosenberg.[55]

OL: You got to know a lot of interesting people, but had no *teacher* in the truest sense?

DG: I learned a lot from a lot of people. But I wouldn't know whom to designate as my mentor teacher. There were, however, a couple of formative books, most prominently Franz Wieacker's history of modern private law,[56] which I read in preparation for the state exam and in which I found answers to questions to which I hadn't found answers during my studies.

OL: But you've spoken most extensively of Mallmann . . .

[49] Peter Lerche (1928–2016), professor of public law at the Free University of Berlin and the University of Munich.

[50] Klaus Stern (1932–present), professor of public law at the Free University of Berlin and the University of Cologne.

[51] Karl Larenz (1903–1993), professor of private law and legal philosophy at the universities of Kiel and Munich. Larenz, Mezger, Maunz, and Hueck were all prominent authors of law books in National Socialist Germany.

[52] Edmund Mezger (1883–1962), professor of criminal law at the universities of Marburg and Munich.

[53] Theodor Maunz (1901–1993), professor of public law at the universities of Freiburg im Breisgau and Munich; Bavarian minister of education (1957–1964).

[54] Alfred Hueck (1889–1975), professor of private law and labor law at the universities of Jena and Munich.

[55] Leo Rosenberg (1879–1963), professor of civil procedure at the University of Gießen, rector of the University of Gießen (1926–1928); professor at the University of Leipzig; 1934 forcefully retired; after the War professor in Munich.

[56] Franz Wieacker, *Privatrechstgeschichte der Neuzeit* (1st ed. 1952, 3d ed. 2016).

DG: His scholarly interests were the closest to mine, but I also valued him personally. I had even asked him for a recommendation for the *Cusanuswerk*. I found that Mallmann was very accessible—and this at a time when most students remained rather anonymous. When I met with him, he was very personable.

OL: Were you shaped less at the time by private law?

DG: My affinity for public law stemmed from my interest in politics, which didn't subside even when I was no longer sure that I wanted to become a politician. That affinity sharpened through my concurrent study of political science. I quickly steered clear of criminal law. In civil law, I derived an aesthetic pleasure from the long chains of reasoning. One of my first articles even dealt with a civil law topic.[57] It was an outgrowth of a memo that I had to prepare as a *Referendar*[58] at the Regional High Court.[59] I found that none of the available theories solved the problem satisfactorily, and I developed a proposed solution of my own. The *Neue Juristische Wochenschrift*[60] accepted the article. Shortly after its appearance, it was cited by the Federal Court of Justice.[61] When I arrived in Karlsruhe as a justice of the Constitutional Court, some of the judges at the Federal Court of Justice, who remembered the paper, told me that I was, so to speak, one of their own. Whether they still thought so later on is less certain. Among the foundational fields, I felt most drawn at the time to legal philosophy. I considered it as a possible second area of emphasis.

OL: Were there other classmates of the time with whom you've remained close? My own circle of friends derives largely from my university days.

DG: Some friends from my student days have remained—above all Norbert Reich.[62] We shared a room in the dormitory. We always read our textbooks together, recommended books to each other, and discussed many things far beyond the curriculum—and with special intensity during the years

[57] Dieter Grimm, "Zur Abgrenzung der Schadensersatzansprüche aus § 635 BGB und aus positiver Vertagsverletzung" (1968) 22 *Neue Juristische Wochenschrift* 14.

[58] The *Referendariat* is a two-year (formerly a three-and-a-half year), state-organized legal traineeship which takes the *Referendar* through all legal professions. It normally includes time at a civil court, at the public prosecutor's office, in the administration, and in a law firm. At the end of the *Referendariat*, the *Referendar* has to take the Second State Examination (cf. above fn. 46).

[59] The Regional High Court (Oberlandesgericht) is the second highest court in the German civil court system.

[60] The *Neue Juristische Wochenschrift* (NJW) is a weekly law journal with the widest circulation. It counts among the most famous and most widely read law journals in Germany. It was founded in 1947 and is published by C. H. Beck.

[61] The Federal Court of Justice (Bundesgerichtshof) is the highest court in the German civil court system.

[62] Norbert Reich (1937–2015), professor of private law at the College of Economics and Politics at Hamburg and at the universities of Hamburg and Bremen.

around 1968, when we were both working at the Max Planck Institute for legal history in Frankfurt. We were the same age, though with the small but exceptionally important difference that he was born after, and I before, 31 July 1937. This meant that he was one of the first to face compulsory military service and so was academically younger than I. But he preceded me at every point: examinations, study abroad in the US, doctorate, post-doc, professorship. He was a bit less picky. In the US, for example, I didn't want to study at any but the four best law schools; he was somewhere in New Jersey. His first professorship was at the College of Economics and Politics in Hamburg; I would never have applied to a non-university. Norbert Reich was also known to leave a bar donning a coat that wasn't his. He didn't care what he wore. His wife made sure his colors matched.

I've also retained some friends from my political science studies. I would mention especially Peter Haungs,[63] with whom I had earlier been on the national board of the *Junge Presse*. He helped me get a job teaching political science in Trier.

Friendships from the *Cusanuswerk* have been especially enduring. Above all others, I would mention Winfried Hassemer,[64] a truly independent, critical spirit—swift, scornful, and witty. When he got tired of Frankfurt and was looking for a change, I did everything I could to get him to come to Bielefeld. He got an offer, but didn't accept it. I was disappointed but not upset. He was a good fit for Frankfurt. It was one of the most stimulating faculties in those years. We were later reunited for a few years in Karlsruhe.

All three of those I have just named are no longer living.

[63] Peter Haungs (1939–1994), professor of political science at the University of Trier.

[64] Winfried Hassemer (1940–2014), professor of criminal law and legal philosophy at the University of Frankfurt am Main; justice on the Second Senate of the Federal Constitutional Court (1996–2008); vice president of the same (2002–2008).

# III.
# Paris, America, and PhD

CW: What happened next after the first state exam?

DG: I found myself at an unexpected crossroads. Carlo Schmid's assistant, Wilhelm Hennis,[1] had completed his *Habilitation*[2] thesis. I had attended his first seminar on political parties. That gave rise to a casual but enduring contact. He quickly received an appointment in Hannover, and soon thereafter in Hamburg. Schmid had his second assistant, Otwin Massing, whom I knew from the *Cusanuswerk*, ask me if I was interested in taking Hennis's place. Interested I certainly was, but at the same time I realized that I now faced a choice between law and political science. I wanted to make use of political science insights to enrich constitutional interpretation, but I didn't want to turn my back on legal scholarship. I would also have had to defer my plans to study abroad. So I declined the offer, and Ingeborg Maus[3] was hired instead.

I then went as planned, and with a scholarship from the French government, to the *Faculté de droit et des sciences économiques* in Paris. I had to sign a document promising to avoid any political activity—and demonstrations in particular—while in France. I did so without any feeling of great sacrifice. After my return from Paris, I began my *Referendariat* (legal traineeship),[4] which at the time still lasted three-and-a-half years. I interrupted that training to study at Harvard Law School, and finally completed the legal traineeship and took the second state exam in 1967. Immediately thereafter I took a research position at the Max Planck Institute for European Legal History in Frankfurt, where I had already worked as a part-time assistant during my legal traineeship. My main objective for my time at the Institute was to write my dissertation.

OL: When exactly were you in Paris?

[1] Wilhelm Hennis (1923–2012), professor of political science at the Pedagogical Academy of Hannover, at the universities of Hamburg and Freiburg im Breisgau.

[2] Cf. Chapter II, fn. 12.

[3] Ingeborg Maus (1937–present), professor of political science at the University of Frankfurt am Main.

[4] Cf. Chapter II, fn. 58.

*Dieter Grimm: Advocate of the Constitution.* Dieter Grimm, Oxford University Press (2020). © in the original German edition, Mohr Siebeck GmbH & Co. KG, Tübingen 2017, © this translation, Justin Collings 2020.
DOI: 10.1093/oso/9780198845270.001.0001

DG: From November 1962 till July 1963. I took the night train to Paris and arrived early on the morning of November 8th at the *Maison de l'Allemagne* in the *cité universitaire*. My first question was where I could get breakfast. "*Au Cambodge*," I was told. The answer left me at a loss, but the solution was really quite simple. It referred to the building next door, *La Maison du Cambodge*.

OL: At the time Paris was still peaceful and civilized.

DG: There was still no thought of unrest, let alone street fighting and barricades.

OL: Was Sartre already holding court on the Boulevard Saint-Germain? Or did that start later?

DG: I would have loved to see him. Existentialism was unavoidable in Germany. I spent considerable time on the Boulevard Saint-Germain, but probably in the wrong cafés. I did, however, get to know another major figure: Raymond Aron.[5] A fellow tenant in the German House was studying under him and took me along to his seminar on the sociology of art.

CW: What were the universities in Paris like?

DG: Even more overcrowded and anonymous than in Germany. I took two lecture courses in legal philosophy from Battifol[6] and Villey,[7] as well as "political institutions" from Duverger.[8] Constitutional law wasn't taught in France. The organizational side of the constitution was taught under "institutions." Fundamental rights weren't dealt with at all. This was a telling comment on the significance of constitutionalism in its European birthplace. I also took part in a seminar with Michel Villey.

The professors delivered their lectures in robes. A uniformed porter escorted the professor into the lecture hall and retrieved him when the lecture was done. There was no provision for discussion or for contact with the teachers outside of class. They didn't even have an office at the university. That is still the case today. Only Michel Villey's seminar departed from the usual pattern. He had come to Paris from Strasbourg and was still familiar with the German seminar tradition. The participants in his seminar were mostly scholars—professors, senior lecturers, etc. Professors often made the presentations. I recall one session in which a row broke out over the

[5] Raymond Aron (1905–1983), philosopher and sociologist in the liberal tradition of Montesquieu and Tocqueville, professor of sociology at the University of Paris (Sorbonne), the École des hautes études en sciences sociales and the Collège de France; father of Dominique Schnapper, sociologist and member of the *Conseil Constitutionnel* (2001–2010).

[6] Henri Battifol (1905–1989), professor of international private law and legal philosophy in Paris.

[7] Michel Villey (1914–1988), legal philosopher and legal historian at the universities of Strasbourg and Paris.

[8] Maurice Duverger (1917–2014), French jurist and political scientist; professor in Bordeaux, Poitiers, and Paris.

meaning of a statement by Kelsen.[9] At that point Charles Eisenmann[10] said, "Let's ask him." He left the room and returned with the answer shortly thereafter. He had phoned Berkeley. There was one other German besides me in Villey's seminar, Friedrich Kübler,[11] who was at work on his *Habilitation* thesis. We met again in Frankfurt later on. Although a scholar of civil law, he did some important work in broadcasting law as well.

OL: How did you land on Duguit[12] as the topic of your doctoral dissertation?

DG: It was Coing's suggestion. He was interested at the time in the history of the notion of subjective right,[13] on which Villey was also working. When Coing accepted me as a doctoral candidate and asked about my dissertation ideas, I expressed my interest in legal philosophy (my last seminar with Coing had been on legal philosophy) and in France, where I hoped to spend the following year. He then suggested that I work on Duguit, whom he regarded as one of the most decided opponents of the notion of subjective right.[14]

In Paris, I went to work. In my presentation for the Villey seminar I undertook a comparison between Duguit and Eugen Ehrlich.[15] But I wasn't exactly thrilled with the dissertation topic. I returned to Germany with a lot of material but without a plan and began my legal traineeship in the fall of 1963. A year later I went to Harvard, and there, of course, constitutional law played an entirely different role. I set Duguit aside for the moment and planned to do something on the intellectual roots of American constitutionalism. That later became my master's thesis at Harvard.[16] In 1966, I resumed my legal traineeship in Frankfurt. Coing had offered me

[9] Hans Kelsen (1881–1973), professor of public and international law, as well as legal theory, at the universities of Vienna, Cologne, Geneva, Prague, and Berkeley.

[10] Charles Eisenmann (1903–1980), legal philosopher, professor at the universities of Strasbourg and Paris; known also for his French translation of Kelsen's *Reine Rechtslehre* ("Pure Theory of Law").

[11] Friedrich Kübler (1932–2013), professor of private law, corporate law, and securities law at the universities of Gießen, Constance, and Frankfurt am Main.

[12] Léon Duguit (1859–1928), professor of administrative law in Caen and Bordeaux; legal theorist—"one of the most revolutionary legal thinkers of his generation" (*Encyclopedia Britannica*).

[13] Subjective right meant in contrast to an objective right or law. A subjective right entitles to an individual claim, an objective right does not. The distinction is prevalent in Continental legal systems.

[14] Cf. Léon Duguit, *L'état, le droit objectif et la loi positive* (1901, reprint 2003); *Souveraineté et liberté* (1921, reprint 2002); *Traité de droit constitutionnel* (3d ed. 1927). The abridged edition of the treatise, *Manuel de droit constitutionnel* (1923, reprint 2007), begins with a distinction between *droit objectif* and *droit subjectif* (§ 1) and a *Critique de la doctrine individualiste* (§ 4). On Duguit, see Fabrice Mellerray (ed.), *Autour de Léon Duguit. Colloque commémoratif du 150e anniversaire de la naissance du doyen Léon Duguit* (2011).

[15] Eugen Ehrlich (1862–1922), Austrian legal sociologist; professor in Czernowitz.

[16] Published in German as Europäisches Naturrecht und Amerikanische Revolution" (1970) 3 *Ius Commune* 120.

a position there in the newly founded Max Planck Institute for European Legal History.[17]

We moved slowly—but in Frankfurt quite perceptibly—toward what today is identified with "1968." All at once, Duguit appeared to me in a new light. His critique of the notion of subjective right was only a byproduct of his much more comprehensive critique of a legal system and a body of legal thought that he regarded as idealistic and individualist, and that he wanted to replace with a realist and social approach rooted in the observation of facts. The core concept was *solidarité sociale*, which I now wanted to write about. I then finished my dissertation relatively quickly after going, at Coing's urging, to Bordeaux to look for illuminating material on Duguit. In my research, I came across a publication of the proceedings of a conference held in 1959 to honor Duguit's 100th birthday.[18] I learned from that volume that Duguit had a son who still lived in his parents' home. A chapter entitled "Léon Duguit et sa famille" even supplied the address. So I wrote to Monsieur Michel Duguit, but initially received no reply. After several months, I got a letter from Madame Duguit, Duguit's daughter-in-law. She apologized for the long delay and explained that my letter had arrived when her husband was gravely ill, and that he had since died. But I was very welcome to come to the house. Duguit's workroom was unchanged. I could work at his desk, and since the house was large enough, I could, if I liked, live there during my stay. Additionally, she put me in touch with an emeritus member of the Bordeaux faculty, Marcel Laborde-Lacoste,[19] who as a young professor had been Duguit's colleague. Madame Duguit explained that the books that were especially important to Duguit were behind his writing desk. I was particularly interested in those books. There were a lot of German books among them, which he had worked through, annotated, and underlined. Duguit himself regarded his 1901 book *L'état, le droit objectif et la loi positive* as a reply to Jellinek's *Allgemeine Staatslehre* of 1900. After the First World War, Duguit had to defend his admiration of German jurists. In 2013, the *Université Paris II* invited me to give a lecture on my engagement with Duguit from a distance of more than forty years.[20] On that occasion, I read my dissertation in full for the first time since it was published.

[17] Cf. Frank L. Schäfer, "Visionen und Wissenschaftsmanagement: Die Gründung eines Max-Planck-Instituts für europäische Rechtsgeschichte" (2009) *Zeitschrift für europäisches Privatrecht* 517.

[18] *Revue juridique et économique du Sud-Ouest, série juridique. Congrès commémoratif du centenaire du Doyen Léon Duguit*, 10 (159), Nos 3–4.

[19] Marcel Laborde-Lacoste (1890–1978), professor of private law at the University of Bordeaux.

[20] Dieter Grimm, "Une lecture allemande de Léon Duguit" (2016) *Revue du doit public* 185.

CW: Coing suggested the topic and also graded the dissertation?

DG: Coing first gave the work to his deputy, Walter Wilhelm,[21] to get his impressions of it. Wilhelm was well acquainted with French legal scholarship of the nineteenth and early twentieth century. Unbeknownst to me, the dissertation then sat on Wilhelm's desk. A year passed before I decided to ask Coing if he had had a chance to look at my dissertation. He was visibly mortified, retrieved the text from Wilhelm, and reviewed and graded it within a very short time.

CW: In effect you presented him with a completed work. Did you discuss it with him at all beforehand?

DG: No, and he didn't expect me to either. I told him only that I had expanded the topic beyond the notion of subjective right. The dissertation was supposed to be published by the Athenäum publishing house, with which I had ties. They even had an appropriate series: "Studies and Texts on the Theory and Methodology of Law," edited by Josef Esser.[22] Esser liked the book, as he informed me in a detailed letter. But I didn't like the outward aspect of the series. The volumes were yellow and black, but the black soon faded into a dark brown, giving the books the appearance of chocolate pudding with vanilla sauce. Only one volume departed (to its advantage) from this format, and that was the volume published by Esser himself: *Prior Understanding and Choice of Method*.[23] That volume was black and orange. I asked the publisher to produce my volume too in orange rather than yellow. But he said no. It was, after all, a series. There was little to be said in response. My only argument was the exception made for Esser, but I wasn't Esser. So I choked down my chocolate pudding. When the book came out, however, it was orange.[24]

OL: Coing and Villey were both students of natural law, so they surely got on well.[25] Natural law, of course, was one possible basis for a European

[21] Walter Wilhelm (1928–2002), legal historian; director of the Max Planck Institute for European Legal History (1980–1987); honorary professor at the University of Frankfurt am Main.

[22] Josef Esser (1910–1999), professor of private law at the universities of Greifswald, Innsbruck, Mainz, and Tübingen.

[23] Josef Esser, *Vorverständnis und Methodenwahl in der Rechtsfindung* (1970).

[24] Dieter Grimm, *Solidarität als Rechtsprinzip: Die Rechts- und Staatslehre Léon Duguits in ihrer Zeit* (1973).

[25] Michel Villey (cf. fn. 7), for example, reviewed Coing's *Grundzüge der Rechtsphilosophie* (1950). Villey celebrated the book as an emblem of the overcoming of relativism, skepticism, and nihilism, but found fault with an extreme individualism "rooted in the Protestant tradition" and opined that the book contained nothing truly novel. He would, however, recommend the book for students as an introduction to political philosophy. The review is published in Michel Villey, *Leçons d'histoire de la philosophie du droit* (1960, reprint 2002) 304––10.

understanding. Did it play a role for you? Did you think of it in that sense? Natural law as an opportunity for a re-founding of Europe?

DG: I don't believe that at the time I connected European integration with natural law. But I did realize during the earlier phases of my studies—which, after all, weren't that far removed from the collapse of the Nazi regime—that a legal order requires ethical foundations. I grew up as a jurist in the conviction of positivism's inadequacy and of its role in the legal order's perversion. But that wasn't the same as a conversion to natural law. I was aware of the ambiguity of "natural law" thanks to Erik Wolf's course in Freiburg and his book *The Problem of Natural Law Doctrine*,[26] in which he elaborated nine concepts of nature and nine concepts of law, resulting in eighty-one possible combinations. I also found that essential propositions of natural law had already found expression in the Basic Law, making resort to natural law redundant for solving acute legal problems. When the Max Planck Institute was founded, Coing also looked more to the *ius commune*[27] than to natural law as a starting point for a new harmonization of private law after its fragmentation at the hands of the nation state.[28]

CW: After your studies in France you first returned to Hesse. Can you tell us something about your legal traineeship days?

DG: I began my *Referendariat* (legal traineeship) in the fall of 1963 at the Hofgeismar District Court in the Kassel administrative district. It wasn't a bad introduction to legal practice. The court consisted of one senior circuit judge and two other judges. The older of the two was an irascible type, much feared in the courtroom. This was ascribed to his War injuries, and everyone tried as much as possible to limit him to cases of non-contentious jurisdiction.[29] The younger one has remained in memory thanks to a bit of wisdom he once shared with me. At the end of a long conversation he asked, "Are you married?"

"No," I said.

"Good!" he replied.

"Why's that?" I asked.

[26] Erik Wolf, *Das Problem der Naturrechtslehre: Versuch einer Orientierung* (2d ed. 1959).

[27] The *ius commune* is based on Roman law as it was rediscovered in Iustinian's Digests. From the twelfth until the in the nineteenth century, it was the basis of legal thought in Western Europe.

[28] Cf. Chapter IV, fn. 10.

[29] This refers to the "Freiwillige Gerichtsbarkeit" which is a civil court procedure that does not fall under the scope of the general Code of Civil Procedure. In this form of procedure, the judge takes a more active role in investigating and solving the case. It is mostly used for family law disputes.

"Look at me," he responded. "I used to have big plans. Then I married early and had kids. Now I'm a first instance judge in Hofgeismar. You might someday make something of yourself. Don't blow it with an early marriage."

The next day he called me over to him again and said, "I've thought it over. You'll probably amount to something. Then you'll only get married because of your position. Now you can still marry for love."

I remember the senior circuit judge, Freiherr von Schlotheim, as an exemplary judge—punctilious, but not rigid or aloof as punctilious people sometimes are. Instead he was a man of broad sympathies (he was also engaged ecclesiastically as chairman of the Synod of the Lutheran Church in Kurhessen-Waldeck) who conducted court proceedings with dignity, treated the participants with respect, and had a sense for language and style. Once during a break between hearings a legal trainee pulled out some buttered toast and started chomping away. The judge expressed his disapproval with the sentence, "*Herr* Colleague, I haven't had breakfast yet either." Mistaking his meaning, the legal trainee asked, "Would you like some of mine?"

I remember two characteristic episodes best of all. In a criminal traffic case, he justified his guilty verdict by saying that the defendant had driven too fast into a left turn and encountered oncoming traffic as a result. The judge was not a driver himself. I was to draft the judgment, and I told him that if you go speeding into a left turn, you don't go into oncoming traffic, you go off the road on the other side. He couldn't dispute that, and told me, "I've already announced the judgment. We can't change it. But when you draft the decision make the mistake obvious so that the defendant can appeal it."

In another case, a lawyer presented a power of attorney that I thought invalid. It did come from the party, but it applied to a previous case. In different handwriting, someone had added, "and also for case X." I rushed in to the senior judge in great agitation. He looked at the power of attorney and then said, "You're probably right. But it's not a sure thing. Now look: we have four attorneys in the district. We've known them for a long time. They do their best, and they're not frauds. The lawyer has represented the client many times. He's in America and now this case comes along. Deadlines are looming, and it can take weeks to process the new power of attorney. I say we overlook it."

I next went to the Kassel regional court. There I was told that I was their first legal trainee in twenty years to have received a "Good" on the state exam.[30] This led the court's president, on my second day at work, to

30 "Good" grades are very rare in German legal exams.

assign me to a new mentor—an experienced regional court judge instead of a young judge. Of the regional court president, I have little good to say. Perhaps my experience is not untypical of the time. He had a long chamber with two doors, one right next to his desk and the other at the far end of the room. Visitors entered through the far door. When I went to introduce myself, he stood up as soon as I entered and extended his hand toward me across his desk. I quickened my step to reach his desk and shake his hand. In that instant, he pulled his hand back. "Do you not know," he said, "that one doesn't greet the *Herr* Regional Court President across his desk?"

"You were standing there with your hand extended," I shot back, "and I didn't want to leave you waiting."

A couple of days later I was in the elevator when he entered. "Do you not know," he immediately began, "that one takes one's hand out of one's pocket when the *Herr* Regional Court President enters the elevator?"

I said that I thought I was there for a *legal* traineeship. Something similar had happened to me earlier when I fulfilled my court-based practice requirement as a university student. I was to introduce myself to a judge, but his door was closed, so I waited. Someone came down the hall and asked for whom I was waiting.

"I'm waiting for *Herr* Wagener," I said.

"No," came the reply, "you are certainly not waiting for *Herr* Wagener. At best you are waiting for *Herr* Regional Court Judge Dr. Wagener."

OL: You then interrupted your legal traineeship to go to Harvard. So you needed to go to America too?

DG: From the outset, I didn't want to limit my foreign studies to France. America was the preeminent power in the Western world, its universities were reputed to be excellent, and I thought I would benefit from getting to know an entirely different legal order—the common law system. So I applied to the four universities which, from all that I had heard or learned, were the best: Harvard, Yale, Columbia, and Berkeley.

OL: What tilted the balance in favor of Harvard?

DG: Its fame. I received acceptances from all four schools and chose the one that enjoyed the greatest prestige. But I did drive a few times from Cambridge to New Haven. A theater scholar whom I met on the ship ride over was studying there. I got the impression that, in light of my interdisciplinary interests, Yale wouldn't have been a bad place for me either. But that shouldn't be viewed as retrospective regret that I chose Harvard.

OL: At Yale they train you to be a politician, at Harvard to be a corporate lawyer . . .

DG: . . . and at Yale they also train you to be a professor.

CW: Didn't Karl Carstens[31] also go to Yale very early on?

DG: Carstens was there shortly after the War. Gerhard Casper[32] was there, Fritz Scharpf[33] was there, and so was my future colleague on the Federal Constitutional Court, Helga Seibert.[34]

OL: What were your impressions of American universities?

DG: I hadn't experienced anything like Harvard, either in Germany or in France. This was true in many respects, beginning with its exterior: a university that filled an entire city district and that featured a stadium, multiple museums, a radio station, newspapers, and its own police. But it was more than that. Harvard gave me for the first time the feeling that students were worth something and that professors cared about them. The professors were accessible. They usually worked with an open door, which signaled that you were allowed to come in. For the first time I also felt challenged. You had to prepare for every lecture with extensive reading. In the lecture hall you had an assigned seat. The professors came with seating charts and they called on you. For the exams that followed every course there was a point scale (today things are different) that theoretically ran from 0 to 100, but in practice most scores fell between 65 and 85. Failing grades were all but unheard of, but your scores mattered. On them depended whether you could join Law Review, what jobs would be open to you, and what your starting salary would be. I was interested to see how I would do in an environment in which all my German merits counted for nothing and in which everyone was decidedly ambitious to achieve. I didn't do too badly.

OL: Were there figures in America that particularly impressed you or from whom you took a lot of classes?

DG: At Harvard, I had the best teachers of all my student years. In my first semester there was a required course for all LLM students from civil law

[31] Karl Carstens (1914–1992), professor of public and international law at the University of Cologne; politician (CDU); *Staatssekretär* at the defense department and at the office of the chancellor (1966–1969), member of the Bundestag (1972–1979); head of the CDU/CSU-parliamentary group in the Bundestag (1973–1976); president of the Bundestag (1976–1979); president of the Federal Republic of Germany (1979–1984).

[32] Gerhard Casper (1937–present), German-American jurist; professor and university administrator; professor at the University of Chicago; president of Stanford University (1992–2000); member of the Order "Pour le Mérite".

[33] Fritz W. Scharpf (1935–present), jurist and political scientist; assistant professor of law at Yale and Chicago (1964–1966); professor of political science at the University of Constance; at the Berlin Social Science Center (*Wissenschaftszentrum Berlin*) (1973–1986); director of the Max Planck Institute for the study of society in Cologne (1986–2003).

[34] Helga Seibert (1939–1999), ministerial official; judge on the Federal Constitutional Court (1989–1998).

countries called "Introduction to American Law" that met each morning before the other classes began. It was taught by John P. Dawson,[35] a passionate and warm-hearted teacher who was exceptionally qualified to teach such a class as a comparatist with a deep knowledge of the German, French, and Italian legal systems. His most important book, *The Oracles of the Law*,[36] was admired in Europe as well as in the United States. Later, when I had long since returned to Frankfurt, he received an honorary doctorate there. When the topic was something other than private law, Dawson invited the law school's other luminaries to come to the class, so we got a good overview of the faculty. The course had the side effect that the European students—rounded out by a few students from South America and Japan—came to know and understand one another like a high school class. There is still an annual meeting of this group. In 2015, the fiftieth anniversary of our graduation, the meeting was held for the first time in Cambridge rather than Europe.

The next teacher whom I remember fondly is Paul Freund,[37] the doyen among constitutionalists and a supremely cultivated and well-read man. Freund was a "University Professor"—a title conferred on a very small number of notables and which authorized them to teach in any department on campus. He often entered the classroom with a stack of books, which he usually left on the table unopened. We studied the great landmark cases of the US Supreme Court, analyzed the reasoning, learned something of the context in which they should be understood, and got to know the most influential justices.

The most brilliant lecturer of all, however, was Al Sacks in "Legal Process."[38]

OL: I was about to ask if you encountered the Legal Process School.

DG: The class was a Harvard specialty, invented and constantly refined by Sacks and Henry Hart.[39] The materials were available only in mimeographed copies. There were two large binders that you had to work through. The two authors, who took turns teaching the course, were constantly asked to turn the materials into a textbook. They even signed a contract with a

[35] John P. Dawson (1902–1985), professor at the University of Michigan and at Harvard Law School.

[36] John P. Dawson, *The Oracles of the Law* (1968).

[37] Paul A. Freund (1908–1992), constitutionalist; professor at Harvard Law School.

[38] Albert Sacks (1920–1991), professor at Harvard Law School, where he was dean from 1971 to 1981.

[39] Henry Hart (1904–1969) and Albert Sacks (1920–1991) taught a legendary class called "The Legal Process." The course materials circulated across the US in mimeographed copies for decades. They were posthumously edited and published in 1994 by William Eskridge and Philip Frickey. Other members of the "Legal Process School" included Herbert Wechsler and Lon Fuller, and its protégés included Alexander Bickel and John H. Ely. Cf. Neil Duxbury, *Patterns of American Jurisprudence* (1995) 251–66.

publisher in 1956, but they never submitted the manuscript. They never thought the work was finished. When it finally came out posthumously in 1994, I secured a copy right away.

The course dealt with the functions of law, the processes through which it is created and applied, the actors—both public and private—who play a role in those processes, the role of institutions, and legal reasoning. You got a sense of the framework within which the legal processes that you studied in other classes unfold—the case law and the statutory law. Sacks lectured brilliantly and was incredibly swift and trenchant in his responses to student comments. At the time I didn't know exactly what "the legal process" was directed against or what specific place it filled in American legal education. But I knew that something like it had been missing from my German education. "If I ever become a professor," I thought, "I would like to teach a similar class." (Something of the sort came about later on in the general section of the *Funkkolleg*,[40] for which I was responsible alongside the public law section, and in my course "Introduction to Legal Science" at Bielefeld.)

The approach to American law stood in sharp contrast to the Continental approach. Individual cases were the object of study. Great importance was attached to a precise understanding of the facts, which was important for "distinguishing." Did a judgment serve as precedent for a current problem or not? Treatment of cases in the exams was entirely different from what was expected in Germany. You didn't have to work out the right answer because there were no right answers. The point was to identify the core problem in a case and to derive a solution from the possible precedents. I never heard anything about a "system." Once when the foreign students invited their host families to an event, I was asked to give the welcome address. I talked about differences between the US and our home countries. Among other things, I noted that, whereas we first learn a system and then proceed to exemplary cases, American students study cases without ever arriving at a system at all. In my view, it was easier to approach cases from the perspective of a system than vice versa. That impression was confirmed when I worked for a time at an American law firm after finishing my studies at Harvard. It was also clear that the guiding model of legal education was much more the lawyer than the judge. After all, American judges were usually drawn from the ranks of lawyers and changed roles only at an advanced

[40] The "Funkkolleg" is a public television program which serves educational purposes. It was founded in the 1960s, consisted of lectures, and was meant to give people at home the opportunity to receive additional education.

age. Most Americans thought it quite strange that in Germany one could become a judge already at the age of twenty-six.

I wrote my master's thesis on "European Natural Law and the American Revolution."[41] The topic was a product of my plan to combine legal philosophy and constitutional law. In fact, however, my time at Harvard marked my farewell to legal philosophy.

OL: What led to that realization?

DG: The course in legal philosophy that I took from Lon Fuller[42] played a part. I got the impression that the problems addressed in legal philosophy were too far removed from the political and social questions that arose in constitutional law and in private law as well. The class on political theory that I took outside the law school with Louis Hartz[43] came much closer to my interests. There were already some indications that history would assume the role that philosophy was supposed to play, but I became aware of that only later on.

CW: You surely had a scholarship of some sort?

DG: A scholarship from the *Cusanuswerk*. My parents were not in a position to pay for my tuition or my travel and living expenses.

CW: How many Germans were there in your LLM class?

DG: There were three of us. One became a notary in Bavaria[44] and the other joined the financial administration after a short stint with the law firm Gleiss Lutz. From that group of LLM students, however, several became professors. Two classmates became president of their countries' supreme courts. For the South Americans, a meteoric rise was almost a sure thing. One classmate, who didn't graduate, later became president of the UN General Assembly. Another became his country's ambassador to West Germany.

MATTHIAS ROSSBACH: In retrospect, what significance did your time in the US have for your life?

DG: I ascribe great importance to my year at Harvard—or rather, to my year and a half in the United States. It was a time of increasing self-awareness and self-assurance—a time of better understanding the familiar by light of the foreign, a season brimming with new impressions.

[41] Cf. fn. 16 above.

[42] Lon Fuller (1902–1978), legal philosopher, natural lawyer, and critic of legal positivism; professor at Harvard Law School.

[43] Louis Hartz (1919–1986), professor at Harvard University and author of *The Liberal Tradition in America* (1955).

[44] In contrast to the United States, a notary in Germany is a fully qualified lawyer who has the special permission to perform official acts. Becoming a notary in Bavaria is extremely competitive.

I haven't said anything yet about the US as a country. Nineteen sixty-four was an election year, Johnson versus Goldwater, so politics had an enhanced presence. It was a year that won me over to America, though I never abandoned a certain critical distance. This was true in legal matters as well. I was later accused by critics of the Constitutional Court's freedom of expression jurisprudence of having been Americanized and of wanting to introduce American relations in Germany. But that was particularly wrongheaded when it came to freedom of expression. *New York Times v. Sullivan*,[45] decided during my studies at Harvard, contains some wonderful lines about the importance of free speech and a free press, but I did not accept its conclusions. By the end of my stay in America, I knew that if I were ever forced to emigrate, I would go there. But absent such compulsion, I would rather remain in Germany. At the end of my stay in America, when I was working for a law firm, this insight gained real-life importance.

MR: Why did you end up working at a law firm after your LLM year?

DG: For various reasons, leaving the US was hard for me. Some of my European classmates were applying to work for a while at American law firms. They would later become partners in those firms' European offices. I asked my American friends which was the best law firm in Boston. The answer was unanimous: Ropes & Gray.[46] So I made my way over to Ropes & Gray and rang the bell. I told the receptionist that I was about to earn an LLM at Harvard and now wanted to work at Ropes & Gray for a while. I could tell she wasn't prepared for such a request. But she asked me to take a seat and presently returned with a gentleman who introduced himself as Maxwell, the office manager. Obviously, my request was unprecedented for him as well. He referred me back to the chair in which I had waited before, and returned shortly with the news that, "Mister Quarrels wants to meet you." When I asked who that was, he answered, "One of the senior partners."

Mr. Quarrels was a tall, elegant man who let me have my say. After a while he asked, "And how am I to know that what you say is true?" I was a little irritated and said that he could either trust me or not trust me. He shook his head and said, "You mistake me. I only want to know whom I can call at Harvard to ask about you." I named a couple of my professors, and

[45] The Supreme Court's decision in *New York Times v. Sullivan*, 376 U.S. 254 (1964), is a First Amendment landmark. It held that a public official could successfully sue a newspaper for defamation only upon showing that the paper had acted with "actual malice." Debate on public affairs, the Court wrote, must be "uninhibited, robust, and wide-open."

[46] Ropes & Gray is a Boston law firm founded by two Harvard alumni in 1865. It now has many offices in the US, Europe, and Asia.

he asked me to wait for a moment in the hallway. He soon emerged, however, and announced, "You are hired. When would you like to start?" When I related my success to my American friends that evening, I could tell from their total disbelief with what naiveté I had plunged ahead.

At the time, Ropes & Gray had seventy lawyers. (Later, when I visited the firm as a constitutional judge, there were seven hundred.) I worked with several lawyers on their cases. Above all, I admired their teamwork—almost always with the involvement of a tax lawyer. I looked forward to the weekly firm lunches, at which one lawyer always presented a problem he was working on and asked the others for comments. I got along well with my work, which was confirmed when Ropes & Gray made me a permanent offer. They wanted to give me a couple months' paid leave to study for the bar exam before bringing me on full time.

This was another crossroads. I would have liked to stay a while longer at Ropes & Gray, but I didn't want to be in the US long term. And since I hadn't yet passed the second state exam in Germany, accepting the firm's offer would have entailed a definitive choice to remain in America. So I returned to Germany toward the end of 1965, now considering that I might become a practicing lawyer if I could find a firm in Germany with a similar model of work.

CW: What happened to this idea of becoming a practicing attorney?

DG: I did a part of my legal traineeship[47] with the law firm of Mueller, Weitzel & Weisner in Frankfurt (now the Frankfurt office of Hengeler, Mueller), a firm with a similar working model to Ropes & Gray, though on a much smaller scale. There were only the three named partners and two younger attorneys. Mueller, Weitzel & Weisner would also have liked to hire me long term after my second state exam, but by then the possibility of an academic career had begun to take shape. I hadn't ruled out the possibility of a job in the civil service, but I hadn't pursued one either. I turned down an offer from Bernhard Vogel,[48] then the minister of culture in Rheinland-Pfalz, which came about through my aforementioned friend, Peter Haungs, who for his part had been with Vogel at the professorial chair of Dolf Sternberger[49] in Heidelberg.

MR: Did you return to Harvard later on?

[47] Cf. Chapter II, fn. 58.

[48] Bernhard Vogel (1932–present), politician and minister; minister president of Rheinland-Pfalz (1976–1988); minister president of Thüringen (1992–2003).

[49] Dolf Sternberger (1907–1989), professor of political science at the University of Heidelberg.

DG: In the following year, 1966, I again spent four weeks in the US. There was to be a *Festschrift* for Carlo Schmid, and Otwin Massing, my fellow *Cusanuswerk* scholar who was involved in the preparations, asked if I would be willing to contribute an article on the Legislative Reference Service of the US Congress. The Friedrich-Ebert-Stiftung[50] would cover the costs of a trip to Washington. After that, it was more than twenty years before I returned.

During this period, however, I had a recurring dream: I was a student at Harvard again, on my way to class, when I noticed I was wearing mismatched socks. By the time I found the match and hurriedly put it on, a lot of time had passed. When I reached the classroom, the lecture was over. Sometimes I was a professor at Harvard and realized on my way to class that I had forgotten my lecture notes. The same result: by the time I found them, the students had lost patience and left the hall. I interpret the dream as one of nostalgic yearning, of *Sehnsucht*. After my next visit to Harvard, it never recurred. But I can't deny the exultant feeling that came, even many years later, when I was given a guest professorship at this university that had played such a huge role in my life. Frank Michelman,[51] who was already a very young professor during my student days at Harvard, has become an important conversation partner. We had become close even before my guest professorship, since we were both engaged with the period of transformation in South Africa.

[50] The Friedrich-Ebert-Stiftung is a foundation that promotes political education and particularly gifted students. It is associated with the Social Democratic Party of Germany.

[51] Frank Michelman (1936–present), professor at the Harvard Law School.

# IV.
# Max Planck Institute and *Habilitation*

OL: After your time in the US, you finished your traineeship and then went to work for Coing at the Max Planck Institute, right?

DG: When I returned from Harvard, I went to the Institute as a part-time assistant (alongside my trainee duties) and then, after the second state exam, as a full-time researcher. When my time at Harvard was nearing its end, I wrote to Coing from America, announced my imminent return, and asked for a position as assistant at his chair in the university. He answered that he had something even better. He was just then founding the Max Planck Institute for legal history: "You're welcome there, if you'd like."

OL: So, you were one of the first crop of researchers at the Max Planck Institute in Frankfurt?

DG: One of the first crop, if you count my time as a part-time assistant.

OL: And you worked there on the public law side of things?

DG: Together with Heinz Mohnhaupt.[1] He had already completed his doctorate and arrived the same day that I took up my position as a part-time assistant. Mohnhaupt focused mainly on the early modern period, whereas I concentrated on the nineteenth century. Coing was the sole director. He was followed by Dieter Simon[2] and Coing's deputy, Walter Wilhelm, a man of great gifts who wrote a brilliant dissertation but was never able to surpass it later on.[3] He was well regarded in the Institute and a popular conversation partner. He helped many people with their work, introducing them to new ideas and so forth. Unfortunately, however, he himself published practically nothing. Simon really valued him and wanted him as co-director. Simon got what he wanted, but it soon became clear that, in the end, Simon was the

[1] Heinz Mohnhaupt (1935–present), legal historian at the Max Planck Institute for European Legal History.

[2] Dieter Simon (1935–present), professor of private law and Roman law at the University of Frankfurt am Main; director of the Max Planck Institute for European Legal History in Frankfurt (1980–2003); chair of the Scientific Council (1989–1992); president of the Berlin-Brandenburg Academy of Sciences (1995–2005).

[3] Walter Wilhelm, *Zur juristischen Methodenlehre im 19. Jahrhundert: Die Herkunft der Methode Paul Labands aus der Privatwissenschaft* (1958).

*Dieter Grimm: Advocate of the Constitution.* Dieter Grimm, Oxford University Press (2020). 
DOI: 10.1093/oso/9780198845270.001.0001

only director. Wilhelm then retired early for health reasons, and Michael Stolleis took his place.[4]

OL: You spent 1968 at the Max Planck Institute, then.

DG: Frankfurt was a center of the student movement, and the MPI was near the university—in the West End of Frankfurt, which was an especially frequent site of demonstrations because property moguls were threatening to destroy the largely intact residential area. You simply couldn't avoid the protesting students. You encountered them in demonstrations, "happenings," sit-ins, banners ("Embrace Academic Freedom—Research What You Like!" hung for a long time on one university building), and classroom walls, which were transformed into protest or announcement boards ("Demonstration today at 4 o'clock—Come *En Masse*!"—no one could tell which day that referred to, but that hardly mattered; it applied to almost every day). One had to position oneself with respect to all of this. I nurtured some sympathy for the initial demands (both the academic and the societal ones), rather less for the forms and means through which they were pursued, although there were some witty ones.

MR: Did your sympathy for the academic and societal demands ever lead you to take part personally in any of the protests?

DG: I personally took part in two follow-up actions, which took up the student demands for transparency and codetermination. One took place in the *Cusanuswerk*,[5] the other in the Max Planck Society.

Things had been festering at the *Cusanuswerk* since the death of Benno Ohnesorg[6] at the anti-Shah demonstrations in 1967. Multiple *Cusanus* groups demanded influence in the choice of scholarship students and in the *Cusanuswerk*'s educational program. By then, I hadn't been a student for a long time, but I still played some role in the *Cusanuswerk*, especially as alumni representative. I was asked to conduct the general meeting of *Cusanus* students at the 1968 annual gathering, at which reforms were to be discussed and decisions made. I was able to guide the rather muddled clamor of the students into the paths of well-justified demands for reform, and at the same time to persuade the reluctant *Cusanuswerk* leadership to consider those demands. As a result, I was placed at the head of

[4] Michael Stolleis (1941–present), professor of public law and legal history at the University of Frankfurt am Main; director of the Max Planck Institute for European Legal History (1991–2009); member of the Order "Pour le Mérite".

[5] Cf. Chapter I, fn. 3.

[6] Benno Ohnesorg (1940–1967), West Berlin student shot by police during a demonstration against the Shah's visit to Berlin. His death helped radicalize the student movement.

the reform commission that within six months produced an "Order of the *Cusanuswerk*" that was implemented by the German Bishops' Conference and still remains in force. The core was a pluralist advisory council with student participation. The Council would be responsible for establishing selection criteria and developing guidelines for the *Cusanuswerk*'s scholarship policy and education program, and it would take part in the appointment of its leader. I was then chosen as the advisory council's first chair. Hans Tietmeyer, no friend of innovations, became deputy chair. When Prelate Bernhard Hanssler,[7] the first head of the *Cusanuswerk*, unexpectedly resigned in 1969, there were even efforts to make me his successor. This confronted me with another difficult decision, which I tried to resolve with a compromise: leadership of the *Cusanuswerk* for a three-year transitional period, after which I would continue my scholarly career with appropriate financial compensation for the professional delay. The plan failed because the Association of German Dioceses wouldn't approve the financial outlays. I can't say that I was unhappy with this outcome.

There were contemporaneous rumblings in a number of Max Planck Institutes. The Max Planck Society was still governed by the so-called Harnack Principle: the preeminent scholar receives all necessary means to pursue his research aims. Among these means were the research assistants. Here too, however, there were demands for codetermination in the aftermath of 1968. Such demands were by no means uncontroversial in the Institutes. Even in the MPI for legal history the demands divided the researchers. There were pan-Institute actions. An assembly of delegates was formed from the ranks of scholarly assistants. There too, thanks to a certain knack for leading assemblies, I was placed at the head of the steering group. The group was to discuss their proposals with the president of the Max Planck Society. Here, as with the *Cusanuswerk*, a codetermination model was successfully adopted. It too is still practiced today.

But my engagement at the Max Planck Society, entirely unlike my engagement with the *Cusanuswerk*, nearly cost me my job. During the 1971 MPS general assembly in Berlin, we held a press conference. And because the press is always more interested in conflict than in harmony, our press conference attracted some attention. At the next Institute meeting in Frankfurt, Coing stood up and said that something outrageous had happened in Berlin. During the general assembly of the Max Planck Society, researchers

[7] Bernhard Hanssler (1907–2005), prelate; university chaplain in the diocese Rottenburg-Stuttgart; founder of the *Cusanuswerk*.

from some Max Planck Institutes had had the temerity to hold an anti-MPS press conference and, as he had learned, a researcher from his own Institute had been involved. "With this researcher," he said, "confidential collaboration is no longer possible." So, I prepared myself to be fired. Then I got a call from Hellmut Becker,[8] who at the time directed the Max Planck Institute for Education Research in Berlin and whom I did not know personally. Becker said that he had heard I might be getting the ax from Coing. "If it comes to that," he said, "you can start with me the next day." But it didn't come to that. Coing shunned personal confrontation. He only relieved me of my role as his personal assistant, but on the ground that I should have more time for my *Habilitation* thesis.

OL: Things were destined to go badly with Coing anyway: he was a private law scholar, you wanted to do public law. Besides, Coing was a devotee of natural law.[9]

DG: Coing was in fact a private law scholar. His specialty in contemporary law was inheritance law. The legal history he did was the history of private law, and his project at the MPI, in which multiple researchers were involved, was a "Handbook of Sources and Literature in the Modern History of European Private Law."[10] It was to serve as the foundation for comparative research that would help restore legal unity in Europe. But Coing was open-minded enough to realize that the nascent constitutionalism would necessarily have repercussions for private law. My assignment at the Institute was to research those repercussions. Only much later, when Coing's memoirs were published in 2014,[11] did I learn that he had initially flirted with public law, but that he didn't want to surrender himself to the public law of National Socialism.

Deeper than our topical differences, however, was our difference in method. Legal history was not unaffected by the historiographical turn toward *Gesellschaftsgeschichte*—the history of society conceived not as a topical history such as military history or economic history, but as a historical method in which historical developments are comprehended and construed in light of the societal structures and processes in which they

[8] Hellmut Becker (1913–1993), jurist and scholar of education; founder and director of the Max Planck Institute for Education Research in Berlin; son of the orientalist and Prussian minister of culture, C.H. Becker.

[9] Cf. Lena Foljanty, *Recht oder Gesetz: Juristische Identität und Autorität in den Naturrechtsdebatten der Nachkriegszeit* (2013) 175–87.

[10] Helmut Coing (ed.), *Handbuch der Quellen und Literatur der neueren europäischen Privatrechtsgeschichte* (6 vols) (1973–1988).

[11] Helmut Coing, *Für Wissenschaft und Künste: Lebensbericht eines europäischen Rechtsgelehrten* (Michael Feldkampf ed., 2014).

are embedded. Discussions arose in the Frankfurt MPI between those who held fast to the traditional understanding of legal history as an internal and decontextualized history of legal ideas and doctrines, and those who maintained that legal phenomena and developments can only be adequately understood through a contextualized approach. The dividing line was similar to the one in the reform discussion between the champions of the Harnack Principle and the advocates of codetermination. Here, too, I was unequivocally on the side of social history. When the journal *Geschichte und Gesellschaft* was founded by Bielefeld historians in opposition to the *Historische Zeitschrift*,[12] I wrote to Hans-Ulrich Wehler[13] that law was an important determinant of historical development to which a historiography attuned to social history must attend, and that therefore law, too, should have a place in the journal's conception (and perhaps a representative on its editorial board). At the time I received no answer. Wehler himself largely ignored law in his efforts to write a history of the whole of society—something for which I later reproached him during a 1996 colloquium at the Center for Interdisciplinary Studies in Bielefeld on the occasion of his sixty-fifth birthday.[14] By then, we knew each other well. Wehler reacted in a characteristically honorable way in the foreword to the fourth volume of his *German Social History*.[15] He acknowledged that the criticism was justified, but that he didn't feel competent to address the legal aspects of the history of society.

MR: As a contribution to the methodological debates and perhaps as a product of the discussions at the MPI, you wrote an essay on "Method as a Power Factor,"[16] which appeared after the end of your Frankfurt years. What sort of reactions did it elicit? There, too, you begin with private law methods and then move into public law.

DG: The essay appeared in the *Festschrift* for Coing's seventieth birthday in 1982. I can't recall that it provoked any reactions at the time. Only recently has it been cited often. At the time of its appearance, all was quiet.

[12] The *Historische Zeitschrift* was founded in 1859 by Heinrich von Sybel and covers all periods of history. The journal *Geschichte und Gesellschaft. Zeitschrift für Historische Sozialwissenschaft* (History and Society. Journal for historical social research) was founded in 1975 by the Bielefeld school. In contrast to the *Historische Zeitschrift*, it focuses on modern times and the relationship to social science.

[13] Hans-Ulrich Wehler (1931–2014), professor of general history with special attention to the nineteenth and twentieth centuries at the University of Bielefeld.

[14] Dieter Grimm, "Die Bedeutung des Rechts in der Gesellschaftsgeschichte: Eine Anfrage" in P. Nolte et al. (eds), *Perspektiven der Gesellschaftsgeschichte* (2000) 47–57.

[15] Hans-Ulrich Wehler, *Deutsche Gesellschaftsgeschichte: Vom Beginn des Ersten Weltkriegs bis zur Gründung der beiden deutschen Staaten, 1914–1949* (vol. 4, 2003).

[16] Dieter Grimm, "Methode als Machtfaktor" in *Festschrift für Helmut Coing*, vol. 1 (1982) 469; reprinted in Dieter Grimm, *Recht und Staat der bürgerlichen Gesellschaft* (1987) 347.

CW: Because it could have been politically explosive as well . . .

OL: And for those familiar with your personal history with Coing, the title had a certain double meaning . . .

DG: That could be. But Coing's deputy, Walter Wilhelm, had already dealt with a similar topic in his dissertation—the origin of Laband's method in private law scholarship.[17]

MR: Discussions about method bring us to the problem of interdisciplinarity, which also occupied you during your time at the MPI.

DG: The push for interdisciplinarity was older than the '68 movement. It was linked to discussions about secondary and tertiary education reforms in the early 1960s. Nineteen sixty-eight gave it greater thrust. It was taken up in calls to reform legal education. Most plans to found new universities stated interdisciplinarity as an aim. I myself had been prepared for interdisciplinary work through my dual studies, and I tried to make it fruitful both for legal history and for public law. But the push was very controversial. Many saw it as an attempt to eradicate the autonomy of law and legal science and to place law and lawyers in the service of societal change and thereby endanger the rule of law itself. I didn't share this concern, though there were in fact such efforts. I addressed the topic in my inaugural lecture in Frankfurt.[18] It seemed to me that, on the contrary, interdisciplinarity expanded the relevance of law and legal science, both with regard to its compatibility with other disciplines as well as its capacity to solve new problems.

I also had a little side job during these years. The previously obscure Gehlen publishing house in Bad Homburg had a new director, Dietrich Pinkerneil, who had big plans—especially in the realm of legal science. Accordingly, he was looking for an advisor. He first asked Wolfgang Kilian,[19] who was then an assistant to the law faculty in Frankfurt, but Kilian didn't think he was up for it. Kilian told Pinkerneil that if anyone could do the job, I could. My task was to generate ideas for legal publications and to suggest appropriate authors. Pinkerneil soon found Gehlen too narrow, and he founded the Athenäum publishing house in Frankfurt. My work as an advisor gave me the chance to bring something into the publication plans myself. Together with Norbert Reich, I launched a series that would place a stronger accent on legal politics, which legal scholars had until then

[17] Cf. fn. 3 above.

[18] Dieter Grimm, "Reformalisierung des Rechtsstaats als Demokratiepostulat? " (1980) *Juristische Schulung* 704; reprinted in O. Eberl (ed.), *Transnationalisierung der Volkssouveränität* (2011) 19.

[19] Wolfgang Kilian (1939–present), professor of civil law and information law at the University of Hannover.

neglected. There were interdisciplinary discussions of important legislative proposals, such as the marriage law reform, the LLC reform, etc.

My own project, however—a project of special importance to me—was "Legal Science and Neighboring Disciplines." My aim was to dispel mistrust of interdisciplinarity and to show that (and how) interdisciplinarity could be practiced to benefit law. Each area of law was to be addressed by one jurist and one representative of a neighboring discipline. I myself wrote the essays on "Constitutional Doctrine and Political Science" with Kurt Sontheimer as coauthor and "Legal Science and History" with Hans Fenske[20] as coauthor. After a long and difficult preparatory period, the first volume appeared with the Athenäum Press in 1973. When the second volume was finished, so was the Athenäum Press, which had gone bankrupt. C.H. Beck then took over the project and published both volumes in 1976 as part of the so-called "Black Series." I made a name for myself with this project. There was a lot of talk about "Legal Science and Neighboring Disciplines."

MR: At the MPI, then, you had time for projects of your own alongside your duties at the Institute?

DG: Yes, though it was never explicitly arranged that way. But Coing, who was himself an extraordinarily disciplined worker, was never one to goad others. There prevailed a certain leisureliness—though not in the sense of lazing about; with the exception of one or two mistaken appointments, all the researchers were thoroughly ambitious. But the *Handbook* project dragged on and on. The researchers' contributions grew longer and longer. The many chapters that had been assigned to foreign scholars arrived haltingly. That left a lot of discretion for disposing of one's own time.

In the end, I stayed too long at the Institute, and that was related to this situation. As a short-term goal, I aimed only at my doctorate. But that was taken care of shortly before the end of the summer semester in 1971. Ilse Staff,[21] the first female member of the Association of Public Law professors, Jaenicke, and Coing were conducting the oral exams for a group of doctoral candidates. I remember the exam with Ilse Staff because we talked about Ernst Forsthoff's recently published book *The State of the Industrial Society*. Forsthoff was a kind of favorite opponent in my early writings.[22]

[20] Hans Fenske (1936–present), professor of modern and contemporary history at the University of Freiburg im Breisgau.

[21] Ilse Staff (1928–2017), professor of public law at the University of Frankfurt.

[22] Ernst Forsthoff, *Der Staat der Industriegesellschaft* (1971). Ernst Forsthoff (1902–1974), professor of public law at the universities of Frankfurt am Main, Hamburg, Königsberg, Vienna, and Heidelberg.

I now needed to make a career choice. My father's most fervent wish was for me to continue the family tradition by going to the railroad. I would have been a counselor for the National Railway and perhaps one day even the president of one of its regional headquarters. But this time I had already decided on an academic career, though without being able to say precisely when this decision matured. My father even played his final trump card in vain. He had hoped to tempt me with a lifetime first-class rail pass, to which every higher-ranking official in the railway administration was entitled. It was satisfying to be able to present him with such a pass after I had been appointed as a constitutional judge. So I stayed at the Institute, now with the goal of writing my *Habilitation* thesis, but that also took longer than planned. I let the *Habilitation* thesis straggle a bit because I assumed that it would be abolished as a requirement for an academic appointment.

On the other hand, I owe a lot to the long period spent at the MPI—not only friendships that endure to this day, such as with Heinz Mohnhaupt and Klaus Luig,[23] but also the leisure to do more than work in a task-oriented way and to be able to establish a relatively broad foundation of knowledge. I should also mention the many international contacts that the MPI made possible. It was not only that the Institute's general orientation was an international one, that many foreign scholars visited it, and that it had a prestigious international advisory council. It was also that legal history as a discipline—particularly its Romanist branch—was much more open at the time than was public law. There were many interesting international conferences. It was at the world conference of comparative law in Pescara in 1970—which also had a legal history section, though I presented in the constitutional law division—that I met my wife,[24] who was an assistant at the Institute for Civil Procedure in Vienna. We were married in 1972 in the hope that soon after my *Habilitation* thesis we would end up at the same university.

OL: What was your *Habilitation* thesis about?

DG: I tried as much as possible to synergize my MPI assignment and my *Habilitation* thesis. At the MPI, I was to write a piece on "Constitution and Private Law" for the previously mentioned *Handbook of Sources and Literature*.[25] With Coing's approval, I made this the theme of my *Habilitation* thesis as well. But the choice of topic was by no means merely

[23] Klaus Luig (1935–2020), professor of legal history at the universities of Passau and Cologne.

[24] Ena-Marlis Bajons (1943–present), professor of civil procedure and comparative law at the University of Vienna and, after retirement, at the University of Trent.

[25] Cf. fn. 10 above.

a pragmatic one. I found the issue attractive. It was, to a certain extent, intradisciplinary, but because of the sharp divide between private law and public law, the question had rarely been raised. There was Leisner's 1960 *Habilitation* thesis on "Fundamental Rights and Private Law"[26] and a few writings on the boundary between private law and public law, whereas my interest lay precisely with their mutual interaction. My contribution to the *Handbook* and my *Habilitation* thesis were by no means the same, however. In the *Handbook*, I had to discuss all of Europe and the entire nineteenth century. It was more a reference work than an analytical one. I condensed the core question into a short introduction, which said, among other things: "Insofar as constitutions claim to be the normative foundation and limit of the entire activity of the state, toward which lawmaking especially must be oriented, they too provide a source for the history of private law. Through constitutions, private law acquires a new dimension. True, private law can never at any time be understood in isolation from social realities and ideas of political order. But constitutions introduce within the legal system itself a factor which, thanks to its status as higher law, exerts a formative influence on private law." Then follows a 150-page depiction of the development in various European states, together with a constitutional chronology for all European states, and forty pages of references. At the time, this was uncharted territory. Such a comparison didn't previously exist, nor had the relationship of constitutions and private law been addressed in the legal-historical literature.

My *Habilitation* thesis, by contrast, was devoted to the question that appeared only in the introduction to my *Handbook* article. I explored the question using France, Germany, and Austria as models, with occasional references to England and America for comparative purposes. My plan required extensive reading in primary sources. I read, for example, the complete constitutional debates of the French revolutionary period, as well as sources on the preparations for the codification of private law. I remember such reading in the sources—as tiring as it sometimes was—with pleasure. The aura of historical events wafts upon you as you follow the debates and as the actors take shape before your mind's eye. I limited my *Habilitation* thesis to the period from the origins of the constitutional state to the Restoration—that is, from 1776 to 1820. I planned a second volume on

[26] Walter Leisner, *Grundrechte und Privatrecht* (1960).

further nineteenth-century developments, but that fell by the wayside—which is why my *Habilitation* thesis was never published.[27]

OL: "Constitution and Private Law" is a broad field. Were you able to concentrate on specific subfields? Such as a stronger emphasis on contracts or torts?

DG: No. I was only interested in the fundamental relationship, and I looked to specialized areas of law only as examples within this framework. It was about the transformation of the legal order from a preexisting, material notion of the public good to a procedural concept of the public good resulting from societal self-regulation, and the related transformation, induced by the constitution, from a legal order of objective duties to one of subjective rights—from a preexisting ideal of virtue to private autonomy—and the associated reversal in the hierarchy between public and private law. The bourgeoisie conceived of its order from the perspective of private law: public law exists only to ensure private law. The constitution, though of a higher rank, holds this rank only for the better security of private law—something that I called "the constitution as private-law accessory."

In all of this, it had to be remembered of course that in Germany and Austria the constitutional state had emerged only reluctantly and in a reduced form. But a bourgeois private law emerged all the same—early on in Austria with the General Civil Code, in Germany more through individual reforms. This raised the question of whether, and to what extent, private law could assume the functions that in France fell to the constitution. France remains, however, the model of an entire renewal of the legal order culminating in a *Code Civil*.

CW: The *Code Civil* is a product of French constitutional change—the Revolution. But in the end, it is still the case that through the *Code Civil* the French revolutionary constitutions brought change to the French regions of Germany.

DG: It is interesting to observe how that comes about. Where German territories became French during the course of the Revolution, the *Code Civil* applied anyway, and the population defended it doggedly after the end of French rule. The introduction of a modern, bourgeois private law was expected by Napoleon in the states of the *Rheinbund*,[28] but only Baden adopted the

[27] But see Dieter Grimm, *Deutsche Verfassungsgeschichte, 1776–1866* (1988). For a concise summary, see also Dieter Grimm, "Grundrechte und Privatrecht in der bürgerlichen Sozialordnung" in G. Birtsch (ed.), *Grund- und Freiheitsrechte im Wandel der Gesellschaft und Geschichte* (1981) 359--75; reprinted in Dieter Grimm, *Recht und Staat der bürgerlichen Gesellschaft* (1987) 192–211.

[28] The *Rheinbund* was a confederation of German states that was formed under the protection of Napoleon in 1806 and fell apart after Napoleon's defeat at the Battle of Leipzig in 1813.

*Code Napoleon*, yet in a strange way. There the introduction of a modern, bourgeois statute book clashed with an only halfway-abolished feudal society. Thus, one finds in Baden's *Code Civil*, printed in small font, those provisions of Baden law that still applied even though they contradicted the code of private law. Austria took another path, receiving a modern codification of private law without Napoleonic pressure in 1811, but without having abolished the feudal system beforehand. Thus, the General Civil Code provided that it would only apply insofar as it didn't conflict with older law.[29] Accordingly, when it entered into force the General Civil Code was largely a promise for the future. It was only realized substantially later when the constitution of 1867 essentially overcame the remnants of the feudal system and established fundamental rights.

OL: The *Code Civil* is also a political law code because it implements ideas of equality and freedom through the means of private law. American private law is also political law because it supplies the central criteria of distribution and liability itself rather than relying on the constitution. By contrast, our German conception of private law produces an unpolitical law—the self-organization of society, represented by the *Bürgertum*—whereas public law must handle the entire unpleasant array of political matters. At the same time, everything that interferes with political affairs is deemed political and therefore classified under public law. This is not the case in either the French or the American or the British tradition. We always think that private law must be unpolitical. The more one looks abroad in a comparative way, the more skeptical one becomes of the perception that the German division of private and public, of unpolitical and political is inevitable. I find that today the German model is rather an outlier among Western legal systems.

DG: But when the *Bürgertum*'s conception of private law took root in Germany in the early nineteenth century, it was a political act to treat private law as unpolitical—and thus to distance private law from politics, which had not yet embraced liberalism. The calculation could succeed because private law scholars of the nineteenth century systematically ignored state law and systematized and elaborated the *ius commune* in a liberal way.

By the way: I have overcome my scruples and decided to publish my *Habilitation* thesis—exactly as it was completed in 1978, however.

[29] General Civil Code § 11: Statutes of individual provinces and regions have force of law only when explicitly affirmed by the territorial prince after the promulgation of this statute book.

OL: We look forward to the book.[30] How did your *Habilitation* defense go and what happened afterward?

DG: Because I wrote my *Habilitation* thesis at the MPI, it made sense—indeed, it had already been arranged—that Coing would be the first reviewer. When I gave him the manuscript, he said, "You want to be a professor of public law. Doesn't it make more sense, then, to have our young colleague, Stolleis, who is a public lawyer, write the first review and for me to take care of the second?" The argument was considerately packaged, but I'm quite sure that he didn't want to be associated with me. Stolleis wrote the first review. To this day, I haven't seen Coing's second review. He excused himself from the *Habilitation* defense, pleading that he had pressing engagements and observing that his teacher, Genzmer,[31] hadn't been present at his *Habilitation* defense either.

The defense took place in the middle of February 1979. Because I hadn't done much in the way of administrative law, it was clear that I would give a lecture on an administrative law topic. It was about the category of "affected party" in administrative law. I never published this lecture either, but this time not because I wanted to expand it, but because I didn't regard it as a masterpiece. It emerged under tremendous pressure, in which my application for a professorship in Bielefeld played a role. I was invited to give a job talk in Bielefeld just a few days before my *Habilitation* lecture in Frankfurt. When I responded that I was at work on my imminently impending *Habilitation* lecture, they said: "Do you want a job in Bielefeld or not?" My own impression was that this lecture was a success. It was later included as part of my article on political parties in the Benda-Maihofer-Vogel Handbook.[32] As soon as the Frankfurt faculty gave me the *venia legendi*[33] for the fields of German

[30] The book has since been published. Cf. Dieter Grimm, *Verfassung und Privatrecht im 19. Jahrhundert* (2017).

[31] Erich Genzmer (1893–1970), professor of legal history at the universities of Königsberg, Frankfurt am Main, and Hamburg.

[32] Dieter Grimm, "Politische Parteien" in Ernst Benda, Werner Maihofer, and Hans-Jochen Vogel (eds), *Handbuch des Verfassungsrechts der Bundesrepublik Deutschland* (2d ed. 1994) § 14 (pp. 599 et seq.).

[33] The *venia legendi* has traditionally been the authority to teach at university and has been conferred by the *Habilitation*. In recent times, new ways to obtain the authority to teach at university (similar to the tenure track model of American universities) have emerged.

and foreign public law, modern legal and constitutional history, and legal theory (to which was added, at the instigation of Kurt Shell,[34] a *venia legendi* for political science from the department of social sciences), I had to call Bielefeld. That same evening, they had made up their list there, and I was in the top slot.

[34] Kurt Shell (1920–2018) professor of political science at the University of Frankfurt am Main.

# V.
# Bielefeld

CW: Was the position you took in Bielefeld the one vacated by Böckenförde?

DG: Yes. Böckenförde had left Bielefeld in 1977. The first effort to replace him was unsuccessful. If I remember right, the faculty's first choice declined the offer, and no other offer was made because the faculty didn't really want the other candidates on the list. They preferred to wait for someone who was well established in the basic fields.

OL: Because the faculty already had an interdisciplinary orientation? After all, a normal law faculty always looks for the perfect colleague for the exercises in administrative law—and you were not yet such a colleague.

DG: Indeed, I was not. But neither was Böckenförde. In terms of contemporary law, constitutional law was in the forefront for both of us. Among the basic fields, we shared an interest in history, but we differed in our second field. For Böckenförde it was philosophy, for me it was political science—a more strongly empirical discipline.

That the faculty could afford to take up members with this inclination surely had to do with its composition. Among the universities founded in the 1960s and 1970s, Bielefeld was the one that started out with the largest number of established scholars. This, in its turn, had to do with the founding history of the university. Bielefeld was planned as a reform university. Part of this plan was to alternate teaching semesters and research semesters. This made a young university attractive for senior professors. And interdisciplinarity played a big role in the plan, which stemmed largely from Schelsky.[1] This influenced appointments as well. The openness to interdisciplinarity was comparatively high. The quality of the law faculty was high too. Think only of the large number of Max Planck directors who previously taught in Bielefeld—Mestmäcker,[2] Frowein,[3]

[1] Helmut Schelsky (1912–1984), professor of sociology at the universities of Hamburg, Münster, and Bielefeld.

[2] Ernst-Joachim Mestmäcker (1926–present), professor of commercial law at the universities of Saarbrücken, Münster, Bielefeld, and Hamburg; founding rector of the University of Bielefeld (1967–1969); director of the Max Planck Institute for Foreign and International Private Law in Hamburg (1979–1994); member of the Order "Pour le Mérite".

[3] Jochen Abr. Frowein (1934–present), professor of constitutional and international law at the universities of Bochum, Bielefeld, and Heidelberg; director of the Max Planck Institute for Foreign

*Dieter Grimm: Advocate of the Constitution.* Dieter Grimm, Oxford University Press (2020). © in the original German edition, Mohr Siebeck GmbH & Co. KG, Tübingen 2017, © this translation, Justin Collings 2020.
DOI: 10.1093/oso/9780198845270.001.0001

Eser.[4] And there was no shortage of predominantly doctrinal faculty members either—initially, Blümel[5] and Brohm;[6] when I arrived, Papier,[7] Steiner,[8] and Skouris;[9] later, Oldiges[10] and Krebs.[11]

CW: That means that you got a permanent position immediately coinciding with the end of your *Habilitation* process. There was no period of temporary work or applications. At the time it was probably even more problematic than it is today to apply before completing the *Habilitation* process.

DG: It was indeed more precarious than it is today. And yet I applied a couple of times—and precisely to newly founded faculties that were experimenting with single-level legal education[12] and that, in addition, placed great weight on interdisciplinarity. I particularly remember my application in Hannover, thanks to its curious conclusion. There, I ended up in second place on their list. But the list was returned without explanation to the committee responsible for planning and establishing the new faculty because, according to research by the *Süddeutsche Zeitung*, the FDP regarded all three individuals on the list as "orthodox communists." I had also applied to Bielefeld, and so was already in the running when the first search for Böckenförde's successor failed.

I already had some teaching experience. My friend, Peter Haungs, whom I mentioned earlier, taught political science in Trier and offered

Public Law and International Law in Heidelberg (1973–1993); member of the European Commission for Human Rights in Strasbourg, which at the time was an organ of the European Council antecedent to procedures before the European Court of Human Rights, but which was abolished in 1998.

[4] Albin Eser (1935–present), professor of criminal law in the universities of Bielefeld, Tübingen, and Freiburg; director of the Max Planck Institute for Foreign and International Criminal Law in Freiburg (1982–2003).

[5] Willi Blümel (1929–2015), professor of public law at the Free University of Berlin, the University of Bielefeld, and the German College for Administrative Sciences in Speyer.

[6] Winfried Brohm (1932–2012), professor of public law at the universities of Bielefeld and Constance.

[7] Hans-Jürgen Papier (1943–present), professor of public law at the universities of Bielefeld and Munich; vice president of the Federal Constitutional Court (1998–2002), chairman of its First Senate (1998–2010), and Court president (2002–2010).

[8] Udo Steiner (1939–present), professor of public law at the universities of Erlangen, Göttingen, Bielefeld, and Regensburg; justice of the First Senate of the Federal Constitutional Court (1995–2007).

[9] Vassilios Skouris (1948–present), professor of public law at the universities of Bielefeld (1979–1983) and Thessaloniki; president of the European Court of Justice (2003–2015).

[10] Martin Oldiges (1940–2016), professor of public law at the universities of Bielefeld (1980–1993) and Leipzig.

[11] Walter Krebs (1946–present), professor of public law at the universities of Bielefeld, Münster, and the Free University of Berlin.

[12] German legal education consists of two steps and is completed by taking two state examinations: The First State Examination is taken after law studies at a German university. The Second State Examination is taken after a two-year legal traineeship (*Referendariat*). However, during the 1970s, some German universities tried a new form of legal education in which the theoretical and the practical parts were combined in one step. This experiment ended in the early 1980s.

me a teaching job there. Coing, who in revulsion at the 1968er events in Frankfurt avoided all contact with the university, was not opposed. Trier was far enough away from Frankfurt. So for a few years I traveled to Trier every Wednesday afternoon, gave lectures or taught seminars there (usually about the Federal Republic's government system or theories of the state), and returned the same evening on the last train to Frankfurt. For one semester, I replaced a political science professor on leave in Trier, and despite Coing's aversion to the University of Frankfurt, I also replaced Dieter Simon in his legal history chair while he was on leave. Some of my MPI colleagues were bothered by this because they thought they were better suited for legal history than I. But I was probably a little closer to Simon's brand of legal history than many of my colleagues at the Institute.

In any case, in February 1979 it was just as you said: the completion of my *Habilitation* in Frankfurt and the decision of the faculty in Bielefeld to place me first on their new list fell on the same day.

MR: How did you like life in Bielefeld?

DG: I didn't particularly care for the city. I didn't actually live in Bielefeld itself, but in Halle—a small, undiluted Westphalian town on the other side of the Teutoburg Forest, but fewer than twenty minutes away from the university. The university, by contrast, suited my inclinations very well. I already mentioned the significance of interdisciplinarity as a founding concept. This was reflected architecturally as well. The university consisted of a single, enormous building that fostered chance encounters. The ground floor comprised the "Great Hall of the People," with several lecture halls, the main auditorium at one end and a swimming pool at the other, a cafeteria, another restaurant, a post office, a bank, some shops, etc. It was as good as certain that when you entered the Hall you'd encounter colleagues from other departments. The university library spread throughout the entire second floor. The subject libraries were located below the relevant departments, but without internal barriers. Institute libraries had been expressly rejected. The university library was open twenty-four hours a day.

CW: As a student once during the holidays—close to home—I wrote a criminal law assignment there. The selection of books was excellent.

DG: Bielefeld was a university of short paths and effortless transitions between disciplines. The Center for Interdisciplinary Research (*Zentrum für interdisziplinäre Forschung* or ZiF), moreover, gave the university a distinctive imprint. I also welcomed the single-level curriculum. I found the teaching in the second study period more relevant after the students had a pair of practical experiences behind them and had gained an impression of how the law works in practice.

MR: How stimulating was Bielefeld from a scholarly perspective?

DG: Without the Bielefeld environment, much of what I did would not have been done at all or would have turned out differently. Despite the considerably increased workload and the pressure of deadlines, the university brought me a release of energy and accumulated potential. This began immediately with a new assignment: the *Funkkolleg* on law.[13] A multi-media educational offering, *Funkkollegs* had been around since the 1960s—initially only on the Hessian state broadcasting, but later on in collaboration with several broadcasting platforms. There had already been a *Funkkolleg* devoted to legal science, organized by Hessian Broadcasting and authored by Rudolf Wiethölter, which aired in the winter of 1967–1968. Its aim was "an exemplary, critical description of modern legal problems and of the problem of 'law' in a political society." It shook up legal science and made Wiethölter a *persona non grata* in many quarters, though not in Frankfurt itself. Now the Southwest Broadcasting wanted to do another legal *Funkkolleg* and had acquired Manfred Löwisch[14] from Freiburg, a civil lawyer emphasizing commercial and labor law, as leader of the scholarly team. For classical civil law, Löwisch recruited Gerhard Otte[15] from Bielefeld, and Otte asked me if I would be willing to handle public law. I was attracted by the assignment and attracted by the large number of registered listeners one would expect. I had no inkling of how much work the project would entail.

In contrast to Wiethölter's *Funkkolleg*, this one was more sharply focused on information about law and understanding legal procedures. But I found that such a *Funkkolleg* also needed to engage with some of lay people's basic questions about law. "Why," for example, "is it possible that one can have a legal right but not receive legal redress? Why can the same provision be applied differently by different courts in similar cases? What is the relationship between law and justice?" The two others agreed. But this meant that I now had two fields to take care of. "To take care of" meant to design the plan, recruit authors, write the script, gather accompanying material, formulate exam questions, etc. Thus, my early days in Bielefeld were strongly shaped by the *Funkkolleg*. Very soon after my arrival in Bielefeld, the plan

[13] Cf. Chapter III, fn. 40.

[14] Manfred Löwisch (1937–present), professor of private law, commercial law, labor law, and welfare law at the University of Freiburg im Breisgau.

[15] Gerhard Otte (1935–present), professor of German legal history, private law, and legal methods at the University of Bielefeld.

to write the second volume of *Constitution and Private Law* fell by the wayside. After extensive preparations, the *Funkkolleg* was broadcast in 1982–1983. The scripts were later published in three Fischer paperbacks;[16] the accompanying material appeared with the University Paperbacks series in five volumes.[17]

But back to the environment in which I now operated. For me, what contributed most to the stimulating atmosphere was the interdisciplinary circle called into being by Reinhart Koselleck,[18] which was already well established when I arrived at the University of Bielefeld during its tenth year. The circle met monthly at the house of one of its members, where a different member presented a work in progress. The historians formed the core of the group. Bielefeld was then the Mecca of modern historiography with the triumvirate of Koselleck, Wehler, and Kocka.[19] But other historians were part of the group as well, as were—to take just a few examples—Luhmann,[20] the sociologist; Offe,[21] the political scientist; and Voßkamp,[22] the literary scholar. There were only a few natural scientists. As Böckenförde's successor, I was coopted rather quickly—the only jurist, as I recall. I benefited greatly from these discussions, but the contacts weren't limited to the evening meetings. They continued in the daily life of the university.

MR: Which topics from other disciplines particularly interested you in Bielefeld? How did your work benefit from these interdisciplinary exchanges?

DG: For the Bielefeld historians of those years, with their society-wide approach, the topic of *Bürgertum* was at the forefront. Jürgen Kocka led a research group in the ZiF, in which I became involved. There was a special research group funded by the German Association for Research (DFG),[23] and devoted to *Bürgertum*, in which I had some projects, and *Bürgertum* was also a topic of the working group "Modern Social History," which was

[16] Dieter Grimm, Manfred Löwisch, and Gerhard Otte (eds), *Funkkolleg Recht* (3 vols, 1985).

[17] Dieter Grimm (ed.), *Einführung in das Recht: Aufgaben, Methoden, Wirkungen* (1985, 3d ed. 1997); Dieter Grimm (ed.), *Einführung in das öffentliche Recht: Verfassungs- und Verwaltungsrecht* (1985); Claus Roxin, Gunther Arzt, and Klaus Tiedemann, *Einführung in das Straf- und Strafprozessrecht* (1983, 6th ed. 2013); Gerhard Otte (ed.), *Einführung in das bürgerliche Recht* (1986); Manfred Löwisch (ed.), *Einführung in das Wirtschafts-, Arbeits- und Sozialversicherungsrecht* (1985).

[18] Reinhart Koselleck (1923–2006), professor of history at the universities of Bochum and Bielefeld.

[19] Jürgen Kocka (1941–present), professor of history at the University of Bielefeld (1973–1988) and at the Free University of Berlin, president of the Wissenschaftszentrum Berlin (2001–2007).

[20] Niklas Luhmann (1927–1998), jurist; administrative scholar; sociologist; after a time in the civil service, professor of sociology at the University of Bielefeld (1968–1993).

[21] Claus Offe (1940–present), professor for political science and sociology at the universities of Bielefeld, Bremen, and the Humboldt University in Berlin, as well as the Hertie School of Governance.

[22] Wilhelm Voßkamp (1936–present), professor of German Studies at the universities of Bielefeld and Cologne; managing director of the ZiF at the University of Bielefeld (1978–1982).

[23] The publicly funded but independent institution that distributes government research funds.

strongly influenced by Bielefeld and which at the time was regarded as the vanguard of historical research in Germany.[24] The group met twice a year at the Reimers Foundation in Bad Homburg. I was invited to participate at the initiative of my Bielefeld colleagues. I remember with particular esteem Rainer Lepsius[25]—your father, *Herr* Lepsius—who belonged to the circle as a sociologist and whose methodological consciousness made him sharp in analysis and relentless in his critiques.

The Bürgertum project aligned well with my legal history research. Through it, my research gained enormously in conceptual clarity and contextual nuance. In preparation for the research group at the ZiF, a conference was held in December 1985 designed to test the viability of *Bürgertum* as a category for further research. I presented a lecture on "*Bürgerlichkeit* in the Law," which was published first in the conference proceedings and later as the introduction to my 1987 essay collection *Law and the State in Bürgertum Society*.[26] Although it met with much criticism on the part of historians, who took issue with the level of abstraction and the shortage of sources, I consider it among my important publications.

My contribution to the ZiF research group itself was a comparative work on "Fundamental Rights in the Context of the Emergence of *Bürgertum* Society." The points of comparison were England, the United States, France, Germany (including Austria), and Poland.[27]

The introductory chapter of my *German Constitutional History, 1776–1866*[28] would have been impossible without the ongoing conversation with my historian colleagues in the university, in the ZiF, in the DFG research group, and in the Modern Social History working group. Indeed, without Bielefeld, the constitutional history might never have come about. In those years Hans-Ulrich Wehler was editing a "New Historical Library" for the Suhrkamp publishing house, and he recruited me to write a German constitutional history. We agreed on two volumes. The first was finished just as I was appointed to the Federal Constitutional Court. It was published

[24] On this working group, cf. Ulrich Engelhardt, *Konzepte der "Sozialgeschichte" im Arbeitskreis für moderne Sozialgeschichte* (2007).

[25] M. Rainer Lepsius (1928–2014), professor of sociology at the universities of Mannheim and Heidelberg.

[26] Dieter Grimm, "Bürgerlichkeit im Recht" in Jürgen Kocka (ed.), *Bürger und Bürgerlichkeit im 19. Jahrhundert* (1987) 149; Dieter Grimm, *Recht und Staat der bürgerlichen Gesellschaft* (1987) 11.

[27] Dieter Grimm, "Die Grundrechte im Entstehungszusammenhang der bürgerlichen Gesellschaft" in Jürgen Kocka (ed.), *Bürgertum im 19. Jahrhundert* (vol. 1, 1987) 340; in English in Dieter Grimm, *Constitutionalism. Past, Present and Future* (2016) 65.

[28] Dieter Grimm, *Deutsche Verfassungsgeschichte 1776–1866* (1988, 4th ed. 2015).

in 1988 and has seen four subsequent editions. Because of my move to Karlsruhe, the second volume never saw the light.

MR: With what concept did you approach your constitutional history? Surely it was never meant to be a second Huber.[29]

DG: For reasons of scope alone that was out of the question. Huber wrote seven volumes of around 1,000 pages each. It is a phenomenal work. It wouldn't miss it. I was to write two volumes in a paperback format of around 270 pages each. But there were other reasons why I didn't want to imitate Huber. Huber often yields to the temptation to explain to the reader the correct legal interpretation of earlier constitutions in cases of conflict. He engages with the historical material in a dogmatic or doctrinal way. I don't see that as the office of a constitutional history. Additionally, I thought Huber paid too little attention to the constitution's societal dimension; his is a very state-centered constitutional history. In connection with the societal side of the constitution, I was also interested in the conditions that allowed this historical novelty to rise and spread—not only the ideas behind the constitution, but the links between the ideas and the interests of various stakeholders in certain negotiation settings, as well as the structures on which constitutions depend and which they in turn influence. My keynote address at the 1986 Conference of Legal Historians in Frankfurt, organized by Dieter Simon, served as a kind of test run.[30] It was criticized by legal historians working in a strongly traditional vein. They wanted to know the sources of my argument. I answered: constitutional proposals, constitutional debates, and constitutional texts. My approach was to identify actors, analyze contextual conditions, and, as much as possible, to compare—for only through comparison do peculiarities become clear.

CW: Were the students in Bielefeld interested in theoretical questions and foundational concepts? Early contact with practical experience can work both ways: it can clarify the relevance of theory at a new level, or it can foster the view that theory is no longer necessary.

DG: It was in Bielefeld as it is in most law departments. The majority of students had little serious interest in foundational questions and attended the relevant lectures when required to do so. At the same time there was—perhaps thanks to the East-Westphalian temperament—a certain sense of duty. One

[29] Ernst Rudolf Huber, *Deutsche Verfassungsgeschichte* (7 vols, 1960–1990).

[30] Dieter Grimm, "Entstehungs- und Wirkungsbedingungen des modernen Konstitutionalismus" in Dieter Simon (ed.), *Akten des 26. Deutschen Rechtshistorikertages* (1987) 45; also in Dieter Grimm, *Die Zukunft der Verfassung* (1991, 3d ed. 2002) 31; in English in Dieter Grimm, *Constitutionalism* (above fn. 27) 41.

didn't simply stay away from the foundational lectures. This was an opportunity for the teachers. One could even count always on a small group with a heightened interest in fundamental questions. In any event, I could never complain about a lack of students when I offered courses that weren't of a doctrinal nature. Even the interdisciplinary seminars—such as with Ingrid Gilcher-Holtey,[31] who took the minutes of the Working Group and after her *Habilitation* in Freiburg received an appointment in Bielefeld; or with Niklas Luhmann—found a considerable reception.

OL: Was there any deeper contact with Luhmann—beyond civilities—when you taught a seminar together?

DG: Long before I came to Bielefeld, I had read a lot of Luhmann. I was very impressed with his core insight about the functional differentiation of society, with its consequences of specialized functional systems that operate according to a logic of their own and are only susceptible for signals from the environment if they are framed in terms of their own logic—with all the attendant consequences for social integration. One can indeed see this in much of my own work. Nonetheless, I was not a card-carrying Luhmannist. I struggled in particular with Luhmann's assumption that the political system was merely one functional system among others and subject, like the others, to the same logic. To me that view didn't do justice to the state's unique role in taming the sub-systems' egotisms for the well-being of society as a whole, or to the state's unique means of fulfilling that role. But being at the same university as Luhmann was very attractive. Yet unlike Koselleck, whom I had also read with great profit before meeting him in Bielefeld, Luhmann didn't approach others of his own accord. He was, however, anything but unwelcoming if you approached him. He agreed without hesitation to the idea of teaching a seminar together.

OL: Were you his only partner or did he regularly team-teach seminars?

DG: I always liked looking in the course catalog to see what the colleagues whom I held in high esteem were teaching. I cannot remember any other interdisciplinary seminars co-taught by Luhmann. But I might be mistaken.

In recalling the seminars, I need to be careful to avoid gossiping because Luhmann supplied ample material for gossip. I think, for instance, of the beginning of our teaching together. Luhmann's seminars lasted three hours. I agreed to this, not wanting to ask him to alter his habits. Accordingly, we met from 6 to 9 p.m. The seminar room was across from my office.

[31] Ingrid Gilcher-Holtey (1952–present), professor of contemporary history at the University of Bielefeld.

The time for the first session had come. Six-fifteen rolled around and there was no sign of Luhmann. I tried calling him, but in vain. Finally, I went into the seminar room to ask the students to be patient; *Herr* Luhmann would be there soon. When I entered the room, the students were sitting in total silence—and at the front of the room Luhmann was sitting in total silence.

"Oh," I said. "You're already here. I thought you would come by my office."

"I thought," he answered, "that the seminar took place here."

At the end of the three-hour seminar, I was thirsty, and suggested that we go to The Greek (a restaurant in the "Great Hall of the People") for a beer.

"A beer?" Luhmann retorted. "Now? I need to go home and do some more work."

But because he was polite and obviously didn't want to disappoint me, he asked if they didn't perhaps serve very small beers. So we had a beer together—he, a small one; I, a large one. And I had something to eat as well. Having learned to be careful, I remarked after the seminar the following week: "*Herr* Luhmann, I'm now going to have another beer." He answered that, given that they also had small beers, he would come along. After the third seminar, he said: "I see that you also get something to eat here. That's very practical. I always have to make myself something when I get home." From then on, we not only drank a beer but also had something to eat. And when I once had to tell him that it wouldn't work that night because I had guests at home, he was visibly disappointed. When I got to know him, his wife was already dead. I gather that she had relieved him of many of the life's quotidian burdens. He stood somewhat aloof from the everyday, but his wants were few. He always wore the same thing.

OL: He once came to give four lectures in Munich. We doctoral and *Habilitation* candidates expected grand theater in the great lecture hall, but he was unwilling to let that happen. He explained the basic concepts of systems theory with a routine that quickly emptied the lecture hall. For the first lecture, there were big problems of space; fewer problems for the second; one easily found a seat for the third; and the fourth time, I didn't go either. He was much more interesting to read.

DG: In the seminar he demanded a lot of contingency from the law students. His pedagogical principle was to call into question apparent givens—in which the law, of course, abounds. "Why exactly are things as they are when they could be completely otherwise?" There were limits to the law students' tolerance for this and they sometimes threatened to become aggressive. One had to show them that such questions also offered opportunities.

When I received the topic for my presentation at the Association of German Constitutional Law Professors and was initially unhappy with it,[32] I hoped for inspiration from Luhmann. I was looking for material in the library, when he came rushing by. "What do you have to say about culture?" I hurriedly asked him. "I avoid it," he answered.

OL: During your university studies you were interested in political science alongside law. At the Max Planck Institute, history was your daily companion. Now you come to Bielefeld and are thrown into a strongly sociological milieu. That marks the third neighboring discipline with which you work intensively.

DG: But it is also the last. And it overlaps with political science. These fields were also very strong in Bielefeld. Besides Luhmann, I was in particular contact with Franz Xaver Kaufmann,[33] who, as someone much occupied with the welfare state, was also close to law. In political science, Claus Offe stood out, along with Helmut Willke,[34] who had received his law doctorate in Tübingen with a dissertation on fundamental rights theory, and who thereafter worked in sociology, without losing his ties to law, but with an emphasis on the sociology of the state.

OL: In the mid-1990s—that's now a little later—two collected volumes appeared, on which you collaborated, dealing with the functions of the state and the overburdening of the state. In their subtext, I found both to be deeply inspired by systems theory.

DG: These volumes, which I edited, also have a Bielefeld background. I was quickly made a co-director of the ZiF and organized, as the directors were expected to do, an annual research group on the topic "Functions of the State." The topic wasn't chosen by chance. I was not persuaded by the replacement of the state—then fashionable among political scientists—with the "political system." It owed something to the Renaissance of Marxist thought, but even more to the empirical observation that the political was no longer captured adequately by the concept of the state. It was clearly more evident to jurists than to social scientists that the state was still an identifiable and relevant actor—more than merely the point of attribution

[32] Dieter Grimm, "Kulturauftrag im staatlichen Gemeinwesen" (1984) 42 *Veröffentlichungen der Vereinigung der deutschen Staatsrechtslehrer* 46–82; reprinted in Dieter Grimm, *Recht und Staat der bürgerlichen Gesellschaft* (1987) 104–37.

[33] Franz Xaver Kaufmann (1932–present), professor of social policy and sociology at the University of Bielefeld (1969–1997).

[34] Helmut Willke (1945–present), jurist and sociologist; beginning in 1983, professor of planning and decision theory in the sociology department of the University of Bielefeld; beginning in 2002, professor of state theory and global governance, also at Bielefeld; since 2008 at Zeppelin University in Friedrichshafen.

for various individual and collective actions. My interest was drawn to what exactly constituted the state and how it had changed since Jellinek.

So it happened that Marigret Meyer-Tabellion, the wife of our colleague, Hans Meyer,[35] who had reanimated the legal program of the Metzner Publishing House with her inimitable vitality, approached me during a conference of the Association of Constitutional Law Professors[36] and asked if I'd be interested in writing a "State Theory"[37] as part of her program. "How do you know my most secret thoughts?" I asked in response.

So it made sense to devote the ZiF research group to the topic of the state. I narrowed this to "functions of the State," in part because the functions of the state had long been regarded as unworthy of scholarly interest, and in part because the question had become extremely relevant thanks to the constant expansion of the state's duties and the increasing difficulty of discharging them. The consequences for law, moreover, were unmistakable: a large part of the state's new duties was not subject to control by imperative law. The research group's project and the list of researchers to be invited arose through close collaboration with the previously mentioned social scientists, Offe, Willke, and Kaufmann, as well as Johannes Berger,[38] a sociologist. Luhmann wasn't interested in such collective activities.

The research group convened in the academic year 1988–1989. By that time, I was already in Karlsruhe—something that had been unforeseeable during the planning period. I discussed with the other ZiF directors and my fellow planners the possibility of canceling the program. But all the invitations had already been made, and we were dealing with a group of twenty-five scholars of some stature. My Bielefeld colleagues were also willing to assume increased responsibility for it. Even so, the research group suffered from my dual engagement. I lived in Karlsruhe. Monday was "functions-of-the-State" day, in which I always took part, but not with anything approaching the level of engagement I had envisioned. Some participants took my absence as license to interpret their own duty to be

[35] Hans Meyer (1933–present), professor of public law at the University of Frankfurt am Main and at the Humboldt University in Berlin, where he was president from 1996 to 2000.

[36] The "Association of Constitutional Law Professors" was founded by Heinrich Triepel in 1922. Only professors and lecturers with a *Habilitation* in German, Austrian, or Swiss Public Law are allowed to join this association. It hosts an annual conference each fall.

[37] German "State Theory" (*Staatslehre*) is closely connected to the German concept of the state. Famous treatises on "State Theory" were written by Johann Caspar Bluntschli, Georg Jellinek, Hans Kelsen, Hermann Heller, and others.

[38] Johannes Berger (1939–present), professor of sociology at the universities of Bielefeld and Mannheim.

present rather liberally. Four members of the research group were unable to contribute to the resulting publication.[39]

Revisited today, the volume contains a series of useful insights. But it is striking how internationalization and its impact on the state had barely been noticed. It would soon press right to the forefront of engagement with the state. This undermined the volume's influence in the relevant disciplines. Recently, however, I received a copy of a book by Andreas Anter and Wilhelm Bleek about conceptions of the state in German political science in which our volume is given an astonishingly positive reception.[40] The second publication to result from the research group's work, *The State's Expanding Functions—and Law's Diminishing Capacity to Control Them*,[41] received considerable attention, especially among scholars of administrative law.

Like my plans for further work on the constitutional history, my treatise on the theory of the state fell victim to my occupation in Karlsruhe. When those twelve years were over, I would have had to write an entirely different book. Internationalization and globalization had rendered the old conceptions obsolete. This quickly became clear to me, but when I was again free for new projects, so much had already been said on the subject that I wasn't sure I had anything new to contribute.

OL: These volumes introduced the rhetoric of a crisis of the state. Until 2010, there was an enduring discussion under the rubric of "from the X-State to the Y-State." Even the successful special research group on the "Transformation of the State" relies on the basic semantics of a systems-theoretical perspective that was then introduced in Bielefeld.

DG: The rhetoric of crisis is older. The term "ungovernability" made the rounds as early as the 1970s. I didn't want to associate myself with that, and the ZiF research group was of a different temper as well. Our aim was to analyze the altered conditions of governance.

CW: You mentioned three of the best-known Bielefeld historians. Was there someone with whom you collaborated especially closely? Because of his conceptual approach, Koselleck has always been particularly congenial for jurists.

[39] Dieter Grimm (ed.), *Staatsaufgaben* (1994).

[40] Andreas Anter and Wilhelm Bleek, *Staatskonzepte: Die Theorien der bundesdeutschen Politikwissenschaft* (2013) 98.

[41] Dieter Grimm (ed.), *Wachsende Staatsaufgaben—sinkende Steuerungsfähigkeit des Rechts* (1990).

DG: With all their differences, I cannot single out one of the three. Koselleck recruited me for the entry under "Constitution"[42] in the lexicon of basic historical concepts that he edited with Brunner and Conze—which drew from Wehler (who didn't care much for conceptual history) the remark, "Why do you put up with such drudgery?" But I found the task of exploring historical change through changes in conceptual understanding interesting enough. I did not, however, feel competent to address conceptual developments prior to the rise of the modern constitution. Accordingly, I recommended my MPI colleague, Heinz Mohnhaupt, as coauthor. Although my contribution was far the smaller of the two, it required an immense amount of work, in which my assistants, Gertrud Lübbe-Wolff[43] and Alfons Hueber,[44] as well as two student researchers had an enormous part. The article later appeared as a book,[45] with Mohnhaupt's part expanded and mine in its original form. There are translations in Italian and Portuguese, and my contribution is now available in English.

Koselleck died in 2006. Kocka left for Berlin in 1988. When I arrived in Berlin at the Institute for Advanced Studies, Kocka was a permanent fellow. When I became rector of the Institute in 2001, he became president of the Berlin Social Science Center. Our contacts were always close—as they were with Wehler, who occasionally lived in Berlin after his retirement.

CW: Did you consistently teach the same subjects or did your courses vary?

DG: I regularly taught constitutional law, divided into organization of the state (federalism, separation of powers, etc.), and fundamental rights. I often taught constitutional history and state theory, and I liked to teach Introduction to Legal Science. Once I taught administrative procedure as well. I also taught some elective courses, such as legislation.

My seminars always dealt with different topics. There were seminars on both foundational questions and doctrinal problems. They usually began with a weekend conference in the neighborhood of Bielefeld and then continued throughout the semester. At the time, however, I published relatively little on doctrinal topics—not because I couldn't do it, but because there

[42] Dieter Grimm, "Verfassung (II): Konstitution, Grundgesetz" in *Geschichtliche Grundbegriffe* (vol. 6, 1990) 863–99; reprinted as "Der Verfassungsbegriff in historischer Entwicklung" in Dieter Grimm, *Die Zukunft der Verfassung* (1991) 101–55; in English in Dieter Grimm, *Constitutionalism* (above fn. 27) 89.

[43] Gertrude Lübbe-Wolff (1953–present), professor of public law at the University of Bielefeld; justice on the Second Senate of the Federal Constitutional Court (2002–2014).

[44] Alfons Hueber (1949–present), jurist; now a notary in Chemnitz. (In contrast to the United States, a notary in Germany is a fully qualified lawyer who has the special permission to perform official acts.)

[45] Dieter Grimm and Heinz Mohnhaupt, *Verfassung: Zur Geschichte des Begriffs von der Antike bis zur Gegenwart* (1st ed. 1995, 2d ed. 2002).

was no shortage of doctrinal writers, whereas my questions of interest were addressed relatively rarely. But I've never looked down on doctrine. In my doctrinal lectures, I always placed great emphasis on understanding, not just knowing. But I also insisted on a methodological approach and sound reasoning. That continued later on at the Court.

OL: I'm now in the mood for a provocative thesis. It strikes me—I hope you won't take offense at this—that at bottom you were never deeply engaged with administrative law. Public law is characterized by the fact that it takes account of normative hierarchies. A constitutionalist needs inferior law, otherwise the constitution as such remains invisible. The constitution is perceptible only through its contrast with ordinary law, and that, for public lawyers, usually means administrative law. But for decades, ordinary law for you meant private law. That gives you, I would say, a unique imprint within the guild. You have a perspective on the constitution in which ordinary law has less to do with the relationship between the citizen and the state than with the processes of societal self-organization. Is that a correct observation? Would you say that this placed you in a position to see things differently from the mainstream—that it pushed you to the forefront of the discussion and made you more accessible? Do you see this biographical development as an advantage or a distinction?

DG: The observation is right. If you look over my bibliography you might find two-and-a-half administrative law articles. This made my appointment in Karlsruhe a surprise to some people, including the Karlsruhe correspondent for *Die Welt*, Henning Frank. As he later told me, in his confusion following my appointment he asked Fritz Ossenbühl[46] who this freshly elected fellow was. His answer: "A pure constitutionalist." For Ossenbühl, this was surely not a purely positive assessment.

There was an opportunity to change this. Wolfgang Hoffmann-Riem[47] conceived the idea for his New Science of Administrative Law very early on. We knew one another from various interdisciplinary projects. He asked me if I wanted to take on the administrative law project with him. At the time I was already in Karlsruhe and couldn't see where I would find the time for such an undertaking.

That private law played a greater role for me than administrative law results from the time I spent at the Max Planck Institute in Frankfurt, which

[46] Fritz Ossenbühl (1934–present), professor of public law at the University of Bonn.

[47] Wolfgang Hoffmann-Riem (1940–present), professor of public law and administrative science at the University of Hamburg; justice senator in Hamburg (1995–1997); justice of the First Senate of the Federal Constitutional Court (1999–2008), successor of Dieter Grimm.

was oriented toward the history of private law. Had I become assistant to a Frankfurt public lawyer, things would probably have turned out differently. But I have always regarded my neglect of administrative law as a shortcoming. At the same time, I was aware that I couldn't have reached the same standard in administrative law as in constitutional law, if I was to hold fast to my interdisciplinary interests.

CW: One of your few administrative law essays—the one on the concept of takings—also views administrative law in conjunction with private law.

OL: I would add that it isn't so important whether one turns for ordinary law to administrative law or to private law—only that one not lose sight of ordinary law. Today, however, public lawyers are all obliged to turn to administrative law, whereas in your generation, *Herr* Grimm, there were a few who embraced a non-administrative law perspective. Häberle[48] and Böckenförde didn't do administrative law either. That is a socialization of the constitutionalist that we barely find today. But what is the consequence of such a socialization for descriptions of the constitution? I can imagine that it might even be an advantage. Those who deal constantly with administrative law might approach the constitution too much from the perspective of fundamental rights because they need the constitution as an individual defense against administrative encroachment. By contrast, you are more strongly interested in functional interrelationships and questions of societal power.

DG: That brings us back, once again, to Luhmann. Luhmann sensitized me to the significance of the relative autonomy of societal sub-systems. For the most part, such sub-systems are ordered through private law. Among other things, that changes the outlook on fundamental rights. It quickly struck me as too one-sided to understand them only in terms of individual liberty vis-à-vis the state. They also had the role of preserving the autonomy (and internal functional logic) of sub-systems that were threatened less by the state than by other powerful systems. Protection against such threats could only come from the state. The objective dimension of fundamental rights—the so-called "duty to protect"—followed ineluctably. I have therefore explained and defended its necessity. The essay in which I did so—early and thoroughly—stemmed from a lecture in Switzerland, where the so-called "horizontal effect of fundamental rights" was subjected to heavy attacks on the part of private lawyers. It appeared in a Swiss journal and therefore went

[48] Peter Häberle (1934–present), professor of public law at the universities of Marburg, Augsburg, St. Gallen, and Bayreuth.

almost unnoticed in Germany. As for your hypothesis that I am more interested in functional interrelationships and questions of social power, my essay "Return to a Liberal Understanding of Fundamental Rights?"[49] might serve as proof. But I did not embrace Luhmann's purely objective interpretation of fundamental rights, under which the individual shrivels, in the end, into a mere agent of system-differentiation. I am much closer to the Court's view that the full power of fundamental rights develops in the synthesis of their subjective and objective dimensions.

OL: By contrast, I would say that Böckenförde's understanding of the constitution is a rather individualistic one, from which you distance yourself. Which is entirely consistent with your socialization—beginning with Duguit, the critic of subjective rights.

DG: My own impression is that there are few breaks, let alone reversals, in my work. There is also no particular inclination to follow scholarly fashions, but yet a willingness to take on questions of very contemporary relevance. In my teaching, I have always felt it my duty to provide scholarly orientation for such situations. But I must also say that much that seems harmonious in hindsight did not spring from any particular plan. Only with the coming together of the volume *Law and State in Bürgertum Society*,[50] for instance, did I realize how, unbeknownst to me, things had organized themselves into a conceptual whole.

[49] Dieter Grimm, "Rückkehr zum liberalen Grundrechtsverständnis? " (1988) *recht, Zeitschrift für juristische Ausbildung und Praxis* 41–50; reprinted in Dieter Grimm, *Die Zukunft der Verfassung* (1991) 221–40; in English in Dieter Grimm, *Constitutionalism* (above fn. 27) 183.

[50] Dieter Grimm, *Recht und Staat der bürgerlichen Gesellschaft* (1987).

# VI.

# Karlsruhe: From Scholarship to Practice

## A. Responsibility for Communicative Fundamental Rights

OL: You then had the good fortune to apply your understanding of fundamental rights in the area of Article 5 GG[1] on the Federal Constitutional Court. Some fundamental rights bear a stronger individualist imprint, others a more functional one. Within the Court's First Senate you were given responsibility for perhaps the most "functional" fundamental right, for which you were especially well equipped.

DG: Constitutional law was also well equipped through five television judgments.[2] I didn't need to be a revolutionary.

OL: You weren't opposed to private television as such, but you resisted attacks on the order of broadcasting law from the private television lobby in conjunction with the CDU/CSU/FDP government and their fellow travelers among the state governments. You solidified the jurisprudence and to a certain extent defended it.

DG: I would not disagree. But perhaps I also moved it in a couple directions that hadn't come up in earlier cases. The *Fees* judgment[3] is one example, as is the

[1] Article 5 of the Basic Law (Grundgesetz [GG]) reads: "(1) Every person shall have the right freely to express and disseminate his opinions in speech, writing and pictures and to inform himself without hindrance from generally accessible sources. Freedom of the press and freedom of reporting by means of broadcasts and films shall be guaranteed. There shall be no censorship."

(2) These rights shall find their limits in the provisions of general laws, in provisions for the protection of young persons and in the right to personal honour.
(3) Arts and sciences, research and teaching shall be free. The freedom of teaching shall not release any person from allegiance to the constitution."

[2] This refers to the judgments of the Federal Constitutional Court that formed the constitutional basis of German public television. The first of those judgments was laid down in 1961 and prohibited the founding of a second public television station by the federal government, thereby giving this competence to the states (12 BVerfGE 205 (1961)).

[3] 90 BVerfGE 60 (1994) (holding that the financing of public broadcasting must conform to the principle of programming neutrality, and that therefore cannot be determined through the parliamentary process but only in a neutral way).

*Dieter Grimm: Advocate of the Constitution.* Dieter Grimm, Oxford University Press (2020). © in the original German edition, Mohr Siebeck GmbH & Co. KG, Tübingen 2017, © this translation, Justin Collings 2020.
DOI: 10.1093/oso/9780198845270.001.0001

decision on short reporting,[4] which bars the commercialization of events and functions that are important for society as a whole. But I have always objected when people have said that I am a friend of public broadcasting. I am a friend of the constitution and of what it has to say about a democratic society's need for information and communication.

OL: You could also have said: No, a spirit of competition now prevails in broadcasting law, and television is to be opened up for free enterprise, such that programming will be successful only when it finds public approval and commercial financing. Wouldn't it be a more democratic approach to treat viewers like voters, allowing them access to the programming they freely choose and, through such competition, affording them a chance to influence programming?

DG: A wonderful brief. I am, of course, familiar with the argument. Indeed, it was the credo of the commercial TV companies and those who supported them in politics and scholarship—including legal scholarship. I had considerable doubts about the argument, and for that reason, as early as my 1983 lecture at the Association of Constitutional Law Professors conference on "Cultural Functions in the State," I used broadcasting as my example in the third part, after exploring historical and systematic considerations in the first two parts.[5] I had characterized culture as the "ideational reproduction of society" and derived therefrom the state's dependence on cultural preconditions, which in their turn needed state support. In the early days of the dual system,[6] it seemed important to understand broadcasting not only as a commercial but also as a cultural undertaking—a view that had consequences for the configuration of the broadcasting order that was then just coming into being. At bottom, I was concerned with refuting the idea that broadcasting funded by advertising was somehow more democratic—better attuned to the wishes of "mature citizens." In the commercial sector, the needs of the advertising industry—which are by no means identical with the interests of citizens—inject themselves between broadcasting and

[4] 97 BVerfGE 228 (1998).

[5] Grimm, Chapter V, fn. 32.

[6] The dual system of public and private television has been existing in Germany since the early 1980s. In its third television judgment, the Federal Constitutional Court said in 1981 (57 BVerfGE 295 (1981)) that private television was allowed as long as the law determined its framework and ensured that all television programs taken together represent the pluralism of opinions in society. Today, public television plays a more important role in Germany than e.g. in the United States. The market share of the two largest public television networks (ARD and ZDF) taken together is around 25 percent. In 2018, they both had a higher overall market share than the most popular private television network. Cf. Statista, *Zuschauermarktanteile ausgewählter TV-Sender in Deutschland im Jahr 2018*, available online: https://de.statista.com/statistik/daten/studie/214350/umfrage/marktanteile-der-tv-sender-in-deutschland/, accessed on December 23, 2019.

the citizen. Above all, though, maturity doesn't materialize automatically with the coming of age. It is a precondition in need of constant buttressing. Broadcasting plays an important role in this respect, but the fulfillment of that role can hardly be expected in a pure market model. I defended myself against the accusation of paternalism, which was often raised later on, with the observation that state regulation only affected the supply side, not the user side.

OL: Where did the orientation toward culture come from? Did your experience as editor of a school newspaper play a role?

DG: That couldn't have been it. There were former student newspaper editors among my opponents as well. There were very similar ideas at the basis of the Court's case law, though without the foundation in cultural theory.

OL: But you are not now saying that it was only the jurisprudence that reinforced you. If you didn't agree with it, you could have changed it.

DG: I was indeed in agreement with the jurisprudence as it had developed from the twelfth through the fifty-seventh volumes of the Court's official reports. It conformed to my conceptions of democracy, in which a society's capacity to discuss and seek agreement about its situation, its available options, and its aspirations plays a big role. A lot of this depends on the media system. It was challenged at the time because the public broadcasting monopoly could no longer be justified by the limited range of frequencies. Digitalization later required a redefinition of broadcasting. Today, it is the Internet for whose problems constitutional law offers, as yet, no answer.

CW: For me, though my basic position differs in part, the last part of your lecture remains the most intelligent and succinct summary of this line in the Court's jurisprudence. Was that a deciding factor in your appointment in Karlsruhe? Before then, you were something of an outsider among constitutionalists. After that lecture, politicians who wanted to preserve a specific model had to pay attention to you. The vacancy in Karlsruhe was not just any vacancy—it was the seat of Konrad Hesse, since portfolios within the First Senate are passed down from one judge to another.[7]

DG: I don't know why I was looked to as Hesse's possible successor. I've never made efforts to find it out. The right of nomination fell to the SPD, but the position had been, since Ritterspach,[8] a "neutral"

[7] The Federal Constitutional Court consists of two Senates. Within each Senate, the justices have responsibilities for specific subject matters for which they are rapporteurs. In the First Senate, those portfolios are traditionally passed down from one justice to his/her successor. In the Second Senate, those portfolios are rearranged according to seniority when a new justice is appointed.

[8] Theodor Ritterspach (1904–1999), Bavarian, then federal ministerial civil servant; justice on the First Senate of the Federal Constitutional Court (1951–1975).

one.[9] I had occasionally spoken at SPD events, but by no means only at SPD events. I had spoken at CDU and FDP events as well. What I am about to say is an unverified hunch. In June 1986, the SPD hosted a conference on legal politics organized by Herta Däubler-Gmelin,[10] then the party's vice chair. I was invited to present at the conference on "interest protection and law enforcement in the society of tomorrow."[11] The foremost question was how to make interests that are incapable of representation both visible in the political process and legally enforceable. The presentation clearly impressed *Frau* Däubler-Gmelin. She told me that she had thoroughly "unboned" me. I remember this because the word left me perplexed. She explained that it was Swabian, and it effectively meant "gutted." It's possible that this gave rise to a recommendation for Karlsruhe. *Frau* Däubler-Gmelin was decisively involved at the time in the selection of constitutional judges. If this interpretation is correct—and I admittedly don't know if it is—then my nomination had nothing to do with broadcasting.

OL: Who was it who asked whether you were willing to become a constitutional judge?

DG: It was Gerhard Jahn,[12] the former federal minister of justice. He called me up at the university and said that he was sure that I was aware (I was *not* aware) that within a year Professor Hesse would be leaving the Constitutional Court, and my name was being considered as his successor. He had been tasked with finding out whether I was available for the job. He added that of course I would need time to think it over and (if I remember correctly) said that he would call again in a couple weeks. I answered that for *this* question I did not need time to consider. I was ready to say Yes immediately. He ended the conversation with the observation that in that case he would get in touch with the CDU. Should they reject me, he would let me know right away. If I didn't hear from him, I could assume that I would

[9] Eight of the sixteen justices of the Federal Constitutional Court are elected by the Bundestag, the other half by the Bundesrat. Each election requires a two-thirds majority in the respective chamber. Due to this supermajority quorum, the largest parties CDU/CSU and SPD have informally divided up the right to nominate a justice between them. That does not necessarily mean that the candidates have to be members of the respective party.

[10] Herta Däubler-Gmelin (1943–present), politician (SPD); member of the German Bundestag (1972–2009); federal minister of justice (1998–2002). In 1987, she was the vice chair of the SPD parliamentary group in the Bundestag.

[11] Dieter Grimm, "Interessenwahrung und Rechtsdurchsetzung in der Gesellschaft von Morgen" in H. Däubler-Gmelin and W. Alderstein (eds), *Menschgerecht: 6. Rechtspolitischer Kongress der SPD* (1986) 392.

[12] Gerhard Jahn (1927–1998), lawyer, politician (SPD); member of the German Bundestag (1957–1991); federal minister of justice (1969–1974); deputy floor manager of the SPD parliamentary group in the Bundestag (1974–1990).

be appointed the following year. He added in closing: "Just before the deadline you will probably see some names in the papers. Yours won't be among them. If that happens, don't worry about it." So it happened. The next that I heard was a call from the Bundesrat a year later: at the end of the week I would be chosen as a justice of the Federal Constitutional Court; they needed my written consent.

OL: This position on the First Senate stands out among the sixteen on the Court because, thanks to the strange division of labor within the First Senate, it entails responsibility for the freedoms of speech, press, and broadcasting under Article 5 GG. What's more, the SPD has the right of nomination for this position, and the SPD naturally has a strategic interest in preserving public broadcasting because, for economic reasons, it would get the short end of private television.

DG: That could be so. But I was not particularly prominent in broadcasting law. All the same, in my Bielefeld colleague, Martin Stock,[13] I had a contact who was entirely at home in broadcasting law and with whom I had even taught a seminar on broadcasting systems in Europe. But my only writing on the topic was my lecture at the constitutionalists' conference and a critical case note[14] on the penultimate *Television* judgment by Hesse in 1986.[15] I rather doubt that politicians were aware of these texts. I don't think politicians read lectures from the Conference of Constitutional Law Professors. But the strangest things happen. The CDU thinks it needs to send another conservative criminologist and sends *Herr* Schluckebier[16] to the First Senate—which doesn't deal with criminal law! One shouldn't overestimate the steadiness of purpose in the political appointment process. Compared with the American praxis, it remains refreshingly unprofessional.

OL: But it is striking that the SPD has a felicitous hand for preservers of public broadcasting. That continues even after you. Such fortune in staffing a position has been rare among politicians.

DG: The effect seems to support that. Incidentally, the division of labor in the First Senate is not unalterable. Hesse was only responsible for Article 5(1) and Article 5(2), as well as commercial law and a few neighboring areas.

[13] Martin Stock (1933–present), professor of public law at the University of Bielefeld.

[14] Dieter Grimm, "Verfassungspolitische Perspektiven einer dualen Rundfunkordnung" (1987) 35 *Rundfunk und Fernsehen* 25.

[15] 73 BVerfGE 118 (1986). This was a decision on the Broadcasting Law of Lower Saxony, which clarified that, even in a dual broadcasting system, public broadcasting retained its function as bundled in the concept of "basic provisioning."

[16] Wilhelm Schluckebier (1949–present), judge on the Federal Court of Justice (1999–2006); justice on the First Senate of the Federal Constitutional Court (2006–2017).

I could round out the portfolio considerably. When Helmut Simon[17] left the Court a few months after my appointment, the freedom of assembly fell to me as well—a collective continuation, in a sense, of the individual right to free speech. When Hermann Heußner left the Court early for health reasons in 1989, I took over data protection. I had already replaced Heußner as judge rapporteur during his illness. Then came freedom of association, thanks to its affinity to Article 8 GG (freedom of assembly), whereas Article 9(3) GG, which is relevant for labor law, remained in the old portfolio. With the departure of *Frau* Niemeyer[18] that same year, I succeeded in taking over the general personality right with the argument that, because free speech often collides with the personality right, the same judge should cover both. Various important cases connected with Reunification fell into my portfolio as part of the responsibility for commercial law that I had taken over from *Herr* Hesse. Only when, for reasons of temporary docket overload, the Second Senate wanted to transfer competence over political parties to the First Senate because I was considered an expert on Article 21 GG did my Senate refuse to go along. The law of political parties belongs decisively to the law of state organization. But even without the law of political parties, one can hardly imagine for a constitutionalist a lovelier portfolio. I don't know what would have become of me had I been responsible for social security law, the importance of which I don't dispute.

OL: Do you think the division of labor in the First Senate makes sense? Or is that of the Second Senate better?[19]

DG: From a newcomer's perspective, the First Senate is surely better. In the Second Senate, new justices get penal institutions and the right of asylum. With every personnel change, the carousel of competences turns too—and it does so before the arrival of the newcomer, who is thus left with only unpopular topics.

MR: Let's go back to the communicative freedoms, especially freedom of speech. There was occasionally strong opposition among experts to the Court's case law on Article 5(1)(1) GG. What was that like for you?

[17] Helmut Simon (1922–2013), judge on the Federal Court of Justice (1965–1970); justice on the First Senate of the Federal Constitutional Court (1970–1987).

[18] Gisela Niemeyer (1923–2012), judge on the Federal Finance Court (1972–1977); justice on the First Senate of the Federal Constitutional Court (1977–1989).

[19] Cf. fn. 7. In the First Senate, a new justice typically assumes the portfolio of his or her predecessor; in the Second, the responsibilities of a departing justice are distributed among the remaining justices according to seniority. The new justices take over what remains following the redistribution. This means that vacancies in the First Senate can be filled with a greater attention to topics than vacancies in the Second Senate.

DG: Ah yes. If one were to list in a footnote all the books, essays, and case notes dealing with free speech jurisprudence, it would be very long. The discussion was also deeply personal. Rüdiger Zuck[20] published an essay in the *Neue Juristische Wochenschrift* with the title, "Justice for Judge Grimm"—which, however, was anything but a plea for understanding. When I presented on "Personality Protection in Constitutional Law"[21] at the Karlsruhe Forum in 1996, the moderator thought it necessary to stress that I was a *member* of the First Senate and not *the* First Senate. As at other conferences, the atmosphere there was chilly. In Karlsruhe, my Bielefeld colleague, Peter Schwerdtner,[22] fired with heavy artillery but little marksmanship. The atmosphere changed only when Claus-Wilhelm Canaris[23] expressed his agreement with my remarks. Thus, even Uwe Diederichsen,[24] in his rhyming synopsis of the conference could ask: "Might Justice Grimm, from what we saw, / Be not so bad for private law?" In fact, the free speech cases had the backing of the entire Senate. What was true of the broadcasting case law was true here as well: the foundations had been laid long before my time. The *"Soldiers are Murderers"* judgment was the only significant exception to the rule that our free speech decisions were unanimous. And even then, one of the four cases was decided unanimously, which meant that the standards were approved unanimously and thus deprived the only dissenting opinion (two of the three judges in the minority declined to write dissents) of much of its fundamental quality.

CW: You were accused of having abolished the protection of honor in favor of free speech.

DG: That was the heart of the critique, sometimes embellished with the charge that I wanted to foist American law on Germany. The critique, however, was misguided in both law and fact. In fact, more ordinary-court judgments giving precedence to the protection of honor were affirmed than were overturned. This, of course, wasn't apparent to everyone because most cases concluded with unpublished chamber decisions. Legally, the accusation was wrong because it had been the Federal Constitutional Court itself that first elevated honor to the status of a fundamental right. In the text of the

[20] Rüdiger Zuck (1932–present), lawyer; longtime chair of the constitutional law section of the Federal Bar Association.

[21] Egon Lorenz (ed.), *Karlsruher Forum 1996: Schutz der Persönlichkeit* (1997) 3–26.

[22] Peter Schwerdtner (1938–2006), professor of private law and legal theory at the University of Bielefeld.

[23] Claus-Wilhelm Canaris (1937–present), professor of private law and legal philosophy at the universities of Graz, Hamburg, and Munich.

[24] Uwe Diederichsen (1933–present), professor of private law at the universities of Cologne and Göttingen.

Basic Law, it is merely a restraint on the freedom of opinion, whereas some critics thought the framers themselves had established the primacy of personal honor in Article 5(2) GG. What most critics failed to understand was that in cases of conflict between free speech and personal honor, one must always consider the consequences for democratic discourse. That had been established as early as *Lüth*.[25] If there was any reliance at all on American jurisprudence, it was here, in the notion of a "chilling effect." The joyful reception of the 1996 *German Society for Humane Death* decision,[26] in which many detected a longed-for change of course, was premature. In that case, the civil courts had interpreted the contested expression in a variety of ways but had not committed any constitutional error. Accordingly, the judgment of the higher court was upheld. But there was no change in the legal standards for interpreting contested expressions. Because the attacks on our case law so often rested upon erroneous assumptions, I thought it necessary to clarify the Federal Constitutional Court's jurisprudence in an NJW essay.[27] I appended a diagram that still plays a role in the teaching and is called the "Grimmian Tree."

## B. 1987 as a Caesura in the History of the Federal Constitutional Court?

CW: When you arrived in Karlsuhe, the president of the Court was . . .

DG: . . . still Zeidler,[28] but only just. He left the Court in November and died in an accident shortly thereafter. He was succeeded by Roman Herzog,[29] who before that was vice president of the Court and presiding judge of

[25] 7 BVerfGE 198 (1958); in a debate about the limits of the fundamental right of freedom of opinion in the criticism of public figures complicit in Nazism—specifically, criticism by the publicist Erich Lüth of the postwar work comeback of Veit Harlan, a film director—the Federal Constitutional Court ruled that fundamental rights, in addition to their defensive function, constitute an "objective order of values" that radiate through the entire legal order and therefore into civil law as well.

[26] 94 BVerfGE 1 (1996); disputes between a disabled persons association and the German Society for Humane Death led to the more concrete interpretation of expressions of opinion by the ordinary courts.

[27] Dieter Grimm, "Meinungsfreiheit in der Rechtsprechung des Bundesverfassungsgerichts" (1995) 48 *Neue Juristische Wochenschrift* 1698.

[28] Wolfgang Zeidler (1924–1987), judge; justice of the First Senate of the Federal Constitutional Court (1967–1970); president of the Federal Administrative Court (1970–1975); justice of the Second Senate of the Federal Constitutional Court (1975–1987); vice president of the Court from 1975 to 1983 and president from 1983 to 1987.

[29] Roman Herzog (1934–2017), professor of public law at the Free University of Berlin and the Speyer College of Administration; politician (CDU); state secretary and *Land* minister in Rheinland-Pfalz and

the First Senate. Ernst Gottfried Mahrenholz[30] became the new vice president and presiding judge of the Second Senate. All told, there were six new justices appointed in 1987. I joined in July, the other five followed in November: Söllner[31] and Dieterich[32] in the First Senate, and Kruis,[33] Franßen,[34] and Kirchhof[35] in the Second.

OL: That is very unusual to have six new justices—almost half the Court—replaced in a single year. Was 1987 a caesura in the development of the Federal Constitutional Court?

DG: As far as numbers go, yes, more than a third of the justices were replaced. But I don't regard it as a substantive caesura. For the veteran judges, it might have represented something else. In the First Senate, one noticed the feeling that two heroes had departed: Simon and Hesse. (Katzenstein[36] was less suited for heroic characterizations.) But it didn't lead to a rupture in the case law.

OL: I will put the question a little more pointedly. Doesn't the latter part of the 1980s mark the beginning of what we might call a doctrinal phase? Earlier, there were different phases, beginning with the formative or "governess" phase of the 1950s and 1960s, followed by an activist phase in the 1970s and 1980s, during which the last reserves of the Basic Law were jurisprudentially filled out.[37] When you joined the Court, there were few free spaces left. There was already case law on every topic, unless you were dealing with

Baden-Württemberg; justice of the First Senate of the Federal Constitutional Court (1983–1994); president of the Federal Constitutional Court (1987–1994); president of the Federal Republic of Germany (1994–1999).

[30] Ernst Gottfried Mahrenholz (1929–present), advisor in the communal and state administration in Lower Saxony; chief of the Lower Saxony state chancellery office (1970–1974); Lower Saxony minister of culture (1974–1976); member of the state parliament (1976–1981); justice on the Second Senate of the Federal Constitutional Court (1981–1994).

[31] Alfred Söllner (1930–2005), professor of private law, labor law, and welfare law at the universities of Kiel and Gießen; justice on the First Senate of the Federal Constitutional Court (1987–1995).

[32] Thomas Dieterich (1934–2016), judge on the Federal Labor Court (1972–1987); justice of the First Senate of the Federal Constitutional Court (1987–1994), thereafter president of the Federal Labor Court.

[33] Konrad Kruis (1930–present), officer in the Bavarian state chancellery beginning in 1960, ultimately as head of the division for legislation and law; ministerial director beginning in 1978; justice of the Federal Constitutional Court (1987–1998).

[34] Everhardt Franßen (1937–present), judge on the Federal Administrative Court (1977–1987); justice of the Second Senate of the Federal Constitutional Court (1987–1991); president of the Federal Administrative Court (1991–2002).

[35] Paul Kirchhof (1943–present), professor of constitutional law, administrative law, financial law, and tax law at the universities of Münster and Heidelberg; justice of the Second Senate of the Federal Constitutional Court (1987–1999).

[36] Dietrich Katzenstein (1923–2008), president of the state ecclesiastical office in Hamburg; justice of the First Senate of the Federal Constitutional Court (1975–1987).

[37] On the periodization, see Justin Collings, *Democracy's Guardians: A History of the German Federal Constitutional Court, 1951–2001* (2015).

entirely new things, such as data protection. The generation that preceded you—the generation of Hesse and Simon—still had the chance to fill out a fundamental right thirty years after the Basic Law's adoption: I'm thinking, for instance, of the *Brokdorf* decision[38] on the freedom of association. These spaces are no longer there in the generation with which you joined the Court. There is case law on every hand, and the objective now is to work new developments into what is already there. So there now begins a doctrinal phase. The cohort that joined the Court in 1987 is thus in a different situation than the one that joined twelve years earlier. The predecessors were essentially freer.

DG: Martin Oldiges, the then-dean of the Bielefeld faculty, made a similar observation when he spoke at a reception occasioned by my appointment. He wished me well; noted that this was also a great honor for the faculty; but then added that this no longer had the significance it once did because by then the Basic Law was already developed. What remained was to apply the conclusions reached by earlier generations of judges. I didn't believe him at the time, and Reunification utterly refuted him later on. Everything that had to be decided then was without precedent and occupied the Court for ten years.

But even setting aside the cases related to Reunification, I can't see that we were only embedding new developments within existing structures. Only now did the right to asylum, after its revision in 1993, become a major theme. The question of how fundamental rights affect contract law now arose for the first time. There were great stirrings in welfare law—tax law too. After the geopolitical convulsions of 1989, the role of the *Bundeswehr* (the national army) needed to be redefined. The overarching importance of questions of European law made itself felt. It is true, however, that with the *Mülheim-Kärlich* decision[39] of 1979, fundamental rights doctrine had taken its last great step and since then stands ready for application before the Court.

If I were to speak of a caesura, it would be a different one from the one you have in mind. The Court's role began to change. The phase in which the Court's principal task was to impress upon political institutions, ordinary

[38] 69 BVerfGE 315 (1985). The Senate established the constitutional prerequisites for dispersing or banning a public assembly and required accordingly a constitution-conforming interpretation of sections 14 and 15 of the Public Assembly Law. Freedom of assembly belongs to the "indispensable functional elements" of a democratic community. On the *Brokdorf* case, see A. Doering-Manteuffel, B. Greiner, and O. Lepsius, *Der Brokdorf-Beschluss des Bundesverfassungsgerichts 1985* (2015).

[39] 53 BVerfGE 30 (1979).

courts, and administrative authorities the meaning of fundamental rights was over. To an astonishing degree, the binding nature of fundamental rights had been internalized. That doesn't mean that infringements of fundamental rights are a thing of the past. But they are less often the result of a deficient sensibility for fundamental rights. Instead, the Court increasingly finds itself in the role of counterweight to politicians' short-sightedness and inattention to principle. The Court must remind politicians of society's long-term aspirations. It has gone, so to speak, from watchman to admonisher.

OL: Take the decision on codetermination.[40] There were previously two decisions on the property guarantee of Article 14 GG on which to build. But in the end the *Codetermination* decision was the leading decision on the legislature's powers of prognosis and on the corresponding scope of the Court's review. This question was first decided in 1979—after twenty-eight years of Constitutional Court case law. After that decision, although the topic comes up repeatedly, there isn't the same freedom of maneuver. The volumes containing the Court's decisions constantly expand; respect for the earlier case law grows, together with self-subjection to the case law of one's predecessors' predecessors' predecessors. Thus, the Court in 1987 didn't have the freedom of decision that it still possessed in 1977. And today it must still "free itself" from some earlier decisions, and it does so by not citing the first hundred volumes of published decisions. Everything before volume 100—and thereby your decisions as well—increasingly drops out of the canon of citation.[41]

DG: The question is not how often the earlier cases are cited, but whether the Court continues to follow the outlines of its earlier case law. The *Television Fees* judgment of 2007[42] follows almost verbatim that of 1994. Thereafter, though, it's no longer necessary to cite the older case. With every volume of decisions, the net undoubtedly grows tighter. But scientific and technological progress and shifts in societal values ensure movement enough.

[40] 50 BVerfGE 290 (1979). The Senate declared that the expansion of employee codetermination after passage of the 1976 Codetermination Law was constitutional.

[41] The hundredth volume of the Court's official reports—the *Entscheidungen des Bundesverfassungsgerichts* (BVerfGE)—appeared in 1999, the year in which Dieter Grimm's term on the Constitutional Court ended. The decisions in which Dieter Grimm took part are printed in volumes 76 to 101.

[42] 119 BVerfGE 181 (2007); a renewed affirmation, in light of advancing technological developments, of the validity of statements about the dual broadcasting system; limitation of the powers of state parliaments with respect to the financing recommendations of the Commission for the Review and Determination of the Financial Needs of Broadcasting Networks.

Occasionally, they even necessitate a "new" fundamental right. I'm thinking of the integrity and confidentiality of information systems.[43]

CW: The phenomenon differs only slightly from that of ordinary politics. In the early days of the Federal Republic, the Bundestag also had many more possibilities. Unless something exceptional happens, the space for decision-making disappears once a constitutional or a political order "comes of age." *Herr* Lepsius looked at you a bit skeptically when you highlighted the Reunification jurisprudence. There were, of course, many important cases, but they only amount to isolated decisions. Haven't most of them been historicized by now?

DG: I would agree with you on that point. These decisions—as important as they may have been and although they continue to have a social impact—had no enduring impact beyond the unique circumstances that evoked them. They gave rise to no doctrinal development. But my time on the Court was strongly shaped by them. There was virtually no problem related to Reunification that did not come before the Court. The Court's influence on the Reunification process still awaits a thorough assessment.

OL: Yes, but then the Court is absorbed in the technical details of regulation flowing from the unification treaties. Couldn't the great societal developments still be accompanied by constitutional law?

DG: The expression "technical details of regulation" underestimates the importance of those decisions. How would Reunification have proceeded if the original electoral law for the first all-German election—determined entirely by the interests of the western parties—had governed the first post-unification parliamentary elections? What would have happened if the question of restitution had been decided differently—the culpability of government criminality, the transition of pensions and old debts, the dismissal of employees who had been members of the East German communist party, etc.? For me personally, these cases were always grounded in the need for integration to succeed, and the need to avoid the impression that the eastern side was being steamrolled by the western. To this end, I would even have accepted a new Basic Law—without fearing that it would be much different from the old one.

[43] 120 BVerfGE 274 (2008); in connection with the assessment of so-called online searches (by the authorities), the Senate developed a new dimension in the protection of preexisting fundamental rights—the "fundamental right to the guarantee of the confidentiality and integrity of information-technical systems."

## C. "Riding in the Woods"

CW: You said that you cultivated continuity in the broadcasting law jurisprudence, and that you dealt with new developments—which were of a rather technological and economic nature—on this basis. But the decision in *Riding in the Woods* with your dissenting opinion[44] is, by contrast, something of a rebellion—an attempt, perhaps, to change a very strong traditional line. Could you say something about this? Given the underlying facts, the case always elicits smirks . . .

DG: Long before I ever even imagined that I would have a chance to influence the jurisprudence directly, I thought that the *Elfes* case[45] had been wrongly decided. I hinted as much to my Senate colleagues and announced my readiness, should an appropriate case come along, to reopen debate about the "catch-all" fundamental right. One day *Herr* Seidl,[46] who was primarily responsible for property rights cases under Article 14 GG, mentioned that he probably had a suitable case. It was *Riding in the Woods*. I remained, however, unsuccessful across the board. The discussion ended in a 7-to-1 defeat. One member of the Senate even charged that my perspective would pave the way for a police state. I could only laugh—*I*, a harbinger of the police state! I still think that things would have come out differently in 1957 if the Senate had seen that there was a middle way between the two extreme positions it discussed—a path that it later took, beginning with the

[44] 80 BVerfGE 137 (1989); in this decision, the Senate stood by its settled case law, under which Article 2(1) GG protects the "general liberty of action in the comprehensive sense" and thereby riding in the woods as well; a state law that banned riding outside established forest paths was nevertheless deemed justified. Dieter Grimm wrote a dissenting opinion in which he championed a narrower understanding of the scope of protection under Article 2(1) GG: "Riding in the woods enjoys no fundamental rights protection. Fundamental rights differ from the host of other rights in that they protect the integrity, autonomy, and communication of the individual in their fundamental instantiations. Precisely because of this fundamental significance of their objects of protection for an order founded on human dignity, fundamental rights have been set apart from the mass of rights and endowed with elevated guarantees vis-à-vis public authority—and, in particular, with binding effect for the legislature. At the same time, conceptions of what the heightened protection of fundamental rights specifically entail can change with historical circumstances. But it is neither historically nor functionally the purpose of fundamental rights to place every imaginable human action under their special protection."

[45] 6 BVerfGE 32 (1957); the Senate here founded its long settled jurisprudence, according to which Article 2(1) GG protects the "general freedom of action" in a comprehensive sense.

[46] Otto Seidl (1931–present); judge on the Federal Court of Justice (1978–1986); justice of the First Senate of the Federal Constitutional Court (1986–1998); vice president of the Federal Constitutional Court (1995–1998).

*Micro-census* decision of 1969,[47] but without correcting its *Elfes* mistake. I thought the matter was worth a dissenting opinion, though my law clerks counseled against it.[48] "The case is over," they said. "It's not worth it." I was pleased that my dissent led constitutional scholars to address the question again in a fundamental way, even though this discussion also ended to my disadvantage. One colleague later wrote that, in the end, I had apparently been converted, since I didn't hold to my position in further dissenting opinions. But that, of course, is nonsense. I'm no Cato, after all.

OL: Can one not say that an administrative lawyer needs the seamless protection of fundamental rights in order to have available an individual counter-right against the potential all-powerful encroachments of the administrative state? The constitutionalist socialized in private law doesn't need the seamless protection of fundamental rights. For him it's a matter of balancing, of relevance, of power.

DG: I didn't need the seamless protection of fundamental rights, not because I had a greater affinity for private law, but because I had a particular—one could even say an *emphatic*—understanding of fundamental rights. It is incompatible with that understanding that every imaginable act or omission enjoys fundamental rights protection and can only be restricted on the basis of some limiting regulation. I oppose the trivialization of fundamental rights expressed in the prevailing conception.

## D. Constitutional Law and Private Law

CW: Let me follow up in the open areas that *Herr* Lepsius has just addressed. The decisions on private law matters—with *Commercial Representative*[49] and *Suretyship*[50] as watchwords—introduced much that was new. Since

[47] 27 BVerfGE 1 (1969) (ruling on the constitutionality of a representative government statistical survey).

[48] Law clerks at the Federal Constitutional Court are typically either judges from lower courts on secondment or junior scholars who pursue an academic career in constitutional law.

[49] 81 BVerfGE 242 (1990); the Senate derived from Article 12(1) GG the duty of the legislature to take measures to protect the freedom of occupation against contractual limitations—in this case a competition ban on commercial representatives without compensation—in the face of an imbalance of power between the parties.

[50] 89 BVerfGE 214 (1993); the Senate required civil courts to take into account the guarantee of private autonomy, which stems from Article 2(1) GG, when applying the general clauses of sections 138

the *Lüth* judgment, a lot had been written about fundamental rights being embedded in private law, but now a different construction was involved. I can still remember how baffled I was by the reasoning in the *Suretyship* judgment. The case could have been resolved with the indirect horizontal effect, but the Court proceeded according to its fundamental rights model: private autonomy must be saved as such, not the individual who had gotten entangled and needed to stand surety. That is a very institutional approach. Private autonomy must be preserved as such, and that applies only when excesses are avoided: the radically anti-individualist approach, that is. Here, in any case, there was still an open area—or was it a paradigm shift from the duty-to-protect argumentation from *Lüth*?

DG: I must say first of all that I was not the driving force in this case. It fell instead within *Herr* Dieterich's portfolio, and for the outcome it is surely no coincidence that Dieterich was, from the bottom of his heart, a labor lawyer.[51] For my part, the case was a source of headaches. The conclusion of a contract is itself an exercise of freedom, and the limitations on freedom to which a contracting party submits are voluntary self-limitations. For that reason, contracts leave little space for the influence of fundamental rights. But I also agreed—naturally—with the proposition that freedom of contract only leads to a just balance of interests when the parties engage with one another from positions of relative equilibrium. Failing that, the state has a duty to protect. On the other side, poor representation of one's own interests during contractual negotiations does not trigger a duty to protect. It is a question of structural disadvantages. When can one assume their existence and how does one identify them?

CW: The *Lüth* case was highly politicized from the outset. And it played out, not in contract law, but in the realm of statutory obligations. But now the heart of contract law was in play.

DG: I was fully aware of the novelties of the set-up. To a labor lawyer, however, they might have seemed entirely commonplace.

OL: For the labor lawyer, it is a fundamental experience that parity of power in a contractual relationship cannot be presumed. But how did the contracts lawyers react? Or was it criticized as an institutional overreach on the part of the Court?

and 242 of the Civil Code, and to engage in substantive review of contracts marked by an unusual strong burden on one of the parties as well as structurally unequal bargaining power.

[51] Cf. Thomas Dieterich, *Ein Richterleben im Arbeits- und Verfassungsrecht* (2016) 193ff.

DG: The *Commercial Representative* case and the subsequent *Suretyship* case revived for a time the battle over the boundaries between the Constitutional Court and the civil courts. For a long time, the Constitutional Court was poorly regarded by private lawyers. The biannual Conference of German Jurists took up the theme. The private lawyers' objection was that one didn't need constitutional law to achieve balance in such settings; private law could achieve that with its own means. My answer was: But you didn't use them, so the impetus must come from without. This didn't, however, disrupt relations between the Constitutional Court and the ordinary courts in any enduring way. In this respect, Germany differs from many other countries in which relatively young constitutional courts must forever battle against ordinary-court opposition. The relaxed relationship in Germany is surely aided by the fact that many judges of the ordinary supreme courts worked previously as law clerks at the Constitutional Court and are intimately familiar with the interplay between constitutional law and ordinary law. Today, all of the presidents of the five supreme federal courts were law clerks at the Constitutional Court for several years. That is not without consequence.

# VII.
# Uproar about the Constitutional Court's Jurisprudence

## A. *Crucifix* and *"Soldiers are Murderers"*

OL: One of the Court's periodic crises vis-à-vis the political branches fell during your term on the bench—a period of intensified political and even societal controversy surrounding the Court's case law. *Crucifix*[1] and *"Soldiers are Murderers"*[2] were two decisions that first met with incomprehension. How did the Court deal with this response?

DG: The decisions provoked the sharpest protest against the Federal Constitutional Court that I experienced during my tenure there—perhaps the largest protest altogether. Because *"Soldiers are Murderers"* raised no new or controversial questions, the reasoning in the chamber decision was relatively brief. The criminal conviction was overturned because the lower court had isolated the expression from its context and hadn't excluded possible interpretations that would *not* have led to a conviction. The chamber decision came down toward the beginning of the 1994 election campaign.[3] That fanned the flames and kept them burning. Politicians seized upon the case or were compelled to take a stand on it.

On the evening of the day the decision was published, the Conference of German Jurists began in Münster. I was sitting in the front row for the

[1] 93 BVerfGE 1 (1995); the Court held that the compulsory affixation of a crucifix on the walls of a non-confessional public school violates the students' negative religious liberty under Article 4(1) GG.

[2] This began with a 1994 chamber decision, 47 *Neue Juristische Wochenschrift* 2943 (1994), followed by a Senate decision, 93 BVerfGE 266 (1995). In response to a constitutional complaint, the chamber annulled a criminal judgment in which the complainant was convicted of incitement (under section 130 of the Criminal Code) for having posted a decal with the inscription "Soldiers are Murderers." In doing so, the chamber relied on settled doctrine, according to which a conviction violates Article 5(1)(1) GG if, "in the face of ambiguous expressions, the interpretation leading to the conviction is chosen without persuasive reasons for excluding other, equally plausible interpretations (cf. 43 BVerfGE 130, 136; 82 BVerfGE 43, 52; 82 BVerfGE 272, 280; 85 BVerfGE 1, 14)." The Senate decision affirmed this jurisprudence.

[3] The chamber decision was dated August 25, 1994. The Bundestag election was held on October 16, 1994.

*Dieter Grimm: Advocate of the Constitution.* Dieter Grimm, Oxford University Press (2020). © in the original German edition, Mohr Siebeck GmbH & Co. KG, Tübingen 2017, © this translation, Justin Collings 2020.
DOI: 10.1093/oso/9780198845270.001.0001

opening session. Roman Herzog, the federal president, was giving the keynote address. While he was still speaking, I was approached by journalists asking for a commentary about the decision. "You know," I answered, "that I don't comment on decisions." They then pulled out agency reports with statements from politicians about the case that had little to do with the decision—"Federal Constitutional Court: German Soldiers are Murderers." My colleague, Renate Jaeger,[4] was seated next to me. I asked her whether, under the circumstances, I ought to make a statement. She thought that I must. So I spoke in the corridors in front of numerous cameras and microphones. My comments aired on the principal news broadcasts.[5] That gave the decision a name and a face.

The next morning the elections for the Permanent Deputation of the Conference of German Jurists took place. *Herr* Kirchhof and I were the candidates for one of the posts. I lost by a mile. I understand that in the personnel debate prominent jurists said that it was unthinkable that the person responsible for such a decision should represent the German Jurists Conference. In a panel discussion, a politician attacked the decision in terms that made it clear he hadn't read it. I objected that his criticism was beside the point; it would be very advisable, I suggested, to first acquire a little knowledge about the object of one's critique. He answered that he didn't have time to read seventy pages overnight. "The decision," I responded, "is only seven pages long."

In the following days and weeks, I was inundated by a flood of letters—among them death threats, which I forwarded to the Federal Criminal Police Office's satellite station at the Federal Constitutional Court. They appointed body guards that very day. The letters were of three kinds: many were insulting; a few expressed agreement. In between there was a group that expressed deep disturbance or injury. Those were the letters I answered. Not infrequently I received a further reply. When they said, "I see now why you did what you did. I still don't think it's right, but I understand it," I felt that it had been worth the effort.

When the chamber decision was published, there were still other soldier cases lying on my desk. After the storm of protest, it seemed obvious that

[4] Renate Jaeger (1940–present), judge on the Federal Welfare Court (1987–1994); justice on the First Senate of the Federal Constitutional Court (1994–2004); judge on the European Court of Human Rights (2004–2011).

[5] An excerpt from the statement was broadcast in the "20 Uhr-Tagesschau" of September 20, 1994, available online: http://www.tagesschau.de/multimedia/video/video-23324.html, accessed on December 23, 2019.

I should forward them for consideration by the full Senate, even though they raised no legal questions in need of clarification. The Senate affirmed the Chamber decision—unanimously in one of the four cases, by a vote of five to three in the others.

OL: Which decision brought you the police protection—the chamber decision or the Senate decision?

DG: The chamber decision. The Senate decision, which followed at a year's distance, unleashed no further tumult. Perhaps there were critics who hoped that the Senate would show the three unhinged judges what was what. But in light of the Court's settled case law, that could hardly be seriously expected. The Senate's decision, moreover, was so composed as to offer few targets for further attack. From the discussions about the Chamber decision, I knew everything that had been perceived as injurious or offensive. I took pains to consider such feelings. I tried, as it were, to speak with the tongue of angels.

That doesn't mean, of course, that the Senate decision met with universal agreement. But there was no repetition of the large-scale assault. If I remember right, there were constitutional complaints against the renewed criminal decisions in two of the cases; one led to the judgment's being overturned, the other was rejected because this time the court had plausibly defended its interpretation.

OL: So the matter became personalized because of your appearance at the Jurists Conference?

DG: That's how it became known who had been the judge rapporteur in the case—something that is otherwise known only by insiders. *Die Welt* went even further, publishing the images and info of the three "perpetrators" on the Federal Constitutional Court in the manner of a wanted poster.[6] A little later, a conference of the Press Law Study Group was held in Weimar. I met with *Die Welt*'s Karlsruhe correspondent in front of the hotel. When he greeted me, he told his wife with an introductory gest, "This is the infam . . . — er, the *famous* constitutional judge Grimm."

CW: Does the *"Soldiers are Murderers"* decision mark the beginning of an enduringly controversial practice by which the Court explains its own decisions? Was that, perhaps unwittingly, the opening salvo in a development that is still much discussed today? The Court often says that it must communicate its judgment to the public because it is so complex and might

[6] An excerpt from the article is reprinted in Michael Hepp and Viktor Otto (eds), *"Soldaten sind Mörder"* (1996) 177ff.

otherwise be misunderstood. I suspect, without being able to prove it just now, that the Court of the 1950s and 1960s said nothing about its decisions and perhaps could not have said anything about them.

DG: No. However, the public statements multiplied in light of the enormous commotion in the aftermath of the *Soldiers* and *Crucifix* decisions. My sense is that the Court assumed a stronger public profile beginning with the presidency of Ernst Benda.[7] Zeidler didn't shun the public gaze either. I remember his mollifying approach following the kerfuffle surrounding the first abortion judgment, when he spoke of a "raspberry-sized" embryo—the outrage in response to which subsided only after conciliatory talks with the German Bishops' Conference. As near as I can judge, Gebhard Müller[8] was the Court's last reticent president. But public appearances of other justices are nothing new either. There was, for example, a long-running show on the South German Broadcasting, in which important judgments—and not only those of the Federal Constitutional Court—were discussed. It was not considered unseemly for the judge rapporteur to appear on the show and explain the judgment in conversation with an editor.

The Court has little reason to complain about media coverage as such. The great daily and weekly newspapers have correspondents in Karlsruhe, as do the public broadcasting networks. These are thoroughly knowledgeable journalists, who have their own point of view but who accurately present the subject matter. However, when cases like *Crucifix* or *Soldiers* come up, coverage falls to journalists who aren't familiar with the material. When that happens, the actual substance of the case disappears swiftly behind what others have said about it. In such cases, I think it is important—within the limits of the judicial role—to offer clarification. That's what happened with the *Soldiers* decision. The Court had neither said itself that soldiers are murderers nor decided that this expression was permitted without qualification. It merely insisted that courts assess such statements carefully before punishing those who make them. If the statement in fact libels people, it can be prosecuted. If it is a rejection—even an exaggerated rejection—of militarism, a denunciation of killing in war, or a plea for pacifism, then it must be allowed. Accordingly, I didn't avoid invitations to discuss the case—such as

[7] Ernst Benda (1925–2009), politician; member of the Berlin House of Delegates (1955–1957); member of the German Bundestag (1957–1971); federal interior minister (1968–1969); president of the Federal Constitutional Court (1971–1983).

[8] Gebhard Müller (1900–1990), chief prosecutor; took part in the reconstruction of the justice system in Württemberg-Hohenzollern (1946); member of the Württemberg-Hohenzollern state parliament (1948–1952); member of the Baden-Württemberg constituent assembly; minister president of the state Baden-Württemberg (1953–1958); president of the Federal Constitutional Court (1959–1971).

at the federal army's Leadership Academy in Hamburg. What one needed to make clear was that it wasn't a question of disparaging soldiers, but of dealing fairly with expressions of opinion.

OL: Was the Court's press office empowered in the aftermath? Was there active press and public relations work?

DG: The press office was established after the *Crucifix* judgment, not after the *Soldiers* decision. The furor over the *Soldiers* decision was over by May 1995 when, in the aftermath of the *Crucifix* decision, the next wave of indignation crashed over the Constitutional Court. It was different from the reaction to the *Soldiers* decision, but no less fierce. The reactions were more geographically limited. Unsurprisingly, the focal point was in Bavaria. After all, the judgment dealt only with Bavarian schools. There was also a lot of protest in the rest of southern Germany and in western Germany. There was little in the north, almost nothing in the east. This time, the criticism wasn't personal. It targeted the Court as an institution. It was better organized. There were mass petitions, such as from Bavarian parishes. There were protest marches in which bishops and ministers took part. The motivations of the protest were also different. As the letters following the *Soldiers* decision made clear, feelings of personal injury played a big role: my father or brother died for the Fatherland, and now he is being defamed as a murderer. Others associated soldiering primarily with a willingness to lay down one's life for higher values and felt themselves or soldiers generally debased by the Tucholsky quotation.

With the *Crucifix* judgment, by contrast, it was more about questions of identity. Even if more and more people are exiting the churches and attendance at Sunday worship service is declining, we still want to understand ourselves openly as a society shaped by Christianity and to see Christian values imparted through the schools. The secular state is generally accepted, but must all of its consequences be accepted as well? In my observation, the level of agitation was higher, on the whole, in Catholic regions. This increased the dismay with the Court. To illustrate with a personal example: a cousin of mine living in Munich disinvited me from his sixtieth birthday celebration—with every indication that it was difficult and awkward for him, but: "You cannot even imagine what is going on here." My mother's youngest sister—the only one of the siblings still living—called me up and said, "I'm only glad your mother doesn't have to experience this." The Constitutional Court was compared to the Nazis. Indeed, the Court was even worse: the Nazis hadn't succeeded in removing the crosses from the schools. Nonsensical consequences were derived from the decision: the crosses at the summits of the Bavarian mountains must disappear; *Nathan the Wise* could no longer be performed in public theaters, since the Templar dons a robe with a cross.

MR: How did politicians react to the judgment?

DG: Politicians proclaimed that the decision was so erroneous that it mustn't be obeyed. If such statements were possible, this was obviously about more than crucifixes. It was about the foundations of the democratic rule of law. How could politicians credibly demand obedience to their laws from those who didn't approve of them if they themselves eschewed obedience to court decisions they didn't like? I couldn't believe that such a self-dismantling of democratic politics hadn't immediately set off alarm signals. But it was so. I had written a short text about this and for days I carried it around with me in my briefcase, reflecting that it must be observed that the controversy had now reached a stage in which it was no longer about crosses in classrooms, but about the fact that democratic politicians, for the sake of short-term popularity gains, were about to sever the branch that was the strongest support of their long-term legitimacy. In the end, I sent the text to the *Frankfurter Allgemeine Zeitung*, which published it the next day.[9]

The Federal Constitutional Court's approval ratings fell rapidly. The Court itself seemed to me more shaken than after the *Soldiers* decision. Böckenförde told me, "After this decision, the Court will never again be what it was before." I doubted that, and only supposed that the Court's recovery in public opinion would take a little longer this time than was usual after controversial decisions. And so it came about.

CW: As far as I know, the rapporteur was Henschel.[10] In my view, the problematic part of the judgment was, *inter alia*, the phrase "Learning under the Cross [*Kreuz*]." This is problematic in two senses: on the one hand, it unilaterally emphasized the alleged burden of sitting and learning "under" the cross; on the other, it echoed the phrase made familiar through historical research, "Learning under the Swastika [*Hakenkreuz*]."

DG: I share your view. Henschel clearly wasn't thinking of National Socialism, but of the decision about the cross in the courtroom, which spoke of the intolerable coercion involved in requiring a Jewish lawyer to conduct his case

[9] Dieter Grimm, "Unter dem Gesetz " *Frankfurter Allgemeine Zeitung* (August 18, 1995) 29; in English in Donald P. Kommers and Russell A. Miller (eds), *The Constitutional Jurisprudence of the Federal Republic of Germany* (3rd ed. 2012) 584.

[10] Johann Friedrich Henschel (1931–2007), lawyer, ultimately with the Federal Court of Justice; justice of the First Senate of the Federal Constitutional Court (1983–1995); presiding justice of the First Senate and vice president of the Federal Constitutional Court (1994–1995).

"under the cross."[11] At the time, I suggested different phrasing for various passages in the draft decision, which were accepted. In hindsight, I have berated myself for not intervening more often. Jurisprudentially, nothing depended on the phrase "under the cross." But one also doesn't want to ask too much of the judge rapporteur.

CW: One thing about the judgment that has always both interested and puzzled me is that the Senate does, in the end, undertake a theological interpretation of the cross. But in two respects this is something that the Court "cannot" do: first, because the justices are not theologians—that is, they lack the necessary theological expertise; and second, because the state cannot decide theological questions without surrendering its religious neutrality. The theological interpretation was also not really necessary. The Senate could have relied entirely on the cross's effect—on the perspective of its reception.

DG: In my view the question was unavoidable. The meaning of the cross was disputed both in the pleadings and within the Senate. Some regarded it as a specifically Christian religious symbol, others as a general symbol of Western culture. The decisions of the administrative courts below maintained that the cross was a religious symbol only for Christian students, not for others. The Bavarian state government argued that the cross's meaning shifted with the subject being taught. During religious instruction, it was a religious symbol; when the math teacher entered the classroom, it became a cultural symbol. The difference was legally relevant because, if the cross had no religious meaning, then it couldn't infringe upon the complainant's religious liberty. You're right, though, that the Court lacks the competence to determine the cross's meaning. For that reason, the Court inquired after the self-understanding of the Christian churches that identify themselves with this symbol. To do so, it drew upon two uncontroversial sources—namely, the respective lexicons of both major churches: the *Lexicon for Theology and Church*[12] and *Religion in History and in the Present.*[13]

At some point, the storm died down. In Bavaria, after all, little changed. Most of the crosses remained on the walls. This was the result of an ambiguity in the decision, which Bavarian lawmakers exploited. It wasn't entirely clear from the judgment whether the crosses had to be removed without exception, or only when a student or parent objected. Behind that lay a doctrinal ambiguity. In the end, was the decisive factor the subjective right of

[11] 35 BVerfGE 366, 375 f. (1973).

[12] *Lexikon für Theologie und Kirche* (3d ed. 1993–2001).

[13] *Religion in Geschichte und Gegenwart* (4th ed. 1998–2005).

religious liberty or the objective principle, derived therefrom, of the state's neutrality with respect to different religions?

The Court's professional PR work stems from discussions about the *Crucifix* decision. *Frau* Limbach[14] called the press office into being. The press releases were to become more media-friendly. The president and the justices were to be relieved of the burden of appearing personally whenever the Court took a position. *Frau* Limbach chose her media spokesperson, Uta Fölster, from her time as a senator in the Berlin government. Fölster had previously been a district court (*Amtsgericht*) judge.

CW: And is now president of the regional appeal court (*Oberlandesgericht*) in Schleswig . . .

DG: Before that, press releases were written by the judge rapporteur. These, of course, were usually short versions of the judgment, but much too long for a press release. Since the Court's public relations work has been professionalized, the press releases are written by the press office and submitted to the rapporteur to correct for errors.

CW: It strikes me that in recent years the press releases have again become more traditional and are written in the style of a judgment. Press statements should instead be written in a journalistic style.

DG: I find them too long and too doctrinal. On the one hand, they shouldn't cloak the fact that they deal with constitutional law. On the other hand, they are press releases for the media. Accordingly, they should account for the fact that the media have different selection criteria than the courts. I myself often thought of this when writing judgments. In important judgments, I aimed for one or two sentences suited for the papers. It usually worked. It got cited.

MR: Apart from the establishment of a press office, is there something to be learned for the work of the Federal Constitutional Court from the debates about the *Crucifix* decision? Can and should a court preempt such controversies over its decisions?

DG: What I learned from the *Crucifix* case is that such an explosive issue should only be decided after oral argument.[15] That way, the public is prepared for the decision; it doesn't come as a bolt from the blue. Those affected have the chance to present their position publicly. One can speculate, based on the questions they ask, how the judges view the case. None of this prevents

[14] Jutta Limbach (1934–2016), professor of private law at the Free University of Berlin; justice senator for the state of Berlin (1989–1994); president of the Federal Constitutional Court (1994–2002).

[15] Most cases are decided by the Federal Constitutional Court without oral argument. Since 1990, each Senate of the Court has conducted fewer than ten oral arguments per year.

disappointment or outrage, but it might well prevent such an outburst as we then experienced.

OL: Today, too, some constitutional justices feel attacked by criticism. But those who hear of your experiences can only conclude that never since has it gone so far. Back then there were concerted press campaigns that led to hate speech among the populace. In response to the *Crucifix* decision, there was a demonstration in Munich of 30,000 people. At the head stood officers of the state, such as the Bavarian minister president, who as state officials can claim no right of protest vis-à-vis the Court. We try to resolve such federal-state conflicts through other means than through the use of fundamental rights, which are not available as such to a minister president—that is a constitutional organ. These are dimensions that we really haven't seen again.

DG: I wouldn't exclude the possibility of something similar being repeated. Readiness to grow indignant has risen sharply in recent years. The new media facilitate the mobilization of great masses of people. There will always be politicians who exploit such currents for their own ends. A high-ranking national CSU politician later told me that his party was actually quite grateful for the *Crucifix* decision. It allowed them once again to rally Bavaria behind the CSU.

MR: How did the churches respond to you personally after the *Crucifix* decision? You've spoken of your engagement with the *Cusanuswerk* and your close contacts with former *Cusaners*. Were there reactions from that quarter?

DG: There was no reaction from the *Cusanuswerk*. But I do remember a conversation following a chance encounter with Cardinal Lehmann,[16] the then chairman of the German Bishops' Conference. I tried to explain to him that the decision was really a consequence of the Senate majority's having taken the cross seriously. The "Church and Politics" forum that Lehmann directed in Mainz invited me to a session on the decision. The hall was jam-packed, the atmosphere palpably hostile. Fortunately, that doesn't make me lose my composure. I don't know whether, in the end, my explanations about the constitutional order of relations between church and state persuaded any of the participants. As this discussion—but not only this discussion—shows, understanding was hindered most by the fact that many viewed the school, not as part of the state, but as an extension of the home. That differentiated this case from the decision about the cross in the courtroom, which provoked no protests.

[16] Karl Cardinal Lehmann (1936–2018), theologian; professor of dogmatics at the University of Mainz; bishop of Mainz (1983–2016); cardinal (2001); chairman of the German Bishops' Conference (1987–2008).

Some years after these events, there was a discussion at the Catholic Academy in Berlin between Father Langendörfer,[17] the secretary of the Bishops' Conference, and me on questions of religious liberty. The *Crucifix* decision came up again, and I was astonished at the unity between us—up to the one point on which Langendörfer dissented. With respect to the crucifix as a symbol of oppression or evangelization, as the complainant had maintained, he said that the church alone decides what the cross means—no one else. "Yes," I answered, "within the faith community, but not with binding effect for society as a whole."

CW: I still remember that from the Catholic side the reaction came very quickly: finally, someone is taking the cross seriously. The cross is not merely a diluted cultural symbol; rather it has a firm theological message.

DG: Yes, but that wasn't entirely agreed upon within the church. A conversation comes to mind that I had with personnel of the Bishops' Conference secretariat, foremost among them a former managing director of the *Cusanuswerk*, whom I knew well from this time. As he said, there were discussions in the Bishops' Conference about whether peace should be made with the cross as a cultural symbol in order to secure its presence in the public. I thought, and said unequivocally, that the church couldn't pay such a price without diluting its religious convictions.

OL: The *BILD* newspaper also agitated against the decision.[18] Peter Badura[19] wrote a brief in behalf of the Bavarian state government. *BILD* kiosks in Munich displayed a lead story with a photo of Badura in a brawny, bellicose posture. The title was, "Stoiber's Task: He Must Save the School Crosses." And the headline below: "The Lord God Remains."[20]

DG: For that, however, the Lord God wasn't dependent on Peter Badura's brief.

[17] Hans Langendörfer (1951–present), Jesuit; secretary of the German Bishops' Conference since 1996.

[18] Cf. *BILD München*, August 11, 1995. The headlines read, "Politicians Call for Revolution. War of the Cross in Bavaria. He [picture of the complainant] brought about the scandalous judgment." There followed on page one the article, "A disgrace for our country," a guest contribution by Dr. Peter Gauweiler. On page 3 there appeared a piece on the complainant with two photos, including his wife and children, all called by name. There was a small, red-lined superscription: "His name is Padranga, the swordsman—compulsory psychiatric custody and the authorities want to incapacitate him." Large superscription: "This weirdo brought Catholic Bavaria to its knees." Under this article there followed the block: "Reactions to the judgment. Stoiber combative. Waigel appalled. Church uncomprehending." On the reactions, *Der Spiegel* wrote on August 14, 1995, "The Cross is the Nerve," among others. Leo Kirch, a major shareholder of the Springer publishing house, demanded that the editor-in-chief of *Die Welt* be fired for having allowed a commentary against the crosses to be published. On the reactions in Karlsruhe, *Der Spiegel* spread rumors: "The Karlsruhe vice-president, Johann Friedrich Henschel, reported that his colleagues 'burst out laughing' when one of them read aloud from Bavarian protest letters printed in *BILD*. The excitement, the judge coolly prophecies, will soon subside. Emotions are always to be expected with 'questions that affect people personally.' "

[19] Peter Badura (1934–present), professor of constitutional and administrative law at the universities of Göttingen and Munich.

[20] *BILD München* (August 17, 1995).

## B. International Subject Matters, International Courts, International Standards

OL: In hindsight, which of your decisions was the most important?

DG: I can't answer that question as unambiguously as, for example, would have been possible for my colleague, Heußner. Heußner's great feat was the *Census* judgment. My first Senate decision came down in January 1988 and dealt with the freedom of the press (*Presse-Grosso*[21]). The last was dated December 1999 and also had press freedom, as well as personality protection, as its topic (*Caroline*[22]). In between there were fifteen Senate decisions on broadcasting freedom, five more on press freedom, ten on free speech, five on the right of assembly, three on personality rights (which was also relevant for several cases on speech or press freedoms), three on data protection and telecommunications secrecy, two on Reunification, one on freedom of information, and eleven others, among them some important ones in the field of commercial law. To a few of these decisions I attribute considerable significance stretching beyond the individual case. But I can't identify one single, most important case.

I'd rather mention, instead, the decision that gave me the greatest difficulty. It came from Jürgen Kühling's portfolio,[23] not mine, and it certainly doesn't rank among the most spectacular of the era. It dealt with a second register of shipping for German vessels.[24] This was supposed to hinder the outflagging of German ships by departing (to the benefit of ship owners and the disadvantage of their crews) from the principle that German law applies on German ships. This affected labor law directly, but it indirectly affected the German standard of fundamental rights as well. The dilemma was clear: if one were to uphold the German fundamental rights standard, there would soon be no cases in which to apply it on the high seas. If one wanted to uphold German shipping on the high seas, one must lower the standard of fundamental rights. The choice posed a severe test for me.

CW: A fundamental problem that we now confront everywhere.

DG: That wasn't clear to us at the time. We assumed that no other industry was as globalized as shipping on the high seas. With some limitations, we declared the law constitutional. But we wrote the judgment in such a way

[21] 77 BVerfGE 346 (1988).

[22] 101 BVerfGE 361 (1999).

[23] Jürgen Kühling (1934–2020) judge on the Federal Administrative Court (1979–1989); justice of the First Senate of the Federal Constitutional Court (1989–2001).

[24] 92 BVerfGE 26 (1995). The Senate declared constitutional, and thus compatible with Article 9(3) GG and 12(1) GG, a statutory regulation under which the compulsory rules of German labor law didn't apply automatically to second-registry ships under the German flag, but the rules of the state with which there is a "closer tie." By contrast, a regulation by which German collective labor agreements only applied when expressly agreed, even for union members on board such ships, was unconstitutional.

that, if the opportunity arose, it couldn't be applied to other branches of the economy.

OL: We haven't discussed *Caroline*[25] yet.

DG: *Caroline* was the last Senate decision that I had to prepare. The judgment was announced just a few days before my departure from the Court. The European Court of Human Rights later found that it violated Article 8 ECHR.[26] In an interview with the *Frankfurter Allgemeine Zeitung*, the first question was, "How does it feel for a former constitutional justice to have his decision censured in Strasbourg?" My answer was: "Unusual, but we in Karlsruhe have so often censured the judgments of other courts that one shouldn't complain if it happens, for once, to one's own Court." The bromide about their being only "the blue heavens above us" no longer applies without qualification in the age of Europeanization and globalization. But I disagreed with the ECtHR's reasoning. The judgment suffered from a cramped and paternalistic view of the democratic public sphere and the function of the press.

OL: The *Caroline* question signals the new conflicts with the ECtHR in Strasbourg. At bottom, and independent of the interpretation of texts, two different conceptions of fundamental rights collide because the protection of privacy is more pronounced in the ECHR than in the Basic Law. The ECHR's individualist conception of fundamental rights collides with the more strongly institutional understanding of the Basic Law: the safeguarding of the freedom of the press is a guiding principle of the Basic Law, as emerges powerfully in your decision. Institutional or individual protection of fundamental rights—these are the respective positions. This is also related to the differing functions of the two Courts. The ECtHR is a human rights court that can merely rebuke fundamental rights violations without, however, annulling the decisions of the offending state. The binding nature of such a decision as a one-off act is different from the binding effect of a Karlsruhe decision strongly attuned to the standard of institutional thinking about fundamental rights. The relations of the two

[25] 101 BVerfGE 361 (1999). Princess Caroline of Monaco brought an unsuccessful civil claim against the publication of photos of her in a tabloid magazine. With the exception of the photos that showed her children (which also implicated Article 6 GG), her constitutional complaint was largely rejected. The freedom of the press also comprises entertaining publications and their illustrations; it also shields the publication of pictures that show public figures in quotidian or private settings.

[26] ECtHR, judgment of June 24, 2004 (application no. 59320/00). The ECtHR saw in the decisions of the German courts a violation of the right to respect for private life (Article 8 ECHR). The decisive criterion for balancing the protection of private life and the freedom of opinion consists of whether the photos contribute to a debate of general interest. That wasn't the case with these purely private photos.

Courts could be more cordial if more attention were paid to the differing effects of their decisions. Instead, it's possible that we exaggerate the binding effect of ECtHR decisions because we interpret their binding effect and thus their scope as we would Karlsruhe decisions.

CW: In my view, the problems arise in their most essential form in "triangle cases." In bipolar fundamental rights cases—Citizen v. State—we have fewer problems with the ECtHR. Precisely when a law limits the citizen's sphere of freedom, and that limit must then be reviewed for conformity with fundamental rights, the relevant cultural background must be of decisive importance. That inevitably poses a problem for a Court that adjudicates for forty-seven member states.

DG: Tensions are inevitable with multi-level fundamental rights protection. The rights texts are not identical; the conception of fundamental rights is not the same—you alluded to this, *Herr* Lepsius; the methods of interpretation are different; and the boundaries between different levels are unclear—this is your point, *Herr* Waldhoff.

Article 53 ECHR forbids the ECtHR to fall short of the national level of fundamental rights protection. However, when the ECtHR censures national judgments in which both parties invoke fundamental rights and thus balancing is necessary, it inevitably narrows the standard of protection for the fundamental right to which the national court afforded precedence and expands the standard of protection for the right that had to yield at the national level. The framers of Article 53 didn't envision this type of case. But that doesn't mean that Article 53 plays no role here. Rather, this provision imposes a duty of special caution when "triangle cases" must be decided in Strasbourg. But the ECtHR has yet to find an appropriate posture toward Article 53. True, it does afford states a "margin of appreciation," but this is too often mere lip service.

When regarding ECtHR jurisprudence at the national level, the differences in binding effect do play a role. The Federal Constitutional Court addressed this—correctly, in my view—in the *Görgülü* case.[27] When, however, the ECtHR finds a violation of fundamental rights based, not on the interpretation of national law, but in national law itself, then the duty to remedy extends to the law and its effects thus reach beyond the individual case.

With respect to the Court of Justice of the European Union (ECJ), things are different. If it finds that national law violates EU law, the national law

[27] 111 BVerfGE 207 (2004).

loses its applicability without bringing the national legislature into play. EU law doesn't recognize a margin of appreciation.[28] On the contrary, the ECJ has developed the principle of *effet utile*—an instrument capable of confining national law considerably. Where fundamental rights are concerned, the European Charter of Fundamental Rights (CFR) has in *its* Article 53 a norm similar to Article 53 ECHR. EU fundamental rights also must not be interpreted in ways that lessen national fundamental rights protection. But this only applies "in their respective fields of application." The Charter's field of application is defined in Article 51, according to which European fundamental rights apply to EU organs always, but to the member states "only when they are implementing Union law." But the ECJ defines the implementation of Union law with extraordinary breadth and thus negates Article 53 CFR. To make matters worse, Article 53 CFR doesn't affect the four economic freedoms, which thus become a kind of super-fundamental rights.

OL: It's possible that, as an organ of the Council of Europe, the ECtHR feels bound by legal politics. From this perspective, it might even be quite convenient for the Court to reprove Germany in order to wield such decisions against the misdeeds of other states. Do you think that the European Courts operate in a manner significantly different from that of the Federal Constitutional Court? The randomness of assignments in the ECtHR has the inevitable result that its jurisprudence can't display the coherence that we have come to expect from German courts. The panels are not as homogeneously composed, are not as stable, and don't share the same background socialization. The European Courts are (they have said so themselves) isolated from the national cultures that can and should have a corrective effect on their jurisprudence. Taken together, shouldn't all this mean that one must approach judicial decisions differently depending on which court hands them down?

DG: The conditions under which international courts adjudicate are starkly different from those of courts in nation states. You allude to the smaller degree of homogeneity within the judicial panels. Of course, national courts are not homogeneous either in the sense that there are no differences of approach or doubts about interpretation. But they are homogeneous in the

[28] Under the margin of appreciation doctrine, the ECtHR allows the convention states of the ECHR to depart from the ECtHR's general standard of human rights when doing so is justified by national peculiarities of a factual, cultural, or regional nature. The states thus enjoy a certain leeway in implementing European human rights standards.

sense that the judges have been reared and socialized in a national legal culture that shapes conceptions of roles, patterns of behavior, and styles of argumentation. That culture often operates unconsciously, but for that reason all the more enduringly. National courts, moreover, are embedded in a thicker network of participation and accountability than are international courts. They work under constant scrutiny, not only from experts but also from the media and from a public informed by the media. Thus, contact between the courts and the society for which they adjudicate is much closer at the national than at the international level. When courts and society fall out of step, it is much easier to correct national than international courts through legislation. On the basis of these differences, I would derive a duty of greater restraint on the part of international courts vis-à-vis national law and its agents, the national courts. But such a duty is not easy to standardize and implement. It remains largely admonitory. For that reason, there is a certain amount of resistance among national courts. On this score, the Federal Constitutional Court said what needed to be said in its *Lisbon* judgment,[29] but then softened its stance in the *Honeywell* decision.[30]

CW: It appears to me that expert observers, and perhaps the "general" public as well, now perceives more friction between the Court and the ECtHR than between the Court and the ECJ (leaving aside the Euro rescue decisions). The ECJ possesses a clear function in a condensed, supranational space that requires a tribunal to resolve functional disputes. At first blush, there is nothing objectionable about minimal standards of fundamental rights, which the ECtHR is supposed to guarantee (though such minimal standards play almost no role in Germany). But I find highly problematic the perpetual, ad-hoc "intermeddling" with special jurisprudence on the basis of barely plausible, or at least anything but compelling, considerations.

DG: I have rather the impression that the mood shifts depending on the case. Sometimes the ECtHR faces stronger criticism, sometimes the ECJ. Think of Herzog's rallying cry from a while back in the *Frankfurter Allgemeine Zeitung*: "Stop the ECJ!"[31] The deeper reasons for wrangling with the European Courts are entirely different. The Council of Europe comprises around twenty more states than the EU. For the most part, the extras are states that lack an established tradition of human rights and the rule

[29] 123 BVerfGE 267 (2009).

[30] 126 BVerfGE 286 (2010).

[31] Roman Herzog and Lüder Gerken, "Stoppt den Europäischen Gerichtshof! " *Frankfurter Allgemeine Zeitung* (September 8, 2008) 8.

of law. There are ECtHR judges with very different backgrounds and qualifications. In light of the crushing load of cases pending in Strasbourg, the Court decides the overwhelming majority of cases in small groups—as panels of three judges or chambers of seven. That makes it easy to have different decisions in similar cases. The judges also don't see the records of the underlying national case but are dependent on the memos of assistants conversant in the relevant language. The judges decide based on this assistant's perception of the case. It would be interesting to see how the relevant assistant prepared the *Caroline* case. The only corrective is the participation of the judge from the country involved, but that is prescribed only for the chambers and the grand chamber. Another serious defect is that, in cases arising from civil proceedings, the party who won at the national level is not represented, since the case in Strasbourg is an action against the state brought by the party who lost at home.

As far as the EU is concerned, yes, it is indispensable that there be a Community court to interpret and apply Union law independent of national self-interests. The problem here lies in the self-understanding of that court. Till now, the ECJ has not understood itself as a neutral arbiter between the EU and its member states, but rather has pursued an integration agenda that leads to the ever more powerful suppression of national law. If one talks about this with ECJ judges, one often hears that this mindset is a thing of the past. And there are in fact an increasing number of judgments that seem to confirm this. But they haven't yet amounted to a change of course.

OL: I find very important your thought that a court stands in a position of societal accountability and understands itself as a national court. Decisions get debated in a national discursive community; they are commented politically and examined scientifically. Such feedback is missing among the European Courts because there is no European discursive community.

CW: Reliance on cultural and contextual factors is essential precisely when it comes to protecting fundamental rights. In the realm of religious freedom, the ECtHR succeeds rather well when, in light of differing basic conceptions of the relations between church and state, it assesses headscarf bans differently in Turkey than in other contexts. This basic conception is very different among the ECHR's forty-seven member states. That is especially clear in the context just mentioned, but in fact it should apply to all fundamental rights—including problems of equality and questions of discrimination—all of which are culturally defined and conditioned to the highest degree. Only by accounting for this fact can this kind of fundamental rights protection function at all. And so I conclude: minimal standards, yes; but everything beyond that becomes problematic.

DG: I agree on both counts, but I want to add a *mea culpa*. My professorial neighbor in Bielefeld was Jochen Frowein, a scholar of constitutional and international law and vice president of the European Commission on Human Rights. When he became director of the Heidelberg Max Planck Institute, he was succeeded in Bielefeld by Meinhard Hilf,[32] who worked primarily on European law and the GATT. I got along well with both of them, but I paid little attention to their activities in European law. That was a discipline of its own that didn't intersect with mine. Or so, at least, I then thought, as did most other constitutionalists. European lawyers, by contrast, largely identified with their subject and took no critical distance toward it, in order not to endanger the European project. Something similar happened in other member states. Thus, in its early days, the ECJ's jurisprudence could develop largely without criticism either from scholars of European law, who gave it their instinctive approval, and without criticism from scholars of constitutional law, who paid it no heed. So, for example, European law scholars never took stock of the legitimacy costs of the ECJ's constitutionalization of the treaties in 1963 and 1964. For that reason, I put them in the foreground of my 2016 book on Europe.[33] For me, and for others as well, *Maastricht*[34] was the turning point. *Maastricht* made clear for the first time that constitutional law could no longer be treated without European law (and that the same was true, incidentally, of international law).

CW: Let's move now from international courts to international standards—or rather, to the reception of foreign law. In the free speech cases you implicitly embrace—please correct me, if my interpretation is incorrect—a strongly American approach, whereas in broadcasting jurisprudence you took a genuinely German path. Am I reading this rightly?

DG: In *Lüth*, the Court's first free speech decision, the US Supreme Court is cited, but only to highlight the special salience of this fundamental right, which in the Federal Constitutional Court's view precluded its being subjected to total relativization by the legislature. But the Court did not embrace the American notion that, in cases of conflict with other fundamental

[32] Meinhard Hilf (1938–present), professor of European law at the universities of Bielefeld and Hamburg.

[33] Dieter Grimm, *Europa ja—aber welches? Zur Verfassung der europäischen Demokratie* (2016). Also available in English as *The Constitution of European Democracy* (2017).

[34] 89 BVerfGE 155 (1993).

rights, free speech usually takes precedence. The Federal Constitutional Court requires, instead, a balancing, in which free speech preponderated in the *Lüth* case but yielded in the next case, decided the same day.[35] I too haven't toed the American line. This is perhaps most evident when one compares the "*Auschwitz Lie*" decision with American cases like *RAV* and *Skokie*.[36] I remember well a discussion with Justice Scalia[37] at the Catholic University in Washington DC. Where the supremacy of free speech is concerned, Scalia was far more radical than I, although in the many other discussions we had over the years I always found myself on the progressive side. There is also no American counterpart to the differential treatment of expressions of opinion and assertions of fact, which was discussed extensively again in the *Helnwein* decision.[38]

Now, where broadcasting freedom is concerned, there is a decision of the US Supreme Court that looks like a model for Karlsruhe: *Red Lion Broadcasting Company*.[39] Broadcasting freedom, that case held, is not guaranteed in the interest of the broadcaster, but in the interest of a democratic society, which is empowered with the media's help to develop informed opinions and to engage in self-government. One almost scents the Federal Constitutional Court's notion of "serving freedom" when one reads this judgment. But the decision dates from 1969. At that point, Karlsruhe's first *Television* judgment had already come down, though the crucial third one was still to come.[40] When this third decision came down, the Supreme Court had already retreated from *Red Lion*, since that singular decision was based on the scarcity of broadcasting frequencies, which had since been overcome. By contrast, the Federal Constitutional Court held fast to its objective interpretation (albeit with an expanded justification) even after the end of scarce frequencies. Above all, however, the Supreme Court never concluded on the basis of its objective interpretation of broadcasting

[35] 7 BVerfGE 230 (1958)

[36] Compare 90 BVerfG 241 (1994) with *RAV v. City of St. Paul*, 505 U.S. 377 (1992) and *Skokie v. National Socialist Party*, 373 NE 2d 21 (1978).

[37] Antonin Scalia (1936–2016), Professor at the University of Virginia and the University of Chicago; judge on the US Court of Appeals for the District of Columbia Circuit (1982–1986); justice of the US Supreme Court (1986–2016).

[38] 99 BVerfGE 185 (1999).

[39] *Red Lion Broadcasting Company v. FCC*, 395 U.S. 367 (1969).

[40] In its third television judgment, the Federal Constitutional Court said in 1981 (57 BVerfGE 295 (1981)) that private television with its shortcomings in terms of diversity and informational programs was allowed as long as there was a competitive public broadcasting existed and the law determined the requirements for the private sector and ensured that all television programs taken together represent the pluralism of opinions in society.

freedom that the legislature *must* regulate broadcasting; only that it *may*. The fundamental difference lies between the "Right to Protect and the Duty to Protect" (thus the title of an essay in which I commented on this difference).[41]

The doctrine on Article 5(1)(1) and 5(1)(2) GG is thus a German product. The accusation of Americanism . . .

CW: . . . I didn't at all intend it as an accusation . . .

DG: . . . No, and I didn't understand it as such, but in the disputes about Article 5 jurisprudence during my term of service the charge was often raised, but it was misguided.

CW: I also didn't at all mean that something quite concrete was received, but rather that one acts with greater openness with respect to the priors on free speech.

DG: That I would not dispute. These priors are democratically justified. And it may well be that American ideas, too, have flowed into my conception of democracy. The legacy of the failed revolution of 1848—the division between democracy and the rule of law—encumbered us too long.

[41] *Dieter Grimm*, "Schutzrecht und Schutzpflicht" in *Gegenrede: Festschrift für Ernst-Gottfried Mahrenholz* (1994) 529.

# VIII.
# Fundamental Rights Doctrine and the Culture of Deliberation

## A. Proportionality and Fundamental Rights Doctrine

OL: You were always a great proponent of the proportionality principle.[1]

DG: Yes, I always defended it.

OL: What do you think accounts for its particular effectiveness? Does it consist in its relationship to judicial review of legislation, in the sense that it allows the Court to calibrate its review from case to case, and thus respect a political decision and practice a culture of restraint? Or does the advantage lie in the process of deliberation within the Court because proportionality review makes it possible to clarify and rationalize matters?

DG: First and foremost, it seems to me that when fundamental rights conflict some form of balancing is inescapable. If that is true, then the principle of proportionality offers the best prospect of rationalizing the balancing process. Balancing could be avoided only if the constitution left the resolution of rights conflicts to political actors, or if it placed fundamental rights in a certain hierarchical order. Both, however, are highly improbable. With the exception of Article 1(1) GG, there is no basis for a hierarchy. In any event, a hierarchical approach would be unfeasible. It would leave one unequipped to handle cases in which the legislature seriously encroaches upon a lower-ranking right in order to secure a small advantage for a superior right. And, in light of the significance that the framers attributed to fundamental rights protection, the idea that they wanted to leave the resolution of rights

[1] The proportionality principle in German constitutional law is a constitutional test of a state measure that causes a limitation of a fundamental right, with the following steps: Firstly, it has to be determined whether the state measure pursues a constitutionally legitimate aim. Secondly, it is asked whether the measure is suitable to reach this aim. Thirdly, the measure must be necessary, i.e. there may not be an alternative available that is less detrimental to the affected right and at least equally effective.

The final step is proportionality in a strict sense which involves the balancing of the affected right and of the aim which the state measure pursues.

*Dieter Grimm: Advocate of the Constitution.* Dieter Grimm, Oxford University Press (2020). © in the original German edition, Mohr Siebeck GmbH & Co. KG, Tübingen 2017, © this translation, Justin Collings 2020.
DOI: 10.1093/oso/9780198845270.001.0001

collisions to political actors is equally implausible. Habermas's proposal for resolving rights conflicts without balancing proves, on closer inspection, merely to defer balancing.[2] One can, of course, limit the need for balancing, such as by defining the scope of protection narrowly or by abandoning the catch-all fundamental right, but only by paying a price elsewhere.

With this proviso, to me proportionality's value lies foremost in its forcing those who apply the law into a controlled process. The freewheel "balancing" that one often encounters particularly in the US is thus avoided. Respect for the legislative decision comes as a byproduct. But I am deeply concerned that the proportionality principle be handled with care. I'm no stranger to the risks it entails.

MR: What are those risks?

DG: The possibility that political priorities and preferences will be established through a judicial rather than a parliamentary procedure. Accordingly, it must be determined as precisely as possible to what extent such decisions are constitutionally conditioned. Of course, the seriousness of the danger varies with the phases of proportionality review. At the first and second step, it doesn't arise at all. That a fundamental rights restriction can be justified only by a legitimate purpose (i.e. one not precluded by the constitution) should be obvious; that a rights restriction must be capable of fulfilling its purpose equally so. Things get more difficult at the third step. The choice of means is a matter for the legislature, and on whether there is some means less restrictive than the one chosen by the legislature, the legislative decision must enjoy the benefit of the doubt. This is especially true when the measure's expected impact depends on prognoses. In that case, the review must be limited to the correct production of the prognoses. The true difficulty, however, emerges at the last step: balancing.

CW: That's why some have said that balancing should be abandoned altogether.

DG: That, however, would seriously weaken the protection of fundamental rights. Many overlook the fact that the relevant right plays no role at all at the suitability and necessity phases. At those steps, the test simply establishes the relationship between the law's purpose and the legislature's chosen means. In this respect, proportionality review remains intrinsic to the law. As a result, the fundamental right (on account of which all this

[2] Jürgen Habermas, *Faktizität und Geltung* (1992) 309 ff. On this point, see Dieter Grimm, "Justiz und Gesetzgebung. Zur Rolle und Legitimität der Verfassungsrechtsprechung" in P. Koller and Chr. Hiebaum (eds), *Jürgen Habermas: Faktizität und Geltung* (2016) 99, 110 ff.

effort is made) enters the picture only at the balancing phase. Which is why that phase can never be relinquished.

Of course, everything depends at that phase on filling both sides of the scale as precisely as possible. And precise does not mean pitting the grand values against one another. True, when reviewing an antiterrorism law—let's take this example, since the relevant line of cases began with one of my last judgments[3]—the tension between security and freedom looms in the background. But reviewing the challenged law does not require one to decide whether to give priority to "Security" as such or to "Liberty" as such. The law, instead, limits a *specific* liberty in a *specific* aspect to a *specific* degree in order to increase security to a *specific* degree in light of a *specific* aspect of a specific *danger*. If these factors have been ascertained carefully, the balancing process doesn't usually present insurmountable problems. It is both comprehensible and replicable in similar cases. Whoever works with large-scale value judgments, such as of the competitiveness of the German economy or the effectiveness of criminal justice, has already abandoned the limits of proportionality review.

OL: When we talked about *Riding in the Woods*, you made it clear that you are entirely in favor of delimiting more sharply the scope of fundamental rights protection.

DG: That, of course, lies in the same direction.

OL: That's what's interesting. With comprehensive rights protection, questions about scope of protection are displaced by questions about proportionality. To the extent that this is true, those who champion broad protection of freedom depend, in the end, on effective proportionality review. Of course, those who work more closely with the contours of the scope of protection can also make concessions to proportionality. Accordingly, proportionality is no longer the sole, decisive level of review.

DG: How are scope of protection and proportionality connected? The more lavish one is with scope of protection, the more cases there are that must be decided based upon rights restrictions—ultimately, upon proportionality. If one narrows the scope of protection, the question becomes how Article 2(1) GG is to be understood. If it remains a catch-all right, the only thing that changes is the entranceway to fundamental rights review, and thanks to the limits of general laws, everything ends in proportionality. If one accepts my dissenting opinion in *Riding in the Woods*, the number of cases that must in fact be reviewed—and, consequently, in which the proportionality

[3] 100 BVerfGE 313 (1999).

principle must be applied—will diminish. But the scheme of proportionality review does not change.

CW: Since the *Pharmacy* judgment,[4] the differentiated limits have been suavely wiped away.

DG: When the *Pharmacy* judgment came down, the proportionality principle had not yet been fully articulated. A few years later the Court would likely have applied the proportionality principle to all the guarantees of Article 12 GG. But I am not of the view that proportionality review flattens out the differing provisions for limiting the various fundamental rights. The written limits, after all, must be considered before engaging in proportionality review. If most cases nonetheless conclude with proportionality review, that is because offenses against the express limits are relatively rare.

OL: It is interesting how we German fundamental rights theorists can locate the same problem at the level of scope of review, of infringement, and of proportionality[5]—often without knowing exactly where we are placing it. Sometimes we do it more in terms of the scope of protection, as with the personality right or the combination of rights in connection with Article 1(1) GG. From an open scope of protection, a core space then emerged. Alternatively, we work with the intensity of the infringement, which then triggers heightened justificatory requirements, or we increase fundamental rights protection through proportionality. Doctrinally, then, we can juggle a bit. There are, potentially, three balls in the air. For an external observer, however, we are able to pitch this flexibility as doctrine or as a stringent approach to fundamental rights theory—which, in the end, it isn't at all.

DG: It seems to me that the different emphasis is a product of the different constellation of problems in fundamental rights cases. Sometimes the difficulty lies in the scope of protection: Is there a right to know one's parentage? Does the exertion of economic pressure fall within the scope of protection of free speech? Other times the question of infringement stands in the

[4] 7 BVerfGE 377 (1958); the judgment introduced the so-called three-level theory for reviewing the justification of restrictions on occupational liberty. The theory differentiated between restrictions on the practice of one's profession as well as subjective and objective conditions for entering a profession. Since this decision, the levels have become increasingly muddled in the Federal Constitutional Court's case law. In place of the different levels according to the reservation of statutory powers under Article 12 GG, the Court substituted a gradual justification of infringement: the more serious the infringement the greater the burden of justification.

[5] In German constitutional law, the standard of review of the violation of a fundamental right usually consists of three steps: Firstly, it has to be determined whether the conduct of the individual is within the scope of protection of the fundamental right (scope of protection). Secondly, it is asked whether the state action/omission infringes this scope of protection (infringement). Finally, it has to be determined whether this infringement is justified (justification).

foreground: Do government warnings about specific products infringe fundamental rights? *Glycol*[6] is an example—a case that I wish I could have brought to judgment myself. But I suspect that *Herr* Hoffmann-Riem was not ungrateful that it fell to him. Does tapping someone's phone line encroach on telecommunications secrecy or does it represent an "immanent" limitation of this right?[7] If the scope of protection and infringement raise no problems, the focus automatically shifts to the question of limitation. Here, again, there are subdivisions. In the realm of free speech, for example, the problem often lies with the interpretation of the incriminated expression. If the interpretation was erroneous anyway, there is no need for proportionality review.

I was concerned, however, that the varying levels of review be clearly divided and logically organized. If, when reading a draft judgment, I had doubts about this, I used to furnish the formal section markers with substantive headings. This often allowed me to discover inconsistencies. Doctrinally correct deduction was always important to me, because it protects the judge against forgetting important questions or deciding too hastily. But in both Senates, there are always great champions of the expansive interpretation of legal texts.

OL: Doctrinal, then, in the sense of an exacting theory of fundamental rights?

DG: As far as fundamental rights are concerned, yes, but no less so with questions of federalism or separation of powers.

OL: Would you consider yourself an adherent of a unitary theory of fundamental rights—a theory that encompasses and abstracts from the fundamental rights and the specific peculiarities of the case law?

DG: When I teach comparative constitutional law in the United States and come to talk about fundamental rights, I always point out that in a German lecture on fundamental rights, half the time is spent on what applies equally to all fundamental rights. In the US, by contrast, there are only the individual rights—no general theory of fundamental rights.

OL: One could indeed agree that one right be dealt with more through the contours of its scope of protection and another more with regard to the severity of the infringement, because it would be more suitable in the case. If we have three balls in the air, we could also play these balls off against particular rights. We'll resolve this constellation with this ball, that one with the other ball.

6 105 BVerfGE 252 (2002).
7 85 BVerfGE 386 (1992).

DG: The general theories of fundamental rights leave room, of course, for the peculiarities of individual fundamental rights. They don't absorb them. But in my view the different stages of fundamental rights review—scope of protection, infringement, limitation, limits to limitation—are not playthings that can be replaced arbitrarily. It is not the fundamental right but rather the cases that condition the point of emphasis.

OL: Is there a single doctrine or are there many doctrines? Do we have an Article 4 doctrine, an Article 5(3) doctrine, an Article 5(1) doctrine, etc.?

DG: Yes, beneath the general theory of fundamental rights. And yet the discretion that these allow for different doctrines in specific areas can be greater or smaller. With the liberty rights, the role of the general theories is greater; with the equality rights, it is smaller.

OL: In 1985, there appeared the extraordinarily successful fundamental rights textbook by Pieroth and Schlink,[8] which seems to me to have brought about the canonization of this pattern of review. If you read the Federal Constitutional Court's pre-1985 decisions, you note a greater flexibility. Sometimes they talk of "needfulness" rather than "necessity," so that aspects of suitability flow into the necessity inquiry. The concepts are not as rigidly fixed. Proportionality in the strict sense sometimes overlaps with needfulness, which for its part blends a bit with necessity as understood today—similar to what happens today among courts in Canada or Israel. In Germany this flexibility has disappeared. Today there is a clear canon, a shelving away of criteria, but no further reflection about the intermediate categories that arise from the case at hand. Several factors come together: the Pieroth/Schlink textbook appeared in 1985; the "heroes" departed from the Constitutional Court in 1987; and, after you have now repeatedly said that you advocated a doctrinally stringent approach, I am tempted to speak of the beginning of a phase of doctrinalization in Karlsruhe.

DG: Without, one hopes (as you suggested earlier) the pattern of review making reflection superfluous.

OL: How can the Senate still preserve sufficient space for reflection in its deliberations? Such reflection, after all, is vulnerable to the accusation that it doesn't fit in the canonized model of review. Argumentative rationality is now predetermined by the matrix of the proportionality standard. An argument that doesn't fit that matrix immediately becomes an incompatible, latently irrational argument. How, then, can the Court ensure its capacity for

[8] Bodo Pieroth and Bernhard Schlink, *Grundrechte: Staatsrecht II* (1985). The textbook has since been updated by Thorsten Kingreen and Ralf Poscher. In 2019, it appeared in its thirty-fifth edition.

reflection when it has committed itself forcefully to the rationalizing grip of proportionality?

DG: In my view, it is the great variety of the cases that shields us against schematism. Sometimes a particular review step doesn't fit the configuration of a given case. An example: the fundamental rights infringement consists of a duty to make a payment. Concretely: the legislature allows employees, for a specific period, to take an educational holiday with full pay.[9] Employers see in this an infringement of their occupational freedom. If the necessity of the means for the achievement of the legislative goal were to be reviewed, there would always be milder means available in such cases: someone else could pay or the employees could bear part of the cost themselves. If milder means are *always* available, review for necessity makes no sense. Accordingly, one must immediately move on to the level of appropriateness.

For me, the abundance of illustrative material that accumulates in the Court was one of the greatest benefits of my years in Karlsruhe. And one perceives it differently when one has cases to decide than when one reads decisions after the fact.

## B. Handling the Facts of the Case and Precedent

CW: Do you read your successors' decisions differently, now that you once again have only filtered access to the case materials?

DG: When I still had to sign them, I read them differently than I do today. I read them in their entirety, since the drafts were reviewed page by page in the reading conference, and I read them twice—once quickly to gain an overall impression and a second time thoroughly to see whether I wanted to request changes during the reading conference. But it was my role as coauthor, rather than my approach to the case material, that required this kind of reading. Today, I usually read the presentation of the case and of course the rationale, but not always the accompanying material—the summary of the briefs and the positions of the parties. For that there must be some special motivation.

CW: As a student, I always read only the C.I. passages[10] of a judgment's rationale. Only when I needed to plumb more precisely did I take a look at the

[9] 77 BVerfGE 388 (1987).

[10] Many decisions of the Federal Constitutional Court are organized according to a unitary pattern: under subheading A are presented the facts of the case; under B, when necessary, questions of standing and jurisdiction are addressed; whereas the actual decision is reserved for subheading C. Here

other parts. And we were also told to read only the C.I. section. "Everything else is just padding. It is too long, and it will only confuse you." In any case, what the Bavarian state government argued and whatever else was in the briefs isn't all that exciting.

MR: What role do the written submissions actually play in the decision? To what extent do they influence the decisions and shape discussions within the Senate?

DG: Most briefs were disappointing. But most briefs also didn't come from lawyers who were established in constitutional law or even in public law generally. But there were also, of course, some extremely careful, knowledgeable, and impressive briefs and expert opinions. Usually more important than the legal arguments were the factual observations in the briefs themselves or in the statements solicited by the Court. That had something to do with the Court's guiding methodological views. The Federal Constitutional Court's approach differs from that of previously prevailing methods of constitutional interpretation in two ways: through a perspective attuned to material, functional, and values-based arguments, on the one hand; and, on the other hand, through the conviction that a norm's meaning must be determined in light of the sector of social reality that it regulates. Because this reality is in constant flux, constitutional interpretation assumes a basically dynamic feature, which requires that reality be constantly reassessed. And then there are normative provisions and doctrinal precepts that refer to social reality. This is most prominent with steps two (suitability) and three (necessity) of proportionality review. In important cases—especially those involving the abstract review of legislation—the briefs usually contain valuable observations on this front.

OL: From the perspective of the deciding Senate, the context of the case is palpable. But from the perspective of scholars and practitioners, it's not clear what role the case materials should play in further engagement with the case law. Here a problem arises. If the decision made depends on the case material, as you have repeatedly underscored, how can the decision's expressive value be honestly assessed by scholars and practitioners—how, in particular, can the case's context be taken into account in further precedential analysis of the decision? Since we're inclined to read only the C.I. section,

the deciding Senate develops under Roman numeral I the relevant standards on the basis of the relevant provisions of the Basic Law, whereas under Roman numeral II it applies those standards to the concrete case. On all of this, see Oliver Lepsius, "The Standard Setting Power " in Matthias Jestaedt, Oliver Lepsius, Christoph Möllers, and Christoph Schönberger, *The German Federal Constitutional Court. The Court without Limits* (2020) ch. 3.

these case-specific elements fall by the wayside. We ought to include C.II. as well, but there too the legal interests being balanced often remain rather abstract. For the factors relevant to the case, one ought to rely on the briefs and on the judgment's statement of facts under "A." But no one reads that. Isn't the problem that the Court makes its decisions in the consciousness of a concrete problem, which then disappears from view in the abstract analysis of the decision's rationale? Or am I looking at this incorrectly?

DG: I think that you're right—with the consequence that scholars often generalize the decisions more strongly than the Court intended. The Court's deliberations always resonate with concern about the hasty generalization of decisions. Who knows what currently invisible aspect of the problem will arise in the next case? Who knows how the social reality will change? For that reason, you often find in the rationale the expression "in cases like this one." That's an attempt to shield the decision from premature generalization. Also, when one encounters elements of reasoning in a decision that seem strange or superfluous, a glance into the case record usually shows that they were occasioned by the briefs or expert opinions.

It's also worth mentioning in this connection that a practice of "distinguishing," as required in England and America by the binding nature of precedent, has not been developed among us. In this respect the Court, which loves to cite itself, doesn't always exercise the necessary caution. Beginning in 1995, *Herr* Hömig[11] was my left-hand neighbor in the conference room. *Herr* Hömig took pains to review the citation chains in the draft judgments, and often enough he came across judgments or decisions that had little to do with the case at hand.

CW: If a precedent seems to stand in the way, an advocate must show why the precedent isn't on point. When it gets really bad, the advocate must even consult the records of the courts below. Students, of course, don't do this on exams, but a lawyer or advocate does so in big cases when there is really something at stake. But what judicial decisions really contain as much material as gets printed in the official reports of the Federal Constitutional Court? In the published decisions of the Federal Court of Justice there is strikingly little about the relevant facts of the case. In the German tradition of judicial publication, there is no other Court that operates as does the Federal Constitutional Court. The expert periodicals, such as the *Neue*

[11] Dieter Hömig (1938–2016), official in the Federal Interior Ministry (1967–1983); judge on the Federal Administrative Court (1983–1995); justice of the First Senate of the Federal Constitutional Court (1995–2008).

*Zeitschrift für Verwaltungsrecht* ("The New Administrative Law Review") or the *JuristenZeitung* ("Jurists Review"), adopt a middle path, providing a paraphrased, small-font summary of the facts, written by the editors.

OL: So we at least make practical, if not scientific, use of Part A.

DG: On this point, I will only say that in the rapporteur's memos these parts are usually even more extensive than in the judgment.

CW: Even in the collection of cases that you edited with *Herr* Kirchhof for the University Paperbacks series,[12] the excerpts are naturally drawn only from the C.I. section.

DG: There is always a concise summary of the facts, printed in italics and written by *Herr* Eichberger[13] before he himself became a constitutional justice. *Herr* Kirchhof and I chose the cases, *Herr* Eichberger prepared and abridged them. Meanwhile no one needs the collection anymore, since everything is available online.

OL: Abridged versions are needed for didactic reasons. If you send students a link to the full judgment, they are overwhelmed by the vast quantity of text. It actually makes a lot of sense to give students a readable excerpt—three pages or so—in the hope that they'll come to class prepared. I think the culture of analyzing cases needs further development and should focus more on facts and context. The Court itself faces a problem in light of the growing mountain of its own earlier decisions. Today the judges must potentially read 140 volumes. You had to have read eighty volumes. Judges today—only twenty years later—have sixty more volumes.

DG: Even though I was a constitutionalist, I hadn't read eighty volumes either. And judges who came to the Constitutional Court from the five federal supreme courts had read even fewer. Two of my colleagues brought this home repeatedly. The first was Helmut Simon, with whom I served for a few months on the First Senate. He had been in office since 1970, and he could tell the Senate, "In volumes 17 and 43, we did such and such. We could change that, but then we must say why the earlier decisions are being overruled." Later on, Helga Seibert took over Simon's part. She had been responsible for fundamental rights in the Federal Ministry of Justice and knew absolutely everything.

[12] Dieter Grimm and Paul Kirchhof (eds), *Entscheidungen des Bundesverfassungsgerichts: Studienauswahl* (2 vols) (1993, 2d ed. 1997, 3d ed. 2007).

[13] Michael Eichberger (1953–present), judge on the Federal Administrative Court (1998–2006); justice of the First Senate of the Federal Constitutional Court (2006–2018).

OL: When a decision doesn't suit, it gets serenely suppressed. There is not even any "distinguishing." An earlier decision gets cited only in passing, or not at all, and this is done as though that decision didn't stand in the way. There is no discussion of why things are now being done differently. One could, of course, simply say that forty years have passed, and that things are different now.

DG: There is in fact a tendency to present a front of continuity when in fact earlier decisions are being departed from. One should always make such changes openly.

OL: Let's take the decisions on the minimum threshold for European elections.[14] The engagement with the earlier decision[15] was somewhat meager. It gets mentioned, but at the decisive point the Senate doesn't engage with it substantively. That needs to change a bit, including in the Court's manner of presentation. If the Court has a self-interest in distinguishing, so as to preserve discretion and avoid falling into path-dependencies pursued without reflection, then it must justify its decisions in such a way that future Senates have some basis for distinguishing. The strange thing is that a legislature can always say, "What the Bundestag did four years ago doesn't interest us. We have a new majority, and we're going to do everything differently." Not so a court. Today's Senate has difficulty reversing a decision of the Senate forty years ago. Judges always hear it said: "We already decided such and such in 1965." And I always ask myself, "Who exactly is 'we'?" Unlike legislation, jurisprudence runs the risk of petrification.

DG: It is true that every judge who wants to alter long-standing case law faces a much higher justificatory burden than the judge who wants to extend it. One could only talk of petrification, however, if this attitude were to suffocate changes. But that isn't the case. We were talking of the lack of transparency in introducing changes. That is something different from timidity about change.

[14] 129 BVerfGE 300 (2011). By a vote of five to three, the Senate declared unconstitutional the 5 percent minimum threshold in elections for the German contingent of the European parliament, ruling that the threshold violated both electoral equality and the equality of opportunity for political parties.

[15] 51 BVerfGE 222 (1979). The Senate saw no constitutional violation in the 5 percent minimum threshold for European parliamentary elections. The bar was compatible with the Basic Law because it aimed to prevent an excessive proliferation of parties—a goal justified by special, compelling considerations—and didn't go beyond what was necessary to achieve that goal. The decision was unanimous.

## C. Culture of Deliberation and Doctrine

CW: Much is being said these days about the "culture of deliberation" in Karlsruhe. I understand that *Frau* Lübbe-Wolff is preparing a comparative study on the matter.[16] All former and active judges, who report on this in different doses, always say that only doctrinal arguments count. If one presses further, however, there are often entirely different impressions—or else doctrine represents an inherently imprecise category and seems open just about anything. Would you dissent if an outsider were to interpret this as meaning that openly political arguments are frowned upon within the Senate and must be cloaked as doctrinal arguments?

DG: Your interpretation corresponds exactly to my experience. In my nearly twelve-and-a-half years in the First Senate I never heard a partisan argument. But I also can't remember any political arguments not linked to a party agenda. Any member of the Senate who were to make such an argument would be disqualified. The arguments were legal arguments—some better, some worse, but still legal—and whether a legal argument is occasionally motivated by politics remains hidden to the rest of the Senate. What one could see was that everyone at some point reaches the limits of one's argumentative willingness or capacity. But that doesn't mean that from then on things proceed politically; only that the legal argumentation has concluded and one can now only repeat oneself.

OL: Such as with questions about the protection of life.

DG: As one example, because these questions reach close to the consciences of some judges. But it was astonishing to me, even in such cases, how far the doctrine carried us before the differences emerged. Thanks to doctrine, everything isn't immediately at stake in the deliberation. There is, instead, a predetermined, multi-stage path to pursue before one must confront questions of conscience. I was always of the opinion that, in the event that I could no longer reconcile conscience and constitution, I ought to resign.

OL: What does doctrinal argumentation presuppose? Knowledge of earlier decisions? What is a doctrinal or legal argument as opposed to a political one? It is clear that one cannot argue in a partisan, result-oriented way. Many areas are entirely unsuited for such an approach. But when a new legal question arises—such as with data protection—what does it mean to

[16] On this topic, see Gertrude Lübbe-Wolff, "Die Beratungskultur des Bundesverfassungsgerichts: Rede zur Verabschiedung aus dem Amt der Richterin des Bundesverfassungsgerichts " (2014) *Europäische Grundrechte-Zeitschrift* 509–12; Gertrude Lübbe-Wolff, *Wie funktioniert das Bundesverfassungsgericht* (2016).

argue doctrinally or "only" legally? To stay with the census and data protection: one begins with a given fundamental right (when in doubt, Article 2(1) GG) and finds very general understandings of liberty. So far, we're are still in navigable legal waters. But what happens next? One must then say how far the freedom reaches. Is that still only a "legal" or doctrinal inquiry? To what extent do a judge's biases also come into play?

DG: We all know that "legal" and "doctrinal" are open concepts. Different eras have thought differently about them, and different legal orders or legal cultures think differently about them at the same time. Within one and the same legal culture there can be intense battles about this question, such as among us during the Weimar Republic or in the United States today. "Open," however, is not synonymous with "arbitrary." "Legal" or "doctrinal"—whether understood broadly or narrowly—precludes "political" (or, in other legal orders, perhaps "religious" or "ideological"). What is contested are the borderlines. If one allows—as the Federal Constitutional Court does allow—the interpretative application of a constitutional norm to facts and circumstances unimaginable at the time the constitution was framed, then what is legal extends to a realm that is already, for an originalist, political. In saying this, however, I don't dispute the importance—even, for some cases, the decisive importance—of prior conceptions. One could dispute it only if one assumed that a constitutional norm's text entirely predetermined the interpreter's application of it to a given case. As absurd as such a claim would be, it would be equally outlandish to suppose that prior conceptions prevail untrammeled in new cases unforeseen by the constitutional framers. Even in new cases one doesn't start from scratch.

I'll use your census example. The judgment came down before my time as a constitutional judge. It built on the long-standing and accepted interpretation that the free development of one's personality under Article 2(1) GG protected a sphere of privacy. Insofar as data from that private sphere were involved, data protection had already been deduced from this guarantee. The question before the Court in the *Census* case, then, was only whether data protection should remain limited to the private sphere or whether it must be expanded. This question arose because of intervening technological advances. Data could now be processed electronically. Whether, in light of electronic data processing (EDP), protecting data from the private sphere sufficed for the free development of the personality depended, therefore, on how the threat to which Article 2(1) GG responds had changed with the transition from index cards or Hollerith machines to EDP. The Court presented the problem lucidly, concluding that, in light of the technical possibilities of EDP, personality protection was incomplete if it didn't extend to personal data generally, regardless of its links to the private sphere.

Certain preconceptions lie behind that decision—such as that the Constitutional Court may adapt the meaning of constitutional norms to changed circumstances; as well as the preconception that the state must not be all-knowing; and further a conception of personal liberty that comprises the internal as well as the external elements of freedom. But these preconceptions, too, are only relevant as mediated by norms.

MR: Are these preconceptions perhaps especially apparent when compared with American debates and case law?

DG: There comes to mind, as a contrast, the first case in which the US Supreme Court had to wrestle with whether wire-tapping phone calls conducted from a phone booth constituted a search and seizure for purposes of the Fourth Amendment. The originalist on the Court responded that intercepting phone calls was only a technologically enhanced form of eavesdropping—an activity known to the founding fathers which it didn't occur to them to forbid. The textualist underscored that phone calls are not among the "persons, houses, papers, and effects" that the Amendment protects. The formalist—who realized, however, that they were dealing with a new phenomenon—sought the solution through an analogy: in the moment of the telephone conversation, the phone booth and the wire through which the conversation are conducted "belong" to the speaker. And only a minority found that "search and seizure" must be understood in terms of its purpose and extended to novel situations of danger.[17]

In dealing with social change, the Federal Constitutional Court's case law relies on a recurring, but little-noticed model that the *Census* judgment exhibits nicely. The point of departure is the preexisting understanding of the fundamental right, particularly its scope of protection. The next question is whether social change has occurred within the scope of protection of the relevant right. If so, the question becomes whether this change would undermine fundamental rights protection should the Court adhere to its previous interpretation. If it would, the interpretation is developed to adapt fundamental rights protection to the new danger.

[17] *Olmstead v. United States*, 277 U.S. 438 (1928). The majority opinion in *Olmstead* became the minority view forty years later in *Katz v. United States*, 389 U.S. 347 (1967).

OL: You published an article in the *Frankfurter Allgemeine Zeitung*[18] (FAZ) on the controversy[19] then current between Lammert[20] and Voßkuhle,[21] in which you said, in effect, that constitutional questions are political questions and that, accordingly, the Constitutional Court decides politically. In a certain sense, you took a position contrary to Voßkuhle's. The phrase "only legal argumentation takes place" could create the impression among outside observers that there is no consideration of consequences, that there is only a competence for doctrinal judgment in the narrow sense. I find the debate we are now having, or even the interest in the culture of deliberation, striking because it addresses the age-old problem of distinguishing law from politics, but tailored now to the Court as an institution. In this setting, the Court doesn't position itself well if it presents itself as overly legal. Many decisions—including some far-reaching ones—can hardly be explained if one insists that it can all be explained legally and doctrinally.

DG: I tried in my FAZ essay to answer the eternal question about the political character of the constitutional adjudication in a more differentiated way. What exactly is political about the Court's work? For starters, the subject matter is political. The constitution imposes conditions on politics. The Constitutional Court must ensure that politicians observe these constraints. The objects of review, then, are decisions that politicians have made (or omitted). Also political are the consequences of the Court's decisions. The unconstitutional decision is annulled. Both political subject

[18] Dieter Grimm, "Was das Grundgesetz will, ist eine politische Frage " *Frankfurter Allgemeine Zeitung* (December 22, 2011).

[19] In a lecture before the legislative reference service (*Wissenschaftliche Dienste*) of the German Bundestag on November 17, 2011, the president of the Federal Constitutional Court, Andreas Voßkuhle, said: "It does not follow from the fact that the Federal Constitutional Court's decisions have political effects that those decisions are themselves of a political nature. The Federal Constitutional Court makes exclusively legal decisions. The decision-making process of a constitutional judge follows an entirely different logic from that of the decision-making process of political actors." The president of the Bundestag, Norbert Lammert, countered: "I want to raise a small objection to the proposition that decisions of the Federal Constitutional Court and their associated interpretation of the Basic Law are exclusively legal and never political. That doesn't make sense to me either in terms of the motives of the individual justices or of the texts that in the end we get to read. . . . The wisdom of the vast majority of Constitutional Court decisions also consists in the fact that they are in fact not limited a purely legal consideration of the matter, but instead are openly and conspicuously conscious of the political implications of decisions that can perhaps be justified in purely legal terms." In *Frankfurter Allgemeine Zeitung* (December 22, 2011), see also https://www.bundestag.de/dokumente/textarchiv/2011/36525489_kw_46_w_forum-206882.

[20] Norbert Lammert (1948–present), politician (CDU) member of the German Bundestag (1980–2017); Bundestag vice president (2002–2005); Bundestag president (2005–2017).

[21] Andreas Voßkuhle (1963–present), professor of public law at the University of Freiburg im Breisgau; justice on the Second Senate of the Federal Constitutional Court since 2008; vice president of the Court from 2008 to 2010 and president until 2020.

matter and political consequences are unavoidable attendants of constitutional judicial review. That's what it's there for. But the proceedings before the Constitutional Court and the criteria by which the Court decides are not political in this sense. Rather, the petition or the complaint effects a change of venue. Different actors now step forth, different rules apply, and different standards are enforced. One can only ask at this point whether the interpretation and application of constitutional norms is inherently political. That view is widespread in the US, but I disagree. One could only regard constitutional interpretation and application as political if the mere fact that the text of the norm does not fully determine its application sufficed to mark it as political. But that view, I think, misses the mark. After all, the interpretive discretion that every norm leaves open—and that fundamental rights leave open in a special way—is filled on the basis of legal considerations. The question that every judge must ask is, "What is the legally correct reading of the norm?", not, "What would be the best political, religious, or economic solution?" One can dispute what is legally correct, and the dispute can remain unresolved at the end of the deliberations, so that the majority decides. But disagreement among the judges doesn't prove that the decision was not based on legal materials; only that reasonable judges can legitimately differ over the legally correct solution. I am speaking, of course, about judges who take their task seriously. Whether there are judges who decide on the basis of political considerations or simply follow their personal preferences is a separate matter.

OL: For decades, we legal scholars have been debating the integration of the social sciences. With the two volumes from the 1970s,[22] you were a leading participant in that debate, and one almost gets the impression that this has been ignored in recent efforts to position the Court.[23] "Decisions are based only on legal criteria," after all, disclaims social-scientific and interdisciplinary observations in law.

DG: I don't get that impression. "Only legal" can mean two things: on the one hand, that judicial decisions may be made only on the basis of legal criteria, not political, religious, economic, or any other criteria; on the other hand,

[22] Dieter Grimm (ed.), *Rechtswissenschaft und Nachbarwissenschaften, Band I: Soziologie, Politik, Verwaltung, Wirtschaft, Psychologie, Kriminologie* (1973); *Band II: Geschichte, Logik, Linguistik, Informatik, Friedensforschung, Finanzen, Didaktik* (1976).

[23] Cf. Gertrude Lübbe-Wolff, "Die Beratungskultur des Bundesverfassungsgerichts" (2014) 41 *Europäische Grundrechte-Zeitschrift* 509; Gertrude Lübbe-Wolff, 'Wie funktioniert das Bundesverfassungsgericht?' (2015) 23–28; Peter Müller, "Heute darf ich das sagen" Interview in *Die Zeit* (April 9, 2015); further statements in Uwe Kranenpohl, *Hinter dem Schleier des Beratungsgeheimnisses* (2010) 163–67.

that legal norms must be understood on their own terms, and that other disciplines therefore cannot contribute to the understanding of legal norms. I affirm the first reading without qualification; the second I think wrong, as the two volumes "Legal Scholarship and Neighboring Disciplines" should prove.

OL: You said that within the Senate you championed the rationalizing force of doctrine and placed great value on observing precise patterns of thought—that is, you were a champion of the doctrinal resolution of legal questions. But previously, as a scholar, you were a proponent of interdisciplinary approaches.

DG: I don't see any contradiction between the two. I advocate legal doctrine informed by the social sciences. I find the justification for this approach in the very characteristics of legal norms. Legal norms are linked to reality. They are formulated with regard to a specific circumstance, which they are designed to influence—sometimes preserving it, sometimes altering it. If that is so, however, then social reality is one element among others that constitutes the meaning of a legal norm. Thus, determining a norm's meaning requires ascertaining the factual circumstances within which it must achieve its purpose. Within the range of possible interpretations, some favor and some threaten the achievement of that purpose. Understanding the factual realm that the norm regulates is thus part of the legal craft. This is even more clear if one bears in mind that social reality is in a state of constant flux. As a result, what had been a sensible interpretation of a legal norm under the original circumstances can, under altered circumstances, become dysfunctional. But this remains hidden to one who applies law without regard to social change. Sometimes social change is obvious, and jurists can incorporate it doctrinally without external aid. Often, though, it isn't obvious, or is only superficially evident. In that case, jurists need the support of social scientific knowledge. But the task remains a legal one. Social scientific knowledge gains legal relevance only when mediated by legal norms. The jurist doesn't change disciplines; he simply avails himself of other disciplines' insights.

MR: What difficulties do you see in this transfer of insights?

DG: I'm very aware that it can be difficult. The social sciences don't see themselves as auxiliary branches of jurisprudence. They ask different questions and use different methods. As a result, the knowledge the jurist needs is often unavailable. When legally relevant knowledge is available, it is often hard to find. When it is found, there can arise uncertainties over its evaluation. I learned that early in my tenure on the First Senate when I tried to bring social science insights to bear on a case in conference. The question was whether a child of legal age had a right to know the identity of his biological father. In this case, the Civil Code precluded a legitimacy challenge, which the Hamburg district court (*Amtsgericht*) deemed unconstitutional. *Frau* Niemeyer (who was responsible for the general personality right until she left the Court and that responsibility fell to me) submitted a short chamber decision rejecting the district court's position. It seemed to me that the case had extensive implications. The decision could quickly become relevant for the developments that at the time were just getting under way—anonymous sperm donation, for example. I thought the case required consideration by the full Senate, and the discussion within the Senate developed in such a way that I suggested holding oral argument.[24] In preparation for the Senate conference, I read various works dealing with the consequences of uncertainty about one's parentage on the development of one's personality. Armed with these books, I went to the Senate conference ready to show that I was arguing with expert knowledge, not with a lay person's understanding. The stack of books, however, had the opposite effect. Doubts arose about whether these books were to be trusted—whether they represented the consensus of the discipline or merely quixotic views. From this experience I concluded, not that I should give up on social-scientific insights, but that I should leave the books at home. When the cases required it, I always took an interdisciplinary approach.

OL: Such as in the broadcasting jurisprudence?

DG: Certainly. A decisive question there was whether the market could produce the good that Article 5(1)(2) GG promoted. There are no legal answers to that question. The meaning of broadcasting freedom is a legal question, as is drawing the relevant consequences on the basis of the knowledge furnished by social science.

CW: What you have just described is a good example of how one function of doctrine is to provide a level playing field for all authorized participants in the debate. Whereas in an interdisciplinary discussion there must first be agreement—including terminological agreement—about what it is even being talked about, legal doctrine offers a platform on which jurists can argue without preliminary determinations.

DG: I agree wholeheartedly with that view. This function of doctrine had not been quite so clear to me before.

[24] 79 BVerfGE 256 (1989).

OL: What mechanisms of self-preservation are developed in a Senate conference in order to avoid the doctrinal trap of saying: "The argument is not doctrinally compatible or cannot be doctrinally reformulated and is therefore latently political and impermissible"? The danger of this platform of which *Herr* Waldhoff spoke is of course that certain strands of argument can be suppressed in the Senate as un-doctrinal.

DG: There are insights that are not doctrinally compatible. To take a contrived example: suppose that within political science the view prevails that the crisis of representative democracy can be cured through plebiscitary decision-making powers—in particular, that the federal president must be popularly elected. One can agree or disagree, but one cannot use these insights to get around Article 54 GG.[25] But what about insights that might be compatible or that can be reformulated in legal terms? I have no good answer to the question of how to prevent their being suppressed. Within the Senate, methodological discussions took place implicitly at best. Some protection comes in the form of the Court's pluralist composition—pluralist in the sense of the justices' different professional backgrounds.

OL: Do tactical alternatives also get discussed? Perhaps along the lines of: Both available decisions are equally correct doctrinally and, according to our own case law, equally defensible; but the first option has very different consequences—both for our own further doctrine and for social reality.

DG: Consequentialist doctrine is common practice on the Federal Constitutional Court. I discussed this once at a conference of the Society of Comparative Law.[26] The consequences that may be considered, however, are not extra-legal consequences (a judgment's likely impact on German exports, for example) but only the consequences for the functioning of the constitutional guarantee. The question to ask is, "Which of the available interpretations best serves the purpose of the relevant constitutional provision?" But one shouldn't think of this as though, at the end of a controversial discussion, there were two available decisions between which the Court must decide on the basis of their foreseeable consequences. The consequences have already been addressed alongside the other considerations.

OL: I am very sympathetic to the way you've described the Court's deliberations—as a great effort to do justice to a legal dispute with

[25] Article 54 Section 1 of the Basic Law (Grundgesetz [GG]) reads: "The Federal President shall be elected by the Federal Convention without debate. Any German who is entitled to vote in Bundestag elections and has attained the age of forty may be elected."

[26] Dieter Grimm, "Entscheidungsfolgen als Rechtsgründe: Zur Argumentationspraxis des deutschen Bundesverfassungsgerichts" in Gunther Teubner (ed.), *Entscheidungen als Rechtsgründe* (1995) 139–59.

a concrete view of the problem. But it is astonishing how, at the end of the day, the concreteness of the deliberation—this case requires a just resolution—results in very general statements about constitutional interpretation. Between the conference and the crafting of the decision there is a shift from the concrete to the general, and this shift is perhaps what is most interesting to scholars. Effectively, this generalizing task gets preempted by the Federal Constitutional Court and the style of its decisions, whereas in common law cultures this is a task for scholars, or at least a task in which many participate. Which cases, then, are fit for generalization? How does generalization work? In my view, this process is consciously assumed in Germany by Karlsruhe, which then defends it as well in the interpretation of its decisions. I find that the way you have described the Court's culture of deliberation stands in a certain disharmony with how it presents the results of its deliberations in the official reports.

DG: The German style of judgment fosters that. It is not discursive, but authoritative. The result comes first; the rationale supporting that result then follows. Reasons that have been considered but rejected can be introduced only through "Yes, but" constructions. But they do at least get introduced, whereas in France they don't appear at all. Sometimes, albeit rarely, the Court itself makes clear that a decision should apply only to "cases like this one." An example, which I mentioned earlier, is the decision about shipping registers. The effort to provide workable standards to other courts for future cases surely plays an important role.

CW: Perhaps this also has something to do with the tradition of specialized courts, in which appellate courts must ensure jurisprudential unity within a pyramidal judicial structure and therefore, whenever possible, supply implicit directions about interpretation that reach beyond the individual case. One would have to think more about whether that gets transposed to the Constitutional Court.

DG: I always found it interesting to see which audience the rapporteur had in mind when she wrote the judgment. My impression is that most rapporteurs are thinking about lower court judges. This was the case with many former appellate judges from the five federal supreme courts. Others think primarily of the loser, who must learn and understand why he lost—indeed, why he had to lose. I myself—although I'm certainly not alone in this—always had the general public in mind as well.

OL: For a court, the choice between a generalized and an individualized result is especially important. Does that get reflected upon within the parameters of the culture of deliberation, or is that something that emerges from the logic of the case?

DG: There are such discussions, but never detached from the case at hand. In the face of uncertainty about future developments, the tendency is to limit statements to the individual case. If one thinks it possible to see beyond the particular circumstance, it is easier to generalize.

One First Senate decision from my last year on the Court (for which I was not the rapporteur) brought home with particular intensity the question of which branches of civil law the constitution should influence. The case dealt with the testamentary incapacity, under sections 2232 and 2233 of the Civil Code, of persons incapable of writing and speech.[27] Was it really necessary to declare this provision unconstitutional because the affected persons could perhaps still express their will through a wink or a nod? A general discussion of this question never took place.

OL: *Riding in the Woods* contained such a discussion.

DG: Yes, but one triggered by the concrete case and incomplete in scope. I already mentioned that one of my Senate colleagues wished to cut short the discussion by charging that my view would foster a police state.

OL: I think *Riding in the Woods* is a wonderful case because the Court, after the passage of thirty years, once more examines first principles in their full breadth. When the occasion arises, the Court should do that more often.

CW: The silly and replaceable subject matter could serve as only a superficial occasion for the Court to engage once more in a fundamental way with the question of the scope of protection under Article 2(1) GG. But is there not a certain element of tragedy in the fact that, even when the Court wants to decide a case narrowly, the decision still gets generalized somewhat through its treatment by scholars and doctrinalists? By now, that's what we're trained to do!

OL: Or let's think of another case: the dispute surrounding the dissolution of the Bundestag in 1983 led to a new standard—namely, when a confidence motion aimed at triggering a dissolution is permissible—even though the case could have been decided in a narrower way.[28] But then it would have had to be decided in a situational way—ultimately in accordance with the political circumstances. In this way, a general constitutional standard is artificially derived in order to produce a result that perhaps was reached already on other grounds. Twenty years later, in 2005, the legal question comes up

[27] 99 BVerfGE 341.
[28] 62 BVerfGE 1 (1983).

again, but this time through the handiwork of Gerhard Schröder[29] in an entirely different context. The Court measured his deeds against a standard that, in its time, had generalized a particular result, even though this generalization didn't fit Schröder's confidence question at all. True, a standard exists; but the political situation is entirely different. At bottom, the new decision undertook a kind of "distinguishing."[30] The Court could have spared itself that effort if it hadn't erected a general standard in 1983. It wanted to erect that standard, however, to shield itself against charges of deciding the case politically. What makes sense for fundamental rights—developing standards—might prove downright harmful for the law of state organization because that law deals with legal questions that can only be assessed on the basis of a concrete institutional context.

DG: I don't want to elaborate here on my opinion that both cases concerning the dissolution of parliament should have come out the other way. I want only to emphasize that a constitutional court is not authorized to decide in a decisionist manner, and this is especially true in questions as highly political as the dissolution of parliament. The court has to show how its decision flows from the general norm, and this requires a certain degree of generalization. How far the generalization should reach is a matter of debate. But it is interesting to note that every judge is sometimes on one side of the divide, sometimes on the other. There isn't a faction of generalizers and a faction of individualizers.

[29] Gerhard Schröder (1944–present), politician (SPD); minister president of the state of Lower Saxony (1990–1998); federal chancellor (1998–2005).

[30] 114 BVerfGE 121 (2005).

# IX.
# Experiences on the Court

## A. Everyday Work and the Shaping of Cases

CW: When you got started in Karlsruhe, were things about as you had expected or was it completely different?

DG: The first thing I did was to rearrange the furniture in my office. As things were previously arranged, secretaries and visitors entered the room from behind Hesse's back. Additionally, it offered a lovely view of the castle gardens, on which Hesse obviously placed little value. Admittedly, he spent less time in the room than I did. As a Freiburger, he didn't move to Karlsruhe. He usually came only for sittings and spent the night in the hotel.

I was very pleased with my eastward-facing office. In the First Senate, one inherits one's predecessors place in the conference room, but not one's predecessor's office. Instead, the other judges have claim, in order of seniority, on the vacated office if they find it more congenial than their own. Fortunately, no one asserted a claim to Hesse's office. I myself never made use of my right to other rooms. Behind my desk, I hung a large engraving of the Paulskirche National Assembly.[1] The other decorative art also had constitutional significance.

That, however, is probably the last thing you had in mind when you asked your question. But one shouldn't underestimate the importance of such things. This was an additional reason for my going gladly to work—because the Court's building gave me a sense of spatial well-being. It is, of course, an unspectacular building—to the disappointment, incidentally, of some foreign visitors who, on the basis of the Court's reputation, expect imposing architecture. But it was fitting for the Bonn Republic, which wanted to do

[1] The Paulskirche Assembly was an elected national assembly which met in the Paulskirche in Frankfurt from May 1848 until May 1949 as a result of the March Revolution of 1848. It adopted a democratic constitution (Paulskirche Constitution) with fundamental rights and a constitutional monarchy. However, the large German states—especially the King of Prussia—refused to accept this constitution, thereby depriving it of practical effect. This was the major defeat for the political efforts of the German *Bürgertum*. In the second half of the nineteenth century, the German Bourgeoisie became decidedly unpolitical, surrendering politics to military elites and to the nobility.

*Dieter Grimm: Advocate of the Constitution.* Dieter Grimm, Oxford University Press (2020). 
DOI: 10.1093/oso/9780198845270.001.0001

anything other than boast and which understood democratic architecture as transparent architecture.

But now, at last, to the work. Even as a constitutionalist, one knows little about the Court's internal procedures. One has a rough idea of the number of petitions, but what that means for the individual justice is far from clear. I experienced my first surprise when, as Hesse was passing his portfolio on to me, he explained that he was leaving behind ninety-eight unresolved cases. Some of them had been "served," if I knew what "served" meant. I did not know,[2] and I was stunned: nearly a hundred unresolved cases! I asked him how long it would take until I reached zero. "You'll never reach zero," he answered.

In December 1999, I bequeathed to my successor, Wolfgang Hoffmann-Riem, nearly twice as many unresolved cases as I inherited. I mention this to highlight that I had no conception of the perpetual quandary of being unable to keep pace with the new petitions. And the number grew during my term in office. The submissions increased from 3,702 in 1988, my first full year, to 4,885 in 1999, my last year. In 1993 the 5,000-mark was surpassed for the first time. The number remained there for five years before the number of submissions fell a bit again in 1998.

I was equally astonished by the number of cases dealing with trivialities or matters without specific constitutional substance. The general image of constitutional jurisprudence is shaped by the Senate decisions that appear in the grey volumes. But Senate decisions make up less than 1 percent of all cases. The lion's share of working time is devoted to chamber cases, which as a rule are not discussed in conference but are disposed of instead by circulating written proposals.[3]

MR: Was the work within the Senate what you had expected it to be?

DG: As far as the Senate is concerned, it quickly became evident that the question of party adherence or affinity did not play a decisive role. This was the question that nearly every group of visitors and every outsider asked.

[2] It meant that the application or complaint had been formally sent to all parties who had a right to be heard before the case was decided. This happened in cases that were to be considered by the full Senate, as well as a few others. Hesse was indicating that among the ninety-eight unresolved cases were some important ones that would require a lot of time and labor to resolve.

[3] The vast majority of constitutional complaint procedures are conducted not by one of the two Senates of the Federal Constitutional Court, but rather by chambers which consist of three judges. A chamber can deny the acceptance of a constitutional complaint or accept it. If the fundamental legal questions of the case have already been decided by the Senate, the chamber may not only accept the constitutional complaint but also render the final decision in favor of the claimant on behalf of the Senate. In such cases, the decision of the chamber has the same effect as a decision of the Senate. However, a chamber may not declare a statute unconstitutional and void. This kind of decision may only be made by one of the two Senates.

Naturally, everyone within the Court knew who had been nominated by which party, but the mere fact that the other party always had to approve prevented the elevation of loyalists who toed the party line. There were not even groups or factions that agreed on a certain line before the Senate conference or who regularly voted as a group. Not that I expected the opposite. I simply didn't know, and I was happy to land in an open setting where arguments truly mattered. None of this changed in the course of my twelve years there.

Senate conferences were distinctive in that—very unlike the US Supreme Court—there was a basic willingness to reach consensus and an attendant willingness (of course) to compromise, since it was rather exceptional that everyone agreed at the outset. This basic willingness to find a consensus solution did not, however, harden into pressure or expectation. Tenacity incurred no displeasure. One had only to sense when further insistence was useless. Dissenting opinions didn't dismay the Senate either. A new member of the Senate, who didn't know this and who hoped to tilt the balance by threatening to dissent, was only told by Herzog, the presiding justice, "That never impressed anyone here."

Members of the Senate often changed their minds as a result of internal discussion. It even happened that at the end of the deliberations the rapporteur backed away from his or her memo. It is also not the case that one always goes to the conference room with one's mind already made up. I tried to work through the cases on the agenda so thoroughly beforehand as to reach a conclusion. But there were cases—mostly such as came from relatively hermetic areas of law that I didn't know well, such as tax law or social welfare law—for which I left things at a provisional opinion in order to see at the conference how the others viewed the problems.

OL: Are there special rules for Senate deliberations?

DG: Special rules for Senate deliberations did not exist. At the beginning, the rapporteur summarized his or her proposal. Then the discussion began, usually oriented to the different parts of the proposal. A queue was kept of those who wanted to speak and those in the queue spoke in turn. Comments tended to be relatively brief, and those who had to wait to speak built upon what had been spoken before. Those who couldn't muster such flexibility might undermine the effect of their own contributions. The presiding judge had to sense when a discussion had exhausted itself and was ripe for decision.

I have often compared Senate conferences with academic discourse and found that, although academic discussions could be intellectually more enjoyable, they fell far short of judicial deliberations in terms of the accountability imposed by the duty to decide and the binding validity of the decision. One didn't merely loose an opinion on the world; one regulated a legal situation with binding force. For twelve years, I attended Senate conferences with undiminished excitement and joy. Sometimes, of course, I left the conference without joy, disappointed by my colleagues' lack of insight or unwillingness to carry the discussion further. But, with a little distance, I could always tell myself that they were probably having the same experience with me.

I give the Karlsruhe culture of deliberation much of the credit for the respect that the Court has earned in German society. It is not without consequence for outcomes and rationales. When I had the chance to speak to the US Supreme Court, I used the occasion to show my American colleagues what an opportunity they were wasting by voting immediately after oral argument rather than deliberating further.

MR: How does the culture of deliberating the merits of the case differ from the later reading conference?[4]

DG: The reading conference was a hard trial for me when I myself was rapporteur because every member of the Senate could suggest changes—stylistic, structural, substantive. In cases where things got complicated, I adopted the practice of skipping lunch to work on a revised formulation in order to retain linguistic sovereignty over my text. Once in a while, someone expressed a desire to abandon the reading conference and leave the work of revision to the chairman and the rapporteur, as is customary with some of the five federal supreme courts. But I always opposed this. Not infrequently, it was the reading conference that first uncovered flaws or gaps—premature conclusions or redundancies. The reading conference sometimes led us to revisit the debate on the merits and took longer than the merits debate itself. When disputes arose about individual sentences or passages, Herzog as chairman was always ready with the question: "Do we even need that?" And if that didn't help, Seidl was the master of formulations capable of commanding a consensus.

Although I wasn't exactly thrilled with revisions to my own drafts, I often asked for changes to others' texts. If I had large reservations, I shared them with the rapporteur before the reading conference. If I wanted to rework entire passages, and not just individual sentences, I always brought

[4] Reading conferences are meetings of the full Senate in which the text of the opinion to be published is reviewed line by line.

a proposed text to the conference, since I had quickly learned that it was useless to criticize a passage without a ready alternative. If the rapporteur insists on his or her version, the reading conference must vote on which text will serve as its basis. Minor changes could be submitted in the conference, as could those of a purely linguistic nature. I'm afraid that in this respect I sometimes annoyed my colleagues. The sense of style was unevenly distributed among my colleagues, and for the rule that infinitive sentences with "in order . . . to" (*um . . . zu*) or "without having/needing to" (*ohne . . . zu*) always take the subject of the main clause, there was no sensibility at all. I practiced patience and tried to avoid accusatory tones, until one day Udo Steiner, who had filled the vacancy created by Alfred Söllner's early resignation, gave voice to his discontent by shouting, "There is no such rule!" I recommended that he take a look at the *Duden*,[5] and at the next sitting he admitted that the *Duden*, alas, was of my opinion.

CW: Let's talk about law clerks. You had three during your tenure?

DG: When I began, there were two. Reunification occasioned a third. Shortly after my departure, it rose to four.

CW: Did you prepare the memos yourself and leave the chamber decisions to your clerks?

DG: That was my plan. But I didn't stick to it entirely. On the one hand, I prepared many chamber decisions myself. These were either those that could be taken care of immediately and effortlessly (some called them "revolving door cases") or those that were particularly important to me—mostly Article 5 cases. On the other hand, the first drafts of various Senate decisions came from my clerks. Without exception, I wrote the judgments and rationales in Senate matters myself.

CW: Your clerks came from both the academy and the judiciary?

DG: The mixture was important to me. I inherited my first two clerks from Konrad Hesse. Michael Knoblich[6] was a civil judge in Baden-Württemberg; Rüdiger Rubel[7] was an administrative judge in Hesse. Thereafter, there was a splendid array of Bielefelders—overwhelmingly my research assistants and my doctoral and *Habilitation* students.[8] These, however, were always

[5] The *Duden* is a dictionary of the German language. It was founded by *Konrad Duden* in 1880 and is regarded as the leading authority on German spelling and grammar.

[6] Michael Knoblich (1952–present), until 2019 presiding judge on the Karlsruhe regional court of appeals (*Oberlandesgericht*).

[7] Rüdiger Rubel (1954–present), until 2019 presiding judge on the Federal Administrative Court; honorary professor at the University of Gießen.

[8] Marion Albers (1961–present), now professor of public law at the University of Hamburg; Frank Hölscher (1964–present), now a lawyer in Bonn; Rüdiger Nolte (1951–present), most recently presiding judge on the Federal Administrative Court; Helge Rossen-Stadtfeld (1955–present), now professor of

joined by judges, mostly from the civil courts[9] because our caseload always featured many cases from the civil judiciary. I usually asked the justice ministry of North-Rhine Westphalia or the president of the Hamm regional court of appeals, where I had often conducted exams, for suggestions. One of my clerks worked as a practicing lawyer[10] before coming to the Court.

Rosemarie Will[11] was a special case. After reunification, a post was created at the Court for a clerk from the former German Democratic Republic (GDR). No one knew jurists from the GDR. But I knew *Frau* Will through my occasional teaching at Humboldt University after the Wall came down and immediately after the transition, including teaching for those professors of public law who hoped to retain their positions.[12] *Frau* Will was the youngest professor on the faculty, appointed shortly before the transition and, under the new circumstances, immediately made dean. She handled in a remarkable way the delicate and difficult task of transitioning the faculty, and she mastered West German public law with exceptional intelligence. I had frequent conversations with her during my sporadic stays in Berlin, and I am indebted to her for many insights into the living conditions, academic situation, and culture of the GDR. I therefore recommended that *Frau* Will, at the end of her deanship, be given the new position and that she be assigned to my chambers. Some members of the Court, however, were opposed. They feared for the Court's reputation should a communist (as they put it) become one of its clerks. The matter was placed on the agenda of a plenary sitting, but Herzog soon put it to rest when he asked, with his Bavarian liberality, "Have we ever discussed in the plenum whom our colleagues hire as clerks?" No one could point to such a case. "Then why," Herzog continued, "are we doing it now?"

MR: How intensive was collaboration within chambers?

public law at the Bundeswehr University in Munich-Neubiberg; Georg Seyfarth (1966–present), now managing partner at the law firm of Hengeler Mueller.

[9] Manfred Heine (1956–present), now presiding judge on the Hamm regional court of appeals (*Oberlandesgericht*); Christian Müller (1947–present), most recently president of the Arnsberg regional court (*Landgericht*); Günter Offczors (1952–present), most recently judge on the regional welfare court in Darmstadt; Martine Stein (1959–present) now presiding judge on the Düsseldorf regional court of appeals (*Oberlandesgericht*).

[10] Ulli F.H. Rühl (1954–present), now professor of public law at the University of Bremen.

[11] Rosemarie Will (1949–present), now emeritus professor of public law at Humboldt University in Berlin.

[12] The professors of the GDR were at first allowed to retain their positions. However, the reunification treaty provided for ways to remove them inter alia for lack of qualifications or lack of character fitness. The new German states implemented those rules differently. In most cases, there was a formal procedure to determine the qualifications and the fitness of the individual candidate. Cf. 95 BVerfGE 193 (1997).

DG: Collaboration with clerks was close—closer than with assistants at the university. We felt we were part of a team with a common task. Even today we get together every year. I never handed over a draft Senate decision without first discussing it with all the clerks. I wanted a critical examination of my proposal. I didn't want to encounter an argument at the Senate conference that I hadn't heard before. Some deliberations with my clerks were the equal of Senate conferences.

OL: What was the relationship between the two Senates like? Do the justices follow the other Senate's case law? At bottom, the Federal Constitutional Court consists of two courts working side by side. But in the public's eye there is this impression of a harmonious tribunal that in reality doesn't exist. As a justice, must one defend outwardly and accept internally a case law that one cannot influence but must know equally well?

DG: There was no contact between the Senates beyond collegial courtesy. There was, however, some contact between individual judges beyond the Senate boundaries, such as when two judges knew each other well from earlier settings. Official contact was limited to the plenum and to Court events or trips. In any event, each Senate is occupied with its own affairs. Notice is taken of the other Senate's case law, not least because one gets asked about it outside the Court. The public generally doesn't know which Senate decided a case. In the event of a jurisdictional conflict, a committee of six justices (three from each Senate) is convened, with the president casting the deciding (i.e. tiebreaking) vote. Jurisdictional conflicts were rare. When they did come up, they dealt with positive conflicts: both Senates thought they had jurisdiction.

OL: Why does the plenum meet so rarely?

DG: The plenum typically meets twice a year to discuss matters of Court business—more often if needed. But you are probably thinking of the plenum in its capacity as a court of law when one Senate wants to depart from the other's case law (section 16 of the Federal Constitutional Court Act).[13] Here there is in fact a *horror pleni*. Deliberations among sixteen judges are naturally harder than those among eight. What's more, the routines and style of discussion that have developed within each Senate can't be used. Nor can one entirely exclude the possibility of rivalries. These are all reasons to avoid plenary decisions through distinguishing. In my

[13] The plenum of the Federal Constitutional Court consists of all judges of both Senates. It is mainly responsible for procedural matters. However, if one Senate wants to depart from the case law of the other Senate, the plenum has to decide this substantive question.

time there was a very controversial case called *Child as Damage*,[14] in which the Second Senate thought that the First was about to depart from its abortion judgment and must therefore invoke the plenum; whereas my Senate thought there was no departure. The Second Senate couldn't force the issue, but it gave formal expression to its protest through an unprecedented resolution, published as an appendix in the official reports.[15]

CW: How many dissenting opinions did you write?

DG: Besides *Riding in the Woods*,[16] only one, which came in a landlord-tenant case.[17] Landlord-tenant law was constitutionally relevant thanks to Article 14 GG, and during the first five years of my term in Karlsruhe, landlord-tenant law—in particular, eviction for personal use—played a big role because the rapporteur was fired up about the subject and brought case after case to the Senate.[18] Many of them ended in five-to-three decisions, in which I was in the minority, in favor of the property owner. In one case, my two colleagues in the minority wanted to write a dissent at all costs. For me the case wouldn't have been sufficiently important, but if the dissent had to be written anyway, I would rather write it myself. The wave of landlord-tenant cases subsided when the rapporteur was converted to the view that Article 14 GG protected the tenant as well as the landlord.[19] This then brought the civil lawyers back on the scene, although the conceptions of private property in civil law and in constitutional law are not identical.

CW: Was the 1970 decision to introduce dissenting opinions correct?

DG: In my opinion, yes. Opponents' biggest fear was that it would undermine the authority of the Court and its judgments. But that hasn't happened. If one abandons the view that there is only one correct solution for each legal dispute and acknowledges instead the existence of interpretive latitude that can be exploited in more than one way, then one should be open about it.

[14] 96 BVerfGE 375 (1997).

[15] 96 BVerfGE 409 (1997).

[16] Cf. Chapter VI, fn. 44.

[17] 81 BVerfGE 29 (1989). In the case, the civil courts had declared the eviction for personal use invalid. There is no justifiable personal need when the landlord has available another home of equal value that doesn't require the eviction of a tenant. The Senate majority deemed this a violation of the property guarantees of Article 14 GG. The dissenting opinion, coauthored by Justices Dieterich, Grimm, and Kühling, said: "The interpretation given by the regional court to Section 564b(2)(2) of the Civil Code does not deprive the landlord of the constitutionally-enshrined core of private use and power of disposition. It neither strips him entirely of the power to dispose of the rented home, since he retains the other legal avenues of eviction and disposition after the end of the rental agreement, nor does it completely deprive him of the proceeds of his property, since he continues to receive the agreed-upon rental fee. That he must forego potentially more profitable uses of the home does not affect this result, since Article 14 GG does not guarantee the most profitable use of property, but rather requires its social use."

[18] Cf. Thomas Dieterich, *Ein Richterleben im Arbeits- und Verfassungsrecht* (2016) 200f.

[19] Cf. 89 BVerfGE 1 (1993).

CW: I want to ask another, more precise question. When a case is particularly divisive within the Senate, I imagine that there are two possibilities: one can either pursue a grand compromise and eschew dissenting opinions by crafting a conciliatory decision, or one can trace the clear division of positions, so that both groups can formulate their view with greater clarity and sharpness. Is that considered in conference?

DG: I've experienced both paths. I've already noted that, unlike the US Supreme Court, there is a basic willingness to seek a solution acceptable to all sides, but no pressure in this direction. If everyone tries to find common ground during the conference, then residual differences are usually accepted without formal opposition in the form of a dissenting opinion. But if the issue remains divisive after the conference, that doesn't mean that the minority automatically writes a dissenting opinion. In Karlsruhe, that option is employed sparingly. My predecessor, Konrad Hesse, made it a matter of principle not to write dissents. And even a great dissenter such as Gertrude Lübbe-Wolff writes barely twelve dissents in twelve years—as many as an American Supreme Court justice writes in a month. A middle path between the two alternatives you describe is to announce the result of the vote, but usually without giving names. This was sometimes done to show a divided society that the Court was united, sometimes to show a divided society that there were differences of opinion within the Court as well.

CW: How do you assess the position of presiding judge and to what extent does that depend on the concrete person?

DG: I experienced four presiding judges: Herzog, Henschel, Seidl, and Papier. With Herzog, it was an eight-year collaboration; the other three split the last four years. Henschel and Seidl had already served as justices on the First Senate before being named as its chairmen. There were naturally differences in how they led discussions, but the presiding judge enjoyed no bonus in conference. The chair's influence depended, like that of the other judges, on the persuasiveness of his arguments. I never saw any of the four try to use his presiding role to privilege his personal view. In this connection, I must single out Henschel for special praise, because as a judge he was a great fighter, but he gracefully assumed his altered role.

OL: How important is the rapporteur? If he or she stakes out the course, is the burden of proof all the higher for the other judges?

DG: The rapporteur's only advantage is her having wrestled with the issue most intensively. She has no informational advantage. Each judge has access to the full record. And there is no rapporteur bonus in the sense that the rapporteur is usually followed. Rapporteurs often didn't prevail. Things look a little different only in areas that are highly specialized. If, for example, a case is about tax law and the rapporteur happens to be a tax lawyer, that gives her a certain advantage, but by no means ensures that her position will be approved. Although after a while, one can surmise who is of which opinion in certain areas, one can never be certain whether the proposed decision or proffered rationale will succeed in the Senate. Herzog used to say that the rapporteur is the loneliest person on the Court.

OL: If the rapporteur is unable to prevail with her proposal, there comes a point at which another member of the Court must produce a counterproposal.

DG: There are two possibilities. The rapporteur is confronted by her critics with an alternative draft at the outset. Or the rapporteur is simply told that her proposed solution or her outcome is untenable. In that case, an alternative solution must be developed in conference.

CW: Other former constitutional judges relate that there is a certain inhibition about presenting one's first case as rapporteur to the Senate.

DG: In my experience it takes about a year for a new judge to bring her first case before the Senate. Usually this is indeed the product of inhibition. But it can also be because many cases await Senate deliberation. This is often so after a change of judges. Departing judges are given chronological priority on the theory that they should be allowed time to bring their last cases before the Senate. The others hold back for a time, but then clog the conferences with their cases in the early months after the new judge's confirmation. My first case came before the Senate five months after I joined it. Incidentally, it had already been prepared by one of Hesse's clerks. I reworked the proposal thoroughly one more time. The Senate accepted it, but abridged the rationale considerably.[20]

CW: There are relatively few oral arguments in Karlsruhe. It is sometimes unclear for outsiders when they are held and when not. Would you say that the oral argument is decisive? The proposal, after all, has already been made. Put differently: What significance does oral argument have when it does take place?

DG: After oral argument, I was almost always smarter than before. The submissions of counsel and of experts, the exchanges between them, the judges' questions—all expand the horizon. Oral arguments should be held

[20] 77 BVerfGE 346 (1988). A press wholesaler was convicted for distributing writings that imperil the young. The Senate deemed the conviction a violation of the freedom of the press.

more frequently. But this would likely require facilitating the preparatory work. Memos in cases with oral argument are considerably more extensive than in other Senate cases. There are additional conferences—one about the questions the Court will ask the parties, the experts, and others authorized to appear. There is a conference the day before argument about what can be regarded as settled on the briefs and other submissions, and what the Senate still regards as especially weighty. Oral argument is required for disputes between constitutional organs, federalism disputes, and abstract review. In other cases, it was usually the case's importance—sometimes legal, sometimes political or societal—that tipped the balance in favor of oral argument. But it's hard to discern a principle behind these decisions. As I said earlier, the *Crucifix* case should absolutely have featured oral argument.

OL: That would likely have eased some of the sharpness of the criticism.

DG: I assume so. There is usually extensive media coverage both before and after oral argument. The public is prepared. The basic views are known. The judgment doesn't come as a bolt from the blue.

OL: Substantive enlightenment through oral argument—is that the point?

DG: As a rule, the need for enlightenment is already satisfied before oral argument through the parties' and other authorized participants' answers to the catalogue of questions. But the chance for judges to ask follow-up questions and the opportunity for rebuttal by the various participants is important. Some things, indeed, can only be said, not written. During oral argument in a case about expanded codetermination in the mining industry, I asked the head of the Mannesmann supervisory board whether the expanded model of codetermination had noticeably obstructed business policy. The answer came somewhat hesitantly and after an exchange of glances with the CEO: "No, not really."[21]

OL: Are there conversations about cases outside the Senate conference? Do judges go to lunch together or simply meet in the hall and ask, "What do you think about the case?"

DG: During the lunch break of an oral proceeding there is naturally further discussion about the case—evaluations of what has been said so far and the questions that still need clarifying. As long as the Court still had a restaurant, we ate in the "judges' room" on conference days as well and could

[21] 99 BVerfGE 367 (1999) at 391.

discuss things further there. The demise of the restaurant—which was also open to the public—was a real loss. The kitchen needed costly renovations, and I thought the Court's president should have fought harder to salvage the restaurant. I've already noted that there were no factions or groups that met before the conference. But that doesn't mean that people didn't discuss pending cases outside the conference room. There were conversations in the hall, and one could stop by colleagues from whom one could expect further enlightenment.

MR: You said that acquiring knowledge from other disciplines is sometimes difficult—especially because it can be uncertain whether the chosen authors' views are reliable or representative. Does the same problem arise when the Constitutional Court chooses outside experts? How does that happen?

DG: Usually it was the rapporteur who suggested seeking expert input and who, if the suggestion was accepted, proposed names. The other members could propose additional topics or experts. But on the whole, things were left to the rapporteur. In the case about the Federal Intelligence Service's expanded surveillance powers, I reached out to the Karlsruhe Technical University and discussed with experts in the subject matter who might be best qualified to testify as experts.

CW: In cases that deal with technical questions, things aren't quite so delicate—we're obviously thinking of political assessments. Here I think it problematic when the parties aren't asked about the choice of experts and aren't even allowed to question them.

DG: The parties, in fact, are not asked. But they are told which experts have been invited and, if they are worried about bias, they can object. And, of course, all the parties to the case are given the experts' testimonies and a chance to respond. Even during oral argument itself, they can join in the questioning. The question is how one could make it better. At a recent conference on the early history of the Federal Constitutional Court, it was reported that in the *Homosexuals* judgment—a judgment that today elicits embarrassment—expert testimony was secured on the differences between male and female homosexuality.[22]

[22] 6 BVerfGE 389 (1957). The conference was held in Berlin on April 7–8, 2016 under the title, "The Federal Constitutional Court and the Constitutional History of the Federal Republic: Toward a History of the Karlsruhe Republic." The proceedings are published in Florian Meinel (ed.), *Verfassungsgerichtsbarkeit in der Bonner Republik: Aspekte einer Geschichte des Bundesverfassungsgerichts* (2019).

## B. The Constitutional Court's Place within the System of Powers

OL: I want to add a few fundamental questions about the Federal Constitutional Court and its place within the system of powers. I sense that the Court's relationship with the Bundestag is in some respects precarious because, in remarks about the consequences of decisions, the Court doesn't differentiate between individual constitutional complaints and abstract review. Instead, the norm itself is made the object of constitutional judicial review in both cases without distinction. I find this problematic because, in the case of abstract review, the individual case can't be processed factually as well as a constitutional complaint against a lower court judgment. The addressee of fundamental rights review is sometimes the first branch but sometimes the third in the form of a specialized court. Does the Court take that into account, or does the legal question as such—the provision of ordinary law in relationship to the constitution—always assume center stage?

DG: I want to make clear at the outset that the Court's relations with the legislature are always present in conference. Everyone is keenly aware that dangers lurk here. Kirchhof's formula—that the legislature is the first interpreter of the constitution, the Court the second—doesn't end the discussion. The democratic difference between the two must be kept in mind. But that doesn't tell us anything about the treatment of abstract review on the one hand and individual constitutional complaints on the other. In reality, the two have different addressees. But the objects of review are, at least in part, the same. Because judicial decisions that encroach upon fundamental rights are only constitutional if the underlying legal basis is constitutional as well, an admissible constitutional complaint always opens the way to review of the norm itself—quite apart from the fact that in exceptional cases constitutional complaints may be raised directly against statutes. I have the impression—I say impression because I've never posed the question directly—that the different procedural paths play no role in reviewing the norm. The fact that the norm comes before the Court directly in one case and indirectly in the other doesn't change the process of review. In this respect, concrete review rests somewhere between abstract review and constitutional complaints.[23] Like abstract review, it is concerned only with the

[23] The five most important procedures of the Federal Constitutional Court are constitutional complaints, abstract review of statutes, concrete review of statutes, *Organstreit*, and disputes between the federation and the states. A constitutional complaint is brought forward by an individual who complains that an act or omission of the state violates his or her individual fundamental rights. It can

constitutionality of the norm; like the constitutional complaint, it emerges from a concrete legal controversy. The case's context is always discussed as well. The referring court must explain not only why it thinks the relevant norm unconstitutional, but also why that is relevant to its disposition of the case.

OL: In the case of a constitutional complaint, the Court can deal with all the nuances of a rights infringement ex post and in the context of a concrete case, whereas with abstract review the facts are rather of a hypothetical nature. How the norm will operate is then the object of a prediction. The legislature's prognosis competes with the Court's evaluation. Over the years, the Court has rather sharpened the review dimension of prognostic assessments. The Constitutional Court has become more intolerant, if one compares it with the largesse that Hesse accorded the legislature in the *Codetermination* case.[24] I regard the *Codetermination* judgment as a wise decision because the facts developed differently both from what the legislature thought and what the challenger feared, and the Court did not interfere with an open development. Today, by contrast, we find numerous decisions in which the legislature's projection is subject to certain requirements of plausibility or proof—in which a procedural review of predictive discretion supplants an evaluation of the facts. The Court makes the legislature's predictive capacity the object of review, and thus makes itself master of shaping the future.

DG: The problem with abstract review is its abstractness. One usually has no material to look at on the norm's interpretation and effect. Many petitions for abstract review are filed as soon as the law is passed. The proceedings before the Constitutional Court then look like a resumption of the political process. It seems more political than other procedures. For that reason, I could easily do without abstract review. Truly important problems would

usually be filed only after having exhausted all other possible legal remedies. The abstract review of statutes can only be initiated by the federal government, a state government, or one-fourth of the members of the Bundestag. In this procedure, the court determines whether the statute is constitutional and valid or unconstitutional and void. The concrete review of statutes can be initiated by any German court of law. If a court determines that a statute the validity of which is material to its decision is unconstitutional, it may not declare the statute void. Rather, the court has to stay its proceedings and refer the matter to the Federal Constitutional Court. In an *Organstreit*, one constitutional organ (e.g. the Bundestag, the Bundesrat, the federal government) or a part of it claims that its constitutional rights/competences have been violated by another organ or part of it. In disputes between the federation and the states, the court determines whether the competences of the federation or the state have been violated.

[24] Cf. Chapter VI, fn. 40.

in any event reach the Court through concrete review or constitutional complaints.

In any case, the dangers are attenuated in practice. For one thing, abstract review is rare—about four cases a year. For another, the petition has no deadline. Laws can come up for abstract review after being in force for a long time. If the petition comes immediately after the law is passed, it is up to the Court to decide how quickly to consider the case. If a lot of time passes between the law's passage and the Court's review, both the abstractness and the pressures of politicization diminish.

But now you sharpen the question to include review of prognoses. The Court knows that it can claim no superior knowledge in the realm of predictions. Accordingly, it places certain conditions on the production of legislative forecasts, but it doesn't replace them with forecasts of its own. In principle, I think this is right because it requires the legislature to be cautious when making decisions about the future that might affect fundamental rights, but without substantively hemming it in. The legislature's assumptions and forecasts are taken as basis of proportionality review. On the other hand, the "duty to monitor"[25] still has no guarantees of fulfillment. It has not been accompanied by a duty to report, nor has provision been made for any temporal limit on the law's remaining in force.

OL: In recent times, there have been increasing complaints about the Federal Republic's development into a judicial state. Rüthers is one example.[26] How do you view this? This is not a development ascribed only to the Federal Constitutional Court. It applies to the ordinary courts and the European courts as well. The growth in the power of judges is, in my view, a reality that the Parliamentary Council did not have in mind. To this extent, the balance of power has shifted toward the third branch—especially toward the apex courts. But it's not as though this development should be regarded only in a negative light. In many respects we wouldn't want to be without the courts' influence. The Federal Republic owes much to the jurisprudence of the Federal Constitutional Court. It has provided enormous impetus for legal scholarship. Even so, if one looks at all three branches, the growth of judicial power is not an unqualifiedly positive development. Do we have to put up

[25] The Federal Constitutional Court imposes the "duty to monitor" upon the legislature as the flipside of the respect for the legislature's prognostic assessments. In this way, the Court imposes upon the legislature a duty to ensure that its decisions are corrected if the prognoses turn out to be wrong.

[26] Bernd Rüthers (1930–present), professor of private law, labor law, and legal theory at the Free University of Berlin and the University of Constance. See his *Die heimliche Revolution vom Rechtsstaat zum Richterstaat* (2d ed. 2016).

with it? Or, as many colleagues maintain,[27] has the Federal Constitutional Court passed its zenith?

DG: One must first note that courts are created and endowed with powers politically—that is by the other branches. And despite awareness of the dangers you depict, the creation of courts and the expansion of their powers proceeds apace. The number of constitutional courts or courts with powers of constitutional review increased considerably toward the end of the last century. And among international courts the development is even more dramatic. Now we are seeing the first setbacks, but not yet a change of course. The third branch is the expanding branch.

Next, one can observe that courts emancipate themselves from the founders in the perception of their duties, and that, in part, they employ the instrument of legal interpretation very aggressively. There are acts of self-empowerment. Like you, I presume that if the Parliamentary Council existed today it would be astonished at its brainchild. In the dispute between Kelsen and Schmitt about constitutional justice in the 1920s,[28] Kelsen emerged after the Second World War as the unequivocal victor. Today some are asking—including Rüthers, a fierce opponent of Schmitt—whether Schmitt's warnings weren't right after all.

I regard a constitutional court as a condition for a constitution's relevance. Fundamental rights, in particular, have no institutional protection without judicial review. The number of states in which rights are respected without mechanisms for their implementation is vanishingly small. But I don't ignore the dangers to which you allude. Accordingly, it is important to me that politicians be able to correct judicial case law by changing the law or (in the case of constitutional courts) amending the constitution. One reason for the interminable American debate about the "counter-majoritarian difficulty"[29] is that in the United States constitutional amendments are all but out of reach. That places on judges the full burden of adapting the constitution to modern conditions and drives judges inexorably into the role of constitutional politicians that should be reserved for the other branches.

[27] See, e.g., Christoph Schönberger, "Notes on Karlsruhe" in Matthias Jestaedt, Oliver Lepsius, Christoph Möllers, and Christoph Schönberger (eds), *The German Federal Constitutional Court. The Court without Limits* (2020) ch. 1. A loss of significance owing to European law is diagnosed in Udo Di Fabio, "Vom Recht, Recht zu sprechen: Die Legitimation des BVerfG" (2011)/35–36 *Aus Politik und Zeitgeschichte* 2–6.

[28] Carl Schmitt, *Der Hüter der Verfassung* (1931, 2d ed. 1969); Hans Kelsen, *Wer soll Hüter der Verfassung sein?* (1931, reprint edited by R.C. van Ooyen published in 2008).

[29] The concept was coined in Alexander Bickel, *The Least Dangerous Branch* (1962).

The problem is exacerbated in the European Union. The European equivalent of constitutional amendments are treaty amendments, but these are all but impossible, especially for narrow problems like correcting a line of case law. The quandary arises because the treaties regulate much more than constitutions do. All these matters, which in the member states are subjects of statutory law, cannot be corrected politically in the EU. The greatest but least-noted democratic problem in the EU is its over-constitutionalization. I've made this a maxim: the more constitution, the less democracy.[30]

When you ask in conclusion whether the Federal Constitutional Court has passed its zenith, I cannot agree so far as German constitutional questions are concerned. But it is true with regard to the list of things that German constitutional law has lost through the overt or stealthy expansion of EU competences—an area in which the Federal Constitutional Court constantly whets its knives but never wields them.[31]

MR: What do you think of Article 79(3) GG against the backdrop of your view that politicians must be able to correct courts?

DG: Article 79(3) GG sets the hurdles of unconstitutional constitutional law very high, and rightly so. In the few cases in which the Federal Constitutional Court has been asked to measure constitutional amendments against the standard of Article 79, it has never found a violation—and again, in my view, rightly so. My sense is that Article 79's symbolic value is greater than its practical significance.

CW: Does its admonitory power collapse if it gets applied?

DG: Not in every case. But if it were applied to prevent the EU's becoming a state, it might just bring the entire Basic Law down with it.[32]

[30] Cf. Dieter Grimm, *Europa ja—aber welches?* (2016) 116. In English: *The Constitution of European Democracy* (2017).

[31] But see now the judgment of May 5, 2020 on the Public Sector Purchase Programme of the European Central Bank (case nr. 2 BvR 859/15, 1651/15, 2006/15, 980/16).

[32] On this thought, cf. 123 BVerfGE 267.

# X. Europe

CW: Let's stick with Europe for a moment. You said earlier that you were "awakened" relatively late—during debates about the Maastricht Treaty. But you then made a very visible appearance on the European stage with your essay "Does Europe Need a Constitution?"[1]

DG: In discussions about European politics, the prevailing view at that time was that with the level of integration reached through the Maastricht Treaty, the treaties no longer sufficed to legitimate the EU. Instead, a constitution was now necessary. The European Parliament decidedly supported the proposal, which found many proponents with the simultaneous assurance that the EU would not become a state. By contrast, little was said about what makes a constitution, what it is supposed to achieve, and whether it could be divorced from the state, for which it was originally invented.

I was invited to lecture at the Siemens Foundation in Munich, and I wanted to use the occasion to address these questions. The lecture took place in January 1994 and provoked a rather irritated response in the press because I questioned the possibility and expediency of a European constitution, whereas the idea had generally found favor. The text appeared in 1995 as part of the Siemens Foundation's lecture series and, additionally, as an essay in the *JuristenZeitung*.[2] It would become my most successful publication. I owe that to a particularly prominent opponent of my views.

It came about like this. I gave the lecture again two months later, this time at the Lutheran Academy in Tutzing in connection with a conference on legal culture in Europe. In the audience sat Jürgen Habermas.[3] He jumped into the discussion with a detailed comment. He agreed with my analysis but thought I drew the wrong conclusions. The conference organizers decided to publish the lectures and asked Habermas to rework his comment into writing. The book appeared that same year,[4] and soon thereafter my

[1] Dieter Grimm, *Braucht Europa eine Verfassung?* (1995).

[2] Dieter Grimm, "Braucht Europa eine Verfassung?" (1995) *JuristenZeitung* 581.

[3] Jürgen Habermas (1929–present), professor of philosophy and sociology at the University of Frankfurt; director of the Max Planck Institute in Starnberg for Research into Living Conditions in a Scientific and Technical World.

[4] Marie-Theres Tinnefeld et al. (eds.), *Informationsgesellschaft und Rechtskultur in Europa* (1995).

*Dieter Grimm: Advocate of the Constitution.* Dieter Grimm, Oxford University Press (2020). © in the original German edition, Mohr Siebeck GmbH & Co. KG, Tübingen 2017, © this translation, Justin Collings 2020.
DOI: 10.1093/oso/9780198845270.001.0001

lecture and Habermas's response were translated into English and published in the new *European Law Journal*.[5]

Habermas carried me along, so to speak, into realms I could never have reached with a publication in a specialized German legal periodical. The essay became known throughout the EU. Its readership was not limited to legal circles but extended to philosophers, historians, and political scientists. There was now "The Grimm-Habermas Debate" and it marked the starting point of a rich literature. The lecture was translated into many languages. There are three versions in English alone.

MR: What do you think of the lecture's reception and the ensuing debates in retrospect?

DG: Many think of the lecture in terms of the "no demos thesis," by which is meant: a constitution presupposes a people as its original source and putative author; there is, however, no European people and can therefore be no European constitution. This was a truncated version of my actual views, for I made the possibility of a constitution depend less on the existence of an ethnic community than on the existence of a discursively capable society—a European public sphere. A constitution, I argued, was the product of such a society's self-determination about the aims and forms of its political rule. Europe lacked the societal preconditions for such a constitution. Under these circumstances, one could speak of a European constitution only by adopting a diluted conception of a constitution—one that scrimped on the democratic element. But if, by contrast, one conceived of a constitution in its full sense as an act of self-determination by the Union's citizens concerning their political existence, then the constitutionalization of the EU would inexorably transform it into a state.

This was the rub of the ensuing discussion. One side sought to prove that there already was—or in any case would soon be—a European public sphere. Another maintained that the constitution could be decoupled from the state—that contrasting the constitution's full versus its attenuated sense posited a false opposition: there are democratic constitutions and rule-of-law constitutions and there need be no categorical or qualitative difference between the two. Many of my original detractors have since agreed with me. Habermas remained in dissent.[6]

[5] Dieter Grimm, "Does Europe need a Constitution?" (1995) 1 *European Law Journal* 282.

[6] Cf. Jürgen Habermas, "Warum der Ausbau der Europäischen Union zu einer supranationalen Demokratie nötig und wie er möglich ist" (2014) 42 *Leviathan* 524.

MR: Apart from all the differences, were these societal preconditions in place at the framing of the US constitution? Was there a discursively capable society? Or in your view are such comparisons unhelpful because of the different historical situations?

DG: In America there was such a society, though of course with the different conditions of communication and educational prerequisites of the eighteenth century. Don't the *Federalist* papers, which first appeared as newspaper articles, prove as much? True, founding-era Americans thought of themselves more as New Yorkers or Virginians than as Americans, and the ratification debates were carried out in the individual states that emerged from the Revolution. But they were conducted everywhere in the same language and with the same arguments. Even more importantly, Americans had broken with their homelands and committed themselves to something new and, after the Revolution, something in common. Europeans, by contrast, find themselves after the founding of the EU exactly where they were before. And they communicate predominately within their political boundaries, which are usually cultural boundaries as well. What's more, they communicate in their respective languages. Yes, discussion about Europe has increased in every member state. But twenty-eight national discourses about Europe don't amount to a Europe-wide discourse.

CW: Am I wrong in thinking that your interventions in European legal matters are marked by a warning against excess euphoria about Europe? Your forthright critique of the ECJ has also received a lot of attention. Do I read too much into your differentiated position on European integration as an effort to preserve the success of the constitutional state in the Federal Republic? You described yourself as a "friend of the constitution."[7] Under the Basic Law and its development by the Federal Constitutional Court, the Federal Republic joined the community of western constitutional states. In part, perhaps, it even surpassed them. Although the progress of European integration didn't launch a countermovement, it did begin a process that could lead, in the end, to a weakening of this achievement. Am I wrong to think that you regard displacement through international and especially European law as a threat?

DG: You're not wrong to the extent that, where the standard of constitutionality is concerned, Germany has more to lose than the other member states. This is true in several respects. It is true first of all in terms of constitutional theory, constitutional interpretation, and constitutional adjudication. One

[7] Supra at Chapter VI.

can say this without hubris, since the other member states also see Germany as a leader in Europe in these areas. But it's also true with regard to the degree of actual compliance with the constitution. It has been mentioned before to what extent the political discourse in Germany is shaped by the constitution. A posture openly indifferent to the constitution is impossible in German politics. And it is true, finally, with regard to the constitution's symbolic impact, which reaches beyond its political validity. Constitutional patriotism is, for entirely comprehensible reasons, something specifically German.

All of this might play a role in my views on Europe, though not to the extent that I deem the German constitutional standard non-negotiable. Just as I view constitutionalism as a great achievement, I also regard European unification as a great achievement. And since this latter achievement would not have been possible had every state held doggedly to its own constitution, I think it reasonable to pay a certain price for it in constitutional autonomy. I am concerned, then, with the optimal balance, and we haven't found that yet in Europe.

MR: In your recent book you speak of the EU's "alienation" from its citizens, and yet you also underscore that what you want is not "less Europe" but a "better Europe."[8] Many see Europe in crisis after the Brexit vote. In your view, how can this crisis be overcome and an "alienation" of the EU from its citizens be avoided? What should a "better Europe" look like?

DG: As I see it, Europe faces a dilemma. The astounding progress of European integration depended on the essential steps of integration being taken by stealth and with soft soles. They took place administratively and judicially, without public attention or public participation. By now, however, integration by stealth has grown so far beyond the common market and reached so far into political and social realms that the public will no longer accept it without resistance. Referenda results confirm this, as does the rise and strengthening of Eurosceptic political parties, which are usually also populist parties. In the future, things won't proceed without enhanced democratic legitimacy. But that will slow the integration process and might even, in part, reverse it. Brexit is the first unequivocally backward step. At the same time, there will always be pushes for further integration—most of them triggered by crises, such as the financial crisis and the banking crisis;

[8] Dieter Grimm, *Europa ja—aber welches?* (2016) 7. Also available in English as *The Constitution of European Democracy* (2017) 22.

or by the threatened departure of individual member states from European values.

How can alienation be counteracted? I have three main ideas. First, the EU's democratically legitimated and accountable organs (the Council and the Parliament) must regain terrain that they have lost to the executive and judicial institutions (the Commission and the Court of Justice). This can only happen by repoliticizing decisions of high political importance that are currently made through non-political means. The current state of affairs was possible only thanks to the "constitutionalization of the Treaties" that the ECJ brought about in 1963 and 1964, not realizing that the treaties had little in common with a constitution. As is well known, they are much more extensive than even the most detailed member state constitutions, because they are full of regulations that in every member state would be ordinary law and could thus be democratically amended at any time. Constitutionalization prevents that in Europe. Europe is over-constitutionalized. The conclusion to be drawn from this is the following: The treaties should be limited to those provisions that are constitutional in nature, whereas all other provisions should be demoted to the level of secondary European law. This would change nothing in the substance of Union law or the ECJ's jurisdiction, but the democratically legitimated and accountable organs would regain access to these materials, and elections—both national and European—would also become more consequential.

At the same time, parliaments should be strengthened—the European Parliament by Europeanizing elections and parties so that voters can make truly Europe-focused, rather than nationally orientated decisions; the national parliaments by ending the perpetual hemorrhage of policy powers through expansive treaty interpretation. Finally, the correct but hitherto utterly ineffectual idea of subsidiarity must be revived by abandoning the heretofore applicable final criterion for dividing competences between the Union and the member states in favor of a division based on subject matter. None of this, however, gets mentioned in the current reform discussions. Instead, the idea is championed of transforming the European Union into a parliamentary system according to the national model. But doing so would not only completely miss the mark with respect to the causes of democratic weakness I've just described, but would also make the EU even more autonomous from the member states without any prospect of how to plug the resultant legitimacy gaps at the European level.

MR: The Brexit vote was only one of many successes for populist and nationalist movements in 2016. Do you see in such trends a profound danger not only for Europe but also—in light of a rhetoric aimed against religious and ethnic minorities as well as against the press—for liberal democracy worldwide?

DG: Yes. One can see that in the populist opposition parties in Western Europe and even more so in the populist governing parties in Eastern Europe. The patterns of argumentation are, after all, the same everywhere. The populist parties are not populist because they focus on the ideas or interests of the people and issue popular demands. All parties do that, and in a democracy that is unobjectionable. Rather, they are populist because they claim for themselves alone the right to represent the people's interest, thereby branding all rivals as "enemies of the people." All sorts of things may be done to enemies that couldn't be done to rivals. The glaring contrasts between their opponents' election results and their own they brush aside with the argument of the seduction of the people, for which "fake news" and the "lying press" are to blame. Governing populist parties maintain that their election victory established the identity between people and party. Accordingly, they think themselves justified in sweeping away everything that stands in the way of that unity—all in the name of an identitarian conception of democracy. This applies to the parliamentary opposition, the judiciary (and constitutional courts in particular), the media, and fundamental rights—everything, in short, that makes up the constitutional state. One can observe such argumentation among opposition parties in many Western European countries—recently in Germany as well. The government argumentation shows up in Hungary, Poland, Turkey, some Latin American states, and in its outlines even in the country where one would have least expected it: the USA. It remains to be seen how resilient against this the oldest constitutionalism in the world will prove to be.

# XI.
# International Constitutionalist: Renewed Ties with the US

OL: The Yale seminar[1] allowed you to cultivate regular contacts with judges on other constitutional courts. That is also a privilege. I know that there is a culture of exchanging visits among European courts, but the Yale forum is stable, more intensive, and also focused on concrete problems.

DG: Initially, the Yale seminar was just one among many undertakings of this sort. But it became for me, later on, the most important. After the upheavals of 1989, and especially after the founding of constitutional courts in the erstwhile socialist states (and in South Africa as well), various American law schools competed for ties with these new courts. Justices of the US Supreme Court proved equally interested in contacts. The center of attention was the Russian Constitutional Court. The Soviet Union had been the only cocqual power in the era of East–West confrontation. For that reason, the prospect of gaining influence over constitutional developments with one's former opponent was especially attractive.

But the Americans were not unaware that at the founding of the new constitutional courts Germany had played a greater role than the US, not only in Eastern Europe, but in South Africa as well. Almost all of them made pilgrimages to Karlsruhe—first came members of parliamentary commissions responsible for crafting new democratic constitutions, and later the judges of the newly founded constitutional courts. Here the Federal Republic could reap the fruits of its cultural foreign policy. Many of the visitors had been recipients of Humboldt scholarships; others had been sponsored by the partisan foundations.[2] The Russian Constitutional Court alone came to Karlsruhe three times. At the initiative of überschär,[3]

[1] Since 1996, the Yale Law School has hosted an annual *Global Constitutionalism Seminar*. Participants are selected constitutional judges from around the world (usually one judge per country) and the constitutional law faculty at Yale.

[2] This refers to the foundations which are affiliated with a political party, like the Konrad Adenauer Foundation, the Friedrich Ebert Foundation and others.

[3] Hans-Christian überschär (1936–present), diplomat; German ambassador in South Africa (1992–1999).

*Dieter Grimm: Advocate of the Constitution.* Dieter Grimm, Oxford University Press (2020). © in the original German edition, Mohr Siebeck GmbH & Co. KG, Tübingen 2017, © this translation, Justin Collings 2020.
DOI: 10.1093/oso/9780198845270.001.0001

the German ambassador in Pretoria, the South African Constitutional Court made its way to Germany immediately after its appointment by President Mandela.[4] It met for the first time at the Federal Constitutional Court. The week-long meeting was marked by intensive work. In the case of László Sólyom,[5] the first president of the Hungarian Constitutional Court, I saw the published reports of the Federal Constitutional Court in his official rooms in the presidential palace even after he had become president of Hungary.

It often came about, then, that in the US there was a three-part constellation—US Supreme Court; Russian Constitutional Court; German Federal Constitutional Court—until it became clear that the Russians, in the end, hadn't much to offer. They had nothing at all to offer when the Court was abolished after overplaying its hand by meddling in the power struggle between Yeltsin[6] and Khasbulatov.[7]

The New York University Law School was particularly active. Its first conference was held in 1995 (a year before the first Yale seminar) in Florence at the *Villa la Pietra*, which had been given to NYU in 1994. I mention this because, although my American teaching engagement soon concentrated on Yale, it began in New York, and the reason for that had to do with this conference. There was an older professor at the conference who seemed to be scrutinizing me constantly. On the second or third day, as we were visiting an exhibit, he approached me and said, "You must absolutely teach at NYU." It was Norman Dorsen,[8] a Harvard graduate, longtime NYU professor, and for many years the president of the ACLU. Dorsen was perhaps the first in the US to realize the implications of the increasing internationalization of law and had established the "global faculty" at NYU—a large-scale visiting professor program for international and comparative law. He later (with the prodding of Juliane Kokott[9]) founded *I-CON*, the first periodical devoted to comparative constitutionalism. Dorsen wanted to recruit me to the global

[4] Nelson Mandela (1918–2013), South African politician and freedom fighter; Nobel Peace Price (1993); president of the Republic of South Africa (1994–1999).

[5] László Sólyom (1942–present), professor of civil law in Budapest; president of the Hungarian Constitutional Court (1989–1998); president of Hungary (2005–2010).

[6] Boris Yeltsin (1931–2007), politician; president of the Russian Federation (1991–1999).

[7] Ruslan Khasbulatov (1942–present), politician; chairman of the Supreme Soviet of the Russian Federation. He was one of Yeltsin's most significant opponents during the constitutional crisis of 1993, in which Yeltsin, among other things, abolished the Supreme Soviet of the Russian Federation.

[8] Norman Dorsen (1930–2017), professor at the NYU School of Law; president of the American Civil Liberties Union (1976–1991).

[9] Juliane Kokott (1957–present), professor of public law, international law, and European law at the universities of Mannheim, Düsseldorf, and St. Gallen and, since 2003, advocate general at the Court of Justice of the European Union.

faculty, but I had to tell him that because of my position on the Court it was impossible. "Well," he said, "then you can come from time to time to give a lecture or lead a discussion with students and start teaching when your term on the Constitutional Court is over." So it came about that in 1996 I became a "Distinguished Global Fellow" at NYU. It was there, too, that I became acquainted with the famous Dworkin-Nagel seminar. I was in constant contact with Dworkin thereafter.[10]

But NYU was by no means alone in its efforts. Also in 1995, Cardozo Law School in New York hosted a conference of courts, in which six constitutional judges from Europe and Israel, headed by Ruth Bader Ginsburg[11] of the US Supreme Court, dealt with a hypothetical case developed by an equally international team of professors (including Bernhard Schlink[12]) who then packaged it in the form of a Supreme Court case and presented it in oral argument. Just before things got started, a conflict over protocol broke out. In the preliminary discussions, the question arose: In what order we should sit on the bench? No one had thought about this. So I said that I had taken a peek in the courtroom and seen that behind the bench were the flags of the participating countries. Why not just take our places in front of our respective flags? That seemed reasonable, but not to everyone. The French judge spoke up saying that she too had happened to look into the courtroom and seen that the French flag had been relegated to the left end of the bench. She was the representative of a great nation, and she was not willing to assume a marginal position. Mystification all around. Then the English judge spoke up and shared that he too had chanced to have a look into the courtroom. The British flag was hanging at the other end of the bench. He too was the representative of a great nation, but it didn't bother him to sit at the end. That put the French judge in an awkward position and she finally declared, after a long resistance, that she would yield under protest. The full case can be read in the *Cardozo Law Review* under the title, "Justices at Work."[13]

OL: How did the Yale seminar differ from these initiatives?

[10] Ronald Dworkin (1931–2013), professor at Yale, Oxford, and NYU.

[11] Ruth Bader Ginsburg (1933–present), professor at Rutgers University and Columbia University; judge on the US Court of Appeals for the DC Circuit (1980–1993); justice of the US Supreme Court since 1993.

[12] Bernhard Schlink (1944–present), professor of public law and legal philosophy at the universities of Bonn, Frankfurt, and Humboldt University in Berlin.

[13] "Justices at Work" (1997) 18 *Cardozo Law Review* 1609–873. The remarks of Dieter Grimm appear there in transcribed, unedited form.

DG: From the outset, the Yale seminar was more broadly conceived. It wasn't concerned only with judges in new democracies, but with bringing such judges together with colleagues from established courts. No continent was excluded. Judges from common law and civil law countries came together for three working days, together with the constitutionalists on the Yale faculty. The Yale seminar was also planned as a series, rather than a one-time event, although no one at its founding thought it would last for twenty years. Finally, it was carefully prepared with a Reader comprising materials—mostly judicial decisions from the participating countries, insofar as these were available in English—on topics chosen by the faculty. This ensured a certain concreteness in the discussions. The readers are a treasure trove of comparative constitutional law. The Yale seminar was the only enduring gathering of its kind. Paul Gewirtz[14] planned and directed the meetings for nearly ten years. Then he became the founding director of Yale's Chinese Law Center and gave up the Global Seminar. We had met several times to discuss possible participants from Europe, and I had helped him get access to the Conference of European Constitutional Courts held in 1996 in Budapest, so that he could form his own picture of the judges.

OL: How would you assess the personal influence of the participants? Were there any particularly prominent colleagues? Could one use the seminar to share ideas from one's own case law with other courts?

DG: With such a diverse group of participants, knowledge and experience were understandably distributed very unevenly. From the beginning, there was a group of judges who set the tone, above all Stephen Breyer,[15] the hometown hero. Then there were Aharon Barak,[16] president of the Israeli Supreme Court, and Frank Iacobucci[17] of the Canadian Supreme Court. They interacted with Yale constitutionalists of the order of a Bruce Ackerman,[18] Owen Fiss,[19] and Robert

[14] Paul Gewirtz (1947–present), professor at the Yale Law School.

[15] Stephen Breyer (1938–present), professor at the Harvard Law School; judge on the United States Court of Appeals for the First Circuit (1980–1994); justice of the US Supreme Court since 1994.

[16] Aharon Barak (1936–present), professor at the Hebrew University of Jerusalem (1968–1975) (dean of the law faculty beginning in 1974); Attorney General of Israel (1975–1978); judge on the Supreme Court of Israel (1978–1995); president of the Supreme Court of Israel (1995–2006). Barak taught at several universities, including Yale.

[17] Frank Iacobucci (1937–present), professor at the University of Toronto (1967–1982); vice president of the University of Toronto (1983–1985); deputy minister of justice of Canada (1985–1988); judge on the Federal Court of Canada (1988–1991); judge on the Supreme Court of Canada (1991–2004).

[18] Bruce Ackerman (1943–present), professor at the Yale Law School and the Yale Department of Political Science. Previously professor at the University of Pennsylvania and Columbia University.

[19] Owen Fiss (1938–present), professor at the Yale Law School; previously professor at the University of Chicago.

Post,[20] who pushed the seminar to high levels where not everyone was ready or able to follow. The English participants—for a long time Lord Woolf,[21] now Lady Hale[22]—distinguished themselves with a deep distaste for all things fundamental. The academics, for their part, lacked the judges' practical experience and, early on, knowledge of other legal orders as well. Mixing professors and judges ensured, however, that the seminar didn't dwindle into a mere informational exchange, on the order of, "This is how we do it in Spain . . ."

For some participants much was new. Not a few judges heard in the seminar for the first time about the duty to protect and the proportionality principle. I was asked I don't know how many times to delineate the precise steps of proportionality review.[23] Without the Yale seminar, it would hardly be imaginable that Justice Breyer should now advocate proportionality review on the Supreme Court in place of the various tiers of scrutiny.[24] In Barak's book on proportionality,[25] there is a map charting the spread, beginning in Germany, of proportionality review.

In my view, the fact that many participants are there for a long time contributes considerably to the seminar's success. Some were not invited again after the first time, in part because either their knowledge of English or their contributions were deemed inadequate. Additionally, the invitations cease when one departs from judicial office. That doesn't apply to Barak and me because we have been teaching at Yale since leaving the bench. In the seminar, you can talk with one another in a very confidential atmosphere and without worrying about indiscretions. Thanks to the seminar, my reservoir of comparative constitutional material expanded enormously. I have become much more sensitive to the importance of context for constitutional law and constitutional jurisprudence. I recognize the peculiarities of my own constitutional order much more sharply in light of other systems as described by practitioners. I've missed the seminar only once—because

[20] Robert Post (1947–present), professor at the Yale Law School; previously professor at the UC Berkeley School of Law; dean of the Yale Law School (2009–2017).

[21] Lord Harry Woolf (1933–present), judge; Master of the Rolls (1996–2000); Lord Chief Justice of England and Wales (2000–2005).

[22] Lady Brenda Hale (1945–present), judge; Lord of Appeal in Ordinary (2004–2009); justice of the Supreme Court of the United Kingdom since 2009, its vice president from 2013 to 2017 and president from 2017 to 2020.

[23] Cf Dieter Grimm, "Proportionality in Canadian and German Constitutional Jurisprudence" (2007) 57 *Toronto Law Journal* 383–97. For an English formulation of proportionality review, see also the so-called "*Oakes* Test" of the Canadian Supreme Court in *R. v. Oakes*, 1 SCR 103 (1986).

[24] See, for example, Breyer's dissenting opinion in *District of Columbia v. Heller*, 554 U.S. 570 (2008).

[25] Aharon Barak, *Proportionality: Constitutional Rights and Their Limitations* (2012).

of illness. The Yale seminar has become the most important conference of the year.

OL: I think Sabino Cassese[26] would say the same thing, at least on the basis of his *Diario*,[27] in which he reports on the seminar every year.

DG: Sabino Cassese became a constitutional judge in Rome at an advanced age and therefore joined the seminar comparatively late. But he immediately became one of the most argumentatively powerful participants. The same was true of Miguel Maduro,[28] who was invited as advocate general of the ECJ, and for a time of Australia's Michael Kirby[29] or Columbia's Manuel Cepeda.[30] From the German Constitutional Court, many are impressed today by Susanne Baer.[31] I can't name everyone who deserves to be mentioned. *Herr* Rossbach, you attended the seminar once and know what it's like.

MR: I too found it very impressive. Another, more general question about your influence in the US: A professor at Harvard Law School once told me: "If you're doing comparative constitutional law, you really only need to talk to Dieter Grimm. Then you'll know everything important." You have a lot of name recognition in the US and have brought a lot of attention there to the proportionality principle and other aspects of German law. But through your seminars at home, you've also led a lot of German students toward comparative constitutionalism. You are one of the few jurists known on both sides of the Atlantic. Do you see yourself as playing a mediating role? Are you pursuing a particular agenda with your teaching in the US?

DG: More than any agenda is the fact that I love teaching and find the ideal conditions for it in the US. At Yale, as well as at Harvard and NYU, the students are uniformly first-class, motivated, and demanding. And the classes are small. At Yale I have around ten participants, usually about two-thirds of them American students and the other third foreign LLM students. At Harvard and NYU, the groups were larger.

[26] Sabino Cassese (1935–present), professor of administrative law at the universities of Urbino, Naples, and Rome; judge of the Italian Constitutional Court (2005–2014).

[27] Sabino Cassese, *Dentro la Corte: Diario di un giudice costituzionale* (2015).

[28] Miguel Poiares Maduro (1967–present), professor of constitutional law and European law at the European University Institute in Florence and at the Universidade Nova de Lisboa; advocate general of the European Court of Justice (2003–2009); minister of regional development for the Republic of Portugal (2013–2015).

[29] Michael Kirby (1939–present), judge; justice of the High Court of Australia (1996–2009).

[30] Manuel José Cepeda Espinosa (1963–present), professor of constitutional law and, from 1996 to 2000, dean of the law faculty at the Universidad de los Andes; justice of the Constitutional Court of Columbia (2001–2009); president of the Court (2005–2006).

[31] Susanne Baer (1964–present), professor of public law and gender studies at Humboldt University in Berlin; justice of the First Senate of the Federal Constitutional Court since 2011.

But I won't give an emphatic No to the question about an agenda. At bottom, there are two motives. The first is not US-specific. It guides me equally, whether I'm teaching in Germany or elsewhere. I find that we take too many things in our legal orders for granted, thinking them self-evident or even inevitable, even though they emerged at specific times and under specific conditions and could very well have come about differently. One can explain why things came about as they did, but they did not necessarily come about as they did. One can only understand legal norms or legal institutions when one knows why things are as they are. Only then can one apply and develop the law rationally even in atypical situations. Knowledge of contingency protects doctrine, so to speak, from petrification. One needn't at all pose this question with a view to effecting change. One might very well conclude that the existing situation is not in need of reform. But one then owes this conclusion to a higher level of reflection. It is a conscious decision to maintain the status quo with an awareness of the alternatives. The conception of fundamental rights in the US strikes me, in comparison with our own, as insufficiently complex. For that reason, I like to confront American students with our conception of fundamental rights, not with the goal of making converts—far from it—but with the aim of helping them take stock of their situation on their own. There might be good reasons not to change anything, but that would then be the result of reflection, not an unreflected "Carry on!"

The second motive, by contrast, is America-specific. In the aftermath of legal realism, there is a widespread conviction in the US that adjudication—especially in constitutional law—is not what it purports to be, namely the derivation of concrete decisions in real cases from an abstract legal norm with due respect for precedent; a juristic process, in other words. Instead, there are many adherents to the "realist" assumption that other motives are really at work, whether interests or ideologies. This view is presented to students as a fruit of scholarly enlightenment, though perhaps somewhat less often at Yale than elsewhere. Accordingly, the primary question that American jurists pose about a case is not, "What is the right solution?" but rather, "How will the court decide?" If one wished to summarize this view concisely, it is a denial of the (relative) autonomy of law and adjudication. In Europe, by contrast, the grounding assumption is overwhelmingly that law is indeed a product of political decisions, but that when it enters into force it is emancipated from politics and is thereafter to be interpreted and applied only according to legal (and not political, economic, or religious) criteria. I have taught and practiced constitutional law under this premise. Without this core conviction, the separation of powers between legislature and judiciary shrivels into a more or less technical prophylactic for hindering the concentration of power. I try, then, to show that law enjoys a (relative) autonomy, and I find that many students, sated with realism, are strikingly receptive to this view.

MR: You experienced Harvard as a young student and are now a member of the faculty at the Yale Law School. When you look at American universities from the perspective of a faculty member, what stands out to you about the intellectual life of law schools there in comparison with German law faculties?

DG: First of all the size, which has an impact on intellectual life. Considered purely numerically, the Yale Law School has three times as many professors and five times fewer students than the law department at Humboldt University. There are around eighty tenured professors, 600 JD students, and around forty (mostly foreign) LLM or JSD students. The Harvard Law School has around half as many students as Humboldt but more than four times as many professors. As a result, the faculty of leading American law schools can cover a much richer array of subjects and it is much easier for individual professors to cultivate their specialty than it is for their German counterparts. This fosters the potential for stimulation within the faculty and expands the range of options for students. The course offerings are overwhelming; the students' freedom of choice is great. At Yale there are only few required courses, most of them in the first semester.

We can't keep up with that, and these things can't be changed quickly, however often one might dream of a German Harvard. On the other hand, an American professor has no secretary, no assistants, no institute. Six or seven professors share a secretary. One can hire research assistants for a specific project. The faculty administration is also much larger than a German faculty administration. This entails additional tasks: assisting alumni, fundraising, career support, etc.

In addition, there is a difference of style. Faculty members—especially at Yale—maintain a constant dialogue with one another. You leave your office to get a coffee and are immediately drawn into a conversation. A majority of the professors attends the weekly faculty workshop. Manuscripts get swapped repeatedly before publication and presented in various forums. We tend rather to shield ourselves from foreign eyes. But I won't deny that with a younger generation of university teachers in Germany this is improving. I think I can observe this on my own Berlin faculty.

MR: What do you make of the way American universities recruit new talent?

DG: The path to professorship is more open than with us because it doesn't depend on a lengthy apprenticeship. The typical career path for a jurist who graduates from a very good law school and wants to teach at a very good law school is to clerk for a Court of Appeals judge for a year following graduation and then for another year at the Supreme Court. The second clerkship, however, marks a narrow path. The overwhelming majority of Supreme Court clerks comes from two law schools: Harvard and Yale. After that a couple years of practice are recommended, either at a law firm or a government institution. In the end one can return to the university. In this regard, the good law schools recruit heavily from their own ranks, something that is frowned on here.

I don't take part in the hiring process at Yale, though every so often someone asks my opinion of a candidate. But I know from reports that the process involves extraordinarily intensive reading. On German law faculties, by contrast, the hiring committee usually divides the applicants among themselves—one committee member per applicant who, as time permits, reads the applicant's publications more or less thoroughly. The process in the US strikes me as more intense. This is also true of the evaluation of pre-tenure professors. The US differs from us entirely in the independence of positions in the budget. If the faculty wants someone at all costs, the position gets created. More precisely, the notion of a "position" does not exist.

# XII.

# Berlin and the Institute for Advanced Study

CW: Before we move on to Berlin, let me ask a question that encompasses both Bielefeld and Berlin: Who are your academic students?

DG: My first *Habilitation* student was Gertrude Lübbe-Wolff. She had received her doctorate in Freiburg and was an assistant to Jochen Frowein in Bielefeld, but didn't feel that that was a good fit and so asked if she could switch to me. This happened when my first Bielefeld assistant, Annette Fugmann,[1] an outstanding graduate of the first cohort educated in a single phase,[2] left the university after receiving her doctorate and joined the civil service where she enjoyed a rapid ascent in communal politics and later in state politics as well. My second *Habilitation* student was Helge Rossen, who also began with a different supervisor but then, thanks to his pronounced theoretical and social-scientific interests, found a more fitting place with me. The third *Habilitation* student was Ulli Rühl. He had nothing to do with Bielefeld. His academic home was Gießen. He did his doctorate under Ridder, but then didn't find a place as an assistant and worked in Karlsruhe as an attorney. He was recommended to me by Brigitte Zypries,[3] who at the time was a law clerk at the Federal Constitutional Court in the chambers of Thomas Dieterich. Rühl did exceptional work at the Court, and it was astonishing how many cases he could take care of quickly, clear-sightedly, and with reliable bench memos. It soon became obvious to me that, despite his practical gifts, he was an academic *manqué*, and so I asked him if he was still interested in an academic career. He was then the last to complete a *Habilitation* in Bielefeld under my supervision. The other two, Marion Albers and Ulrich Haltern,[4] took their *Habilitation* already in Berlin. That

[1] Annette Fugmann-Heesing (1955–present), jurist and politician (SPD); Hessian finance minister (1991–1994); finance senator in the Berlin government (1996–1999); member of the Berlin house of delegates (1999–2011).

[2] Cf. Chapter V, fn. 12.

[3] Brigitte Zypries (1953–present), jurist and politician (SPD); state secretary in the federal interior ministry (1998–2002); federal minister of justice (2002–2009); parliamentary state secretary to the federal minister for economy and energy (2013–2017); federal minister for economy and energy (2017–2018).

[4] Ulrich Haltern (1967–present), professor of public law and European law at the universities of Hannover, Freiburg im Breisgau, and Munich.

*Dieter Grimm: Advocate of the Constitution.* Dieter Grimm, Oxford University Press (2020). © in the original German edition, Mohr Siebeck GmbH & Co. KG, Tübingen 2017, © this translation, Justin Collings 2020.
DOI: 10.1093/oso/9780198845270.001.0001

doesn't amount to a school. They were all too independent for that. They are only united by a common grounding in theory and a shared interdisciplinary approach.

Marion Albers stood out to me early as an outstanding student in a Bielefeld seminar. She was, moreover, pursuing a dual program of study: law and sociology. She was subsequently a regular participant in my seminars and wanted to do her doctorate with me after her exams. She was certain of a position as an assistant, but when I became a constitutional judge, the second assistant position fell to my promoted successor, Joachim Wieland.[5]

The remaining position was held by Helge Rossen, who was working on his *Habilitation*. Marion Albers wrote a dissertation about data protection and developed a number of pathbreaking insights in her very long work, which was also very long in the making. Accordingly, I tried to persuade her to submit this work as her *Habilitation* and to churn out a relatively quick dissertation in between. I first met Ulrich Haltern at Yale and later saw him again by chance at the Steuben parade in New York. He had done his doctorate with Ipsen[6] in Bochum, but at the time was unsure whether to pursue his future career in the US or in Germany. Whether he would join the legal traineeship (*Referendar*) also depended on his answer to this question. I counseled him at the time to join the traineeship service if he wasn't entirely sure that he wanted to remain in the US. He then became my assistant at Humboldt University. He was followed by Lars Viellechner,[7] another discovery of my seminar, who submitted a dissertation that I certified in my report as being of *Habilitation* quality. This of course was at a time when I had long since assumed emeritus status. My last assistant, who after my retirement from Humboldt University followed me to the Institute for Advanced Study, was Laura Schopp,[8] who, in addition to providing scholarly assistance and taking care of the compact seminars[9] (which mostly dealt with comparative constitutional matters), was my constant source of information for the exhibitions and recitals that I simply couldn't miss.

[5] Joachim Wieland (1951–present), professor of public law, finance law, and tax law at the universities of Bielefeld, Frankfurt am Main, and Speyer.

[6] Knut Ipsen (1935–present), professor of public law and international law at the University of Bochum; president of the German Red Cross (1994–2003).

[7] Lars Viellechner (1976–present), junior professor of public law at the University of Bremen.

[8] Laura Schopp (1977–present); research assistant to Dieter Grimm at Humboldt University and at the Institute for Advanced Study in Berlin (2004–2012); attorney since 2013.

[9] This refers to a series of seminars which have been offered primarily to students and PhD candidates at Humboldt University, but in which also students from other universities have participated. They take place once per semester at the Institute for Advanced Study and usually start on a Friday in the afternoon and end on the following Sunday at noon.

CW: After Karlsruhe, then, your Bielefeld period ended as well?

DG: Both, in fact, coincided. I was prepared to return to Bielefeld. My ties there, Karlsruhe notwithstanding, had not been severed. My service as director of the ZiF extended into my earlier days in Karlsruhe, and with the exception of a single semester I had continued to teach regularly in Bielefeld—lecture courses early on, but soon only compact seminars.

CW: How did your contact with the Institute for Advanced Study come about?

DG: The Institute for Advanced Study had invited me to be a fellow during the 1987–1988 academic year. I had to decline. The response from Berlin was, “We'll be in touch in twelve years.” I took that as an especially original way to express regret, but I didn't take it seriously. Nonetheless, an invitation came in the meantime to join the Institute's advisory board. The advisory board is the basic decision-making council for the selection of fellows. It meets twice a year to discuss candidates. If I remember correctly, Werner Maihofer was my predecessor on the board.[10] I was in good contact with him when he resumed teaching in Bielefeld after his term as federal interior minister. I suspect that I am also indebted to him for my commission to write the article on political parties in the Benda-Maihofer-Vogel Handbook on constitutional law. That was long ago, but I still consider that article to be one of my finest.

A term on the advisory council lasts three years, with the possibility of a one-time renewal. During my second term, I chaired the council. At the end of my tenure in Karlsruhe, I was in fact invited again to join the Institute, but after the *intermezzo* on the advisory council, this no longer came as a surprise. I *was* surprised, however, that the invitation came with the offer of becoming a permanent fellow. The Institute for Advanced Study has six permanent fellows, typically three who teach at Berlin universities and three from outside. This would require, of course, a long-term move to Berlin, but that didn't bother me at all. I had already considered moving to Berlin and keeping a small second apartment in Bielefeld for my remaining three years there. I accepted the offer on the condition that the permanent fellowship be combined with a professorship at Humboldt University. On that point, the Institute and the HU quickly reached an agreement.

At that point, there was no talk of my becoming rector at the Institute. Wolf Lepenies[11] was leading the Institute with extraordinary success

[10] Werner Maihofer (1918–2009), professor of criminal law, legal sociology, legal theory, legal philosophy, and social philosophy at the universities of Saarbrücken and Bielefeld; politician (FDP); federal minister for special tasks (1972–1974); federal minister of the interior (1974–1978).

[11] Wolf Lepenies (1941–present), professor of sociology at the Free University of Berlin; rector of the Institute for Advanced Study in Berlin (1986–2001).

in his third term in office, and I assumed he would do so for another five years. I was not keen on the rectorship. I had already told a search committee looking for a president of the WZB Berlin Social Science Center that I wanted to work again on my own scholarly work, not organize the scholarly work of others. And, when asked if I was willing to be considered as a candidate for the presidency of Humboldt University, I had declined. Thus, with the dawn of the new millennium, I began a new chapter of my life as a Berliner: professor at Humboldt University and permanent fellow of the Institute for Advanced Study.

OL: But in the end you became rector after all, and with that you once again assumed an entirely new responsibility. One carries responsibility for the institution and must look after multiple fields, cultivate international contacts, and perhaps worry about money as well. One's plate is piled with administration and scholarly organization, choice of topics, and scouting for talent.

DG: It didn't happen without hesitation. But the Institute for Advanced Study is smaller than the other organizations. I knew, moreover, from my time on the advisory council that it was blessed with a highly efficient administration and staff that did their work with joy—all thanks to an incomparable head of administration with the humble title of "secretary," Joachim Nettelbeck.[12] I was hopeful, then, that I could combine the job with my own scholarly work. It was important to me that I still be regarded as a scholar.

In addition, the Institute for Advanced Study is a truly beautiful institution—a place where outstanding scholars can concentrate entirely on what drove their choice of vocation in the first place: research. The Institute gives scholars what they most lack in times of seeking third-party funding, evaluating and being evaluated, filling committee assignments, and composing interim reports and final reports: time for undistracted work on projects that promise new insights and that they choose for themselves. Forty scholars from all disciplines and all corners of the globe live and work here, come in contact with one another across disciplinary boundaries, and, through discussions in the Institute, expose themselves to surprises that not infrequently result in changes to the research project.

A rector's principal task consists in ensuring an interesting, well-balanced, and highly communicative cohort of fellows. This is not an unmixed pleasure. The number of candidates far exceeds the available

[12] Joachim Nettelbeck (1944–present), administrative manager of the Institute for Advanced Study from 1981 to 2012.

positions, and there are lovelier things to read than application prose. But one is certainly rewarded for the effort. One gets an impression of the questions posed at the cutting edge of scientific inquiry—and not only in those fields one is independently aware of. One is exposed to topics and discussions that one would have otherwise avoided. The potential for stimulation is very high—much higher than one's capacity to use it all in one's own research.

But there is a lot less time for this than expected, because in addition to choosing fellows there is a plethora of other rectorial duties, each negligible on its own but cumulatively very time-consuming. I therefore resisted all efforts to persuade me to add a second term. I conceded only a single year because my successor, the archeologist Luca Giuliani,[13] was not immediately available. In 2007, I left the office after six years but remained a permanent fellow—a fact not without significance, since in 2005 I became emeritus at the university and lost the perks of my professorial chair. The Institute compensated for that.

MR: In retrospect, what do you make of your time as rector of the Institute for Advanced Study? What were your points of emphasis?

DG: I liked leading the Institute, even though I fell short of my own plans for that time. For that, however, I don't blame the Institute; only myself. And they couldn't have been entirely bad years for the Institute either, otherwise I wouldn't have been pressed so hard to stay on for five years more. There were some new areas of emphasis, such as the study of images—not only artistic images, but also media images and image-producing procedures in the natural sciences. This point of emphasis endured for several years with constantly rotating fellows.

Because of this theme, it was important to me to bring Horst Bredekamp[14] to the Institute as a permanent fellow. This developed into a very inspiring liaison—for the Institute, for the fellows of almost all disciplines, and for me personally. It continued after Horst Bredekamp didn't renew his permanent fellowship. It even led to a collaborative seminar on "Form and Law" at Humboldt University. Today, Christoph Möllers[15] is the permanent fellow with whom I am most actively in contact.

[13] Luca Giuliani (1950–present), professor of classical archeology at the universities of Freiburg, Munich, and Humboldt University in Berlin; rector of the Institute for Advanced Study in Berlin (2007–2018).

[14] Horst Bredekamp (1947–present), professor of art history at the University of Hamburg and Humboldt University in Berlin; member of the Order "Pour le Mérite".

[15] Christoph Möllers (1969–present), professor of public law and legal philosophy at the universities of Münster, Göttingen, and Humboldt University in Berlin; permanent fellow of the Institute for Advanced Study since 2012.

I don't want to draw an overall balance here. But I would like to mention an idea whose realization misfired. I have long lamented the mutual alienation, even disparagement and sometimes even contempt that sours relations between different functional sectors of society—politics, the economy, the media, the academy—each of which holds its own logic of behavior to be rational, considers other approaches to be irrational, and thus misconstrues a basic feature of a functionally differentiated society. When this leads to powerful subsystems seeking to impose their own internal logic on other spheres, it endangers the performance capacity of society as a whole. It was an earlier insight of Luhmann's to derive from this danger the function of fundamental rights: to prevent undifferentiation.[16] It seemed to me that the Institute for Advanced Study could become a place where this alienation could be overcome if one invited into the reflective space it offers leading personnel from businesses and ministries that stand just below the highest reaches of governance. The vertical term "highest" is no accident, since the relevant forces from the economy almost all turned me down with an interesting metaphor of ascent: "If I do that, I'll miss the elevator." There was a greater willingness within the ministerial bureaucracy, but when things got serious, the chosen person was somehow just then unavailable. By contrast, the effort with journalists occasionally succeeded. The *Frankfurter Allgemeine Zeitung* and the *Süddeutsche Zeitung* were willing to give outstanding editors a couple of months free.

OL: Does legal scholarship fit well or ill in such a conscientiously interdisciplinary setting?

DG: For legal scholarship as a field that's hard to say. Even if the number of legal scholars increased slightly during my rectorship, on the whole it remained small. The average was about three per year. These are predominantly jurists whose work is not limited to the doctrine of a specific area of law and who also come with projects that can be built upon. Those who were invited usually had little trouble attracting the attention of other disciplines and integrating themselves within broader communities. The focus group that I organized in 2007–2008 on the topic of "Constitutionalism Beyond the Nation State" had an inherently interdisciplinary orientation.[17] My general impression is that social science literature gets cited more often in legal science than the reverse. There remains a discrepancy between the significance

[16] Cf. Niklas Luhmann, *Grundrechte als Institution* (1965).

[17] The working group resulted in the volume: Petra Dobner and Martin Loughlin (eds), *The Twilight of Constitutionalism?* (2010).

of law for the objects of sociology, political science, economics, history, etc. and the utilization of scholarly legal literature in these disciplines. The reasons must be sought on both sides.

OL: I sometimes get the impression that the sociopolitical influence of legal science is less than it was in, say, 1990. Hardly any lawyers sit on the boards of German-Index corporations anymore. That wasn't so in 1990. Haven't prominent positions of societal decision-making shifted away from lawyers, often to economists but also to fields one wouldn't have anticipated? I can't really prove it. It is more an impression I have felt than something proven empirically. This development naturally doesn't make me happy—that legal science no longer plays the role it once played. Nor does the fact that we legal scholars often attracted society's attention only in the wake of court decisions. As a scholar, then, one is sought out only during the course of some case or in its aftermath. But when it comes to genuine, legal-scientific discourse: who outside the guild is still interested?

DG: It's difficult for me to say something well supported about this. Your impression about leadership positions in corporations is surely right. The diplomatic service would confirm your suspicion, perhaps even the ramified realm of public administration as a whole. From time to time, the magazine *Cicero* publishes a list of the "500 most important intellectuals" on a purely quantitative basis.[18] Among them are usually ten to twelve jurists—public law scholars almost without exception—but decidedly more economists and historians. On the other hand, thanks to the paramount role of the Federal Constitutional Court in the German political system, we have a powerfully legalized political discourse. This has considerably enhanced the practical and publishing significance of constitutionalists. It is probably no accident that most of the jurists in the *Cicero* list are former or current constitutional judges. Another index for this significance is surely the fortnightly "State and Law" page in the *Frankfurter Allgemeine Zeitung* and the law column in *Merkur*.

OL: When you look back on certain developments over the *longue durée*—from Frankfurt to Berlin—are there particular things that stand out to you? Have things changed a lot between the university where you studied and the university where you taught in the end? Have the students or your colleagues changed? In the field of legal scholarship in the German university, what has changed over your nearly sixty years there? Were there some factors, for better or worse, that would be important to you?

[18] Most recently in February 2019.

DG: Of the university in general, I would go back to what I said about the attempts of some functional systems of society to instrumentalize others for their own interests. Scholarship risks becoming a victim of such attempts. I have in mind the pressure on scholarship—stemming from the economy, fostered by the state, and insufficiently resisted by university leaders—to adopt an entrepreneurial or corporate self-understanding. The means of applying such pressure are the methods of scholarly funding. The share of institutional funding is in decline, whereas the share of project-specific funding—usually dispersed on a competitive basis—is on the rise. This, however, augments the risk that research aims are driven by non-scientific considerations. Scholars who can promise commercially useful knowledge have better odds than those engaged in foundational research or those working in smaller disciplines. Individual salary incentives that turn on quantity rather than quality point in the same direction. In saying this, however, I'm well aware that, thanks to the system of foundations that mediate between state and scholarship, Germany is better off than many other European countries.

As far as legal science in particular is concerned, I see between 1957, when I began my studies, and 2017 a series of profound changes, most of them products of changes in the social environment. With the growth in the number of students and the expansion of some universities and the founding of others, the ranks of legal scholars have also grown tremendously. The Free University of Berlin had twelve professorships when I spent a semester there in 1959–1960. At all three of my German universities, the three main areas of public law had one professor each. With the expansion of scholarly personnel came also an increase in specialization. Teaching materials multiplied. In my student years, practically the only constitutional law textbook was Maunz's. The periodicals branched endlessly out. At the same time, the shelf-life of scholarship grew shorter. An author like Ulrich Scheuner,[19] whom I greatly esteem, barely gets cited anymore. Specialization, however, is not only the product of growth in the scholarly sector. It has its roots in the continual rise of new areas of law, which is explained in turn by the regulatory needs driven by scientific and technical advances. This becomes a problem for curriculum as well as for the traditional state exams. Effectively, this has led to an expansion of doctrinal

[19] Ulrich Scheuner (1903–1981), professor of public law at the universities of Jena, Göttingen, Strasbourg, and Bonn.

subjects at the expense of foundational subjects. Under current conditions, however, this strikes me as the wrong path to take.

Among those conditions, alongside expansion and specialization, is internationalization. For a long time, legal science was a national science. No more. But this too has been only partially accommodated. Considerably more international law gets taught than before. But the permeation and permutation of national law through international law has yet to be adequately considered. But most of all, the mounting abundance of legal materials, the mounting acceleration of legal changes, and the mounting influence of foreign and supranational law requires knowledge of how to orient oneself much more than it requires knowledge of positive law. Not that I am opposed to knowledge of positive law. But the difficulty of legal work today consists in finding one's bearings in an ever more confusing field, rather than in mastering the positive law of a new field.

In particular, increasing internationalization necessitates greater knowledge of context. That didn't play a big role so long as law was overwhelmingly national law because one was socialized in the context of national law and always thought in its terms. But as one leaves the realm of national law, that is no longer the case. Knowledge of context must be made explicit and transmitted because even identical legal norms and legal institutions operate differently in different contexts. All of this points to the foundational subjects, and for that reason I brought into being, with the help of the Institute for Advanced Study, the Berlin research association "Law in Context," now headed by Christoph Möllers. For the same reason, I also welcome the 2012 recommendations of the Scientific Council (Wissenschaftsrat) on the Study of Law.[20] But they haven't yet been implemented in legal education.

I should also mention how male the world of law and legal science was. One can get a sense of this from the names that have come up in this interview. In none of the five places where I studied was there a female law professor. The first woman to complete a *Habilitation* in public law was the previously mentioned Ilse Staff. My assistant, Gertrude Lübbe-Wolff, was the fourth. The second and third both did their *Habilitation* work in Switzerland. There was, of course, a female judge on the original

[20] Wissenschaftsrat, Perspektiven der Rechtswissenschaft in Deutschland. Situation, Analysen, Empfehlungen (Drs. 2558-12), November 2012, available online: https://www.wissenschaftsrat.de/download/archiv/2558-12.pdf, accessed on December 23, 2019. English: Prospects of Legal Scholarship in Germany. Current Situation, Analyses, Recommendations.

Constitutional Court: Erna Scheffler.[21] But for a long time there remained only one woman on the Court. A second joined the Court a year before I did. When I left there were five. Today, after some brief backpedaling, there are nine. In the US, where the starting situation was no better (Sandra Day O'Connor[22] became the first female justice of the Supreme Court in 1981), there has been greater progress in the universities than there has been here. I think only of the women on the Yale faculty.

MR: You said that as a student the division of Germany was an important topic that especially interested you. You were then in Berlin as a student and later, after your time in Karlsruhe, you returned to Berlin. Apart from the Institute for Advanced Study, does it have a special significance for you to now be in the capital city of a reunited country?

DG: For me, it is an essential part of the Institute for Advanced Study that it is located in Berlin. The Institute wouldn't be the same if, though otherwise unchanged, it were located in Delmenhorst or Greifswald. But I would have moved to Berlin even without the appointment at the Institute and at Humboldt University. Because I had only three years left until my retirement in Bielefeld (in Berlin, much to my delight, it was six), I had already planned to make Berlin my principal place of residence. That plan was surely influenced by the fact that Germany was now reunited and that Berlin was the capital once more. I remember well how happy I was when the Bundestag decided in favor of Berlin. I even supposed that politics would become somewhat more urbane and a bit less self-absorbed than in the Bonn hothouse where politicians dwelt among themselves. What I didn't foresee was that media coverage of politics would expand to an extent that didn't at all help politicians' public image.

OL: I never understood the argument that politics coming from Berlin is somehow more cosmopolitan than what was done in Bonn. Members of parliament are out among the people in their electoral districts. The idea that in Berlin they are somehow more "in touch" presupposes that they never show their faces in their electoral districts and that these are politically less relevant. That can't be right.

DG: If you compare how many politicians you encounter in Bavaria or how many I saw in Bielefeld or Karlsruhe with how many you come across in Berlin on the street, in the theater, at concerts, at exhibitions, at the countless

[21] Erna Scheffler (1893–1983), justice of the First Senate of the Federal Constitutional Court (1951–1963).

[22] Sandra Day O'Connor (1930–present), justice of the US Supreme Court (1981–2006).

events put on by all sorts of associations and societies in Berlin—even the big corporations that didn't move their headquarters back to Berlin but maintain an extensive presence here—all of that has an impact.

OL: But all of that was no different in Bonn. When I studied in Bonn, there were naturally incessant invitations—ministers came to the student associations, etc. This is simply the presence of the personnel, whether in Bonn or Berlin. It's not a privilege of the place, but an incident of the presence there of these officeholders. In my view, the dilemma in Berlin is this: There are so many observers that politicians only feel themselves observed, whereas in Bonn, in the absence of observers, politicians stay focused on their basic task—and it then gets called a hothouse.

CW: *Herr* Grimm's hope was that in this milieu politicians would not only "sit around" together, which of course happened by necessity in Bonn—hence Koeppen's "Hothouse"[23]—but that they would be absorbed into the city.

OL: For me it was actually clear from the outset that the move to Berlin would lead to a flattening of politics—to an acceleration. Decisions must be quicker. Less remains secret. Compromise faces tougher conditions in Berlin because compromise presupposes a cloakroom and also requires a little time. These conditions are harder to obtain in a city like Berlin than in Bonn. I never entertained the idea that the outcomes of the political process would in any way be qualitatively better because of the move.

DG: In that you were the more prescient. I had hoped, naturally, that here they would go to the museums more often.

OL: Yes, but they still go to the museums at home.

DG: Here they are confronted with much richer offerings.

OL: We can't take Berlin's excess as a representative barrier to entry. That would be entirely un-federal. Isn't it a structural principle of federalism that the city that houses the political organs is not the largest city? That's the case in Switzerland, in the US, in Canada, Brazil, or even Australia. It is only the mistake of regarding German history from a Prussian perspective that leads to this fixation with Berlin. Historically, Berlin is not the German capital. It became the capital only in 1871 and only by force.

MR: Were the personal hopes that you associated with the move to Berlin fulfilled?

DG: Sometimes when I drive or walk through Berlin, I am overcome with the feeling that I have finally arrived where I always wished to come. But you shouldn't mistake that feeling for unmitigated content. As much as I feel

[23] Wolfgang Koeppen, *Das Treibhaus. Roman* (1st ed. 1953).

that I belong in Berlin, I also suffer because of it. I suffer because of a lot of architectural mediocrity—a lack of sensibility for urban spaces and places. How many places are there in which one can turn 360 degrees and meet with aesthetic successes all around? There are a few. But there were many more before the War, as one acknowledges with sadness from the old photos. I also suffer under the provinciality of capital-city politics. But the cultural scene is the opposite of provincial, as is the serenity of Berliners toward the plethora of idiosyncrasies offered by the streetscape. No, I wouldn't know which German city I might prefer to Berlin. Not even the two semesters I spent in Munich at the invitation of the Siemens Foundation could change that.

# XIII.
# Public Intellectual

CW: There are only a handful of constitutional judges who are perceived as public figures: Böckenförde, Paul Kirchhof, Di Fabio,[1] and you. One would have to think a bit to decide who else might or might not belong to this group.

DG: Hesse, for example, would not.

CW: No, Hesse would not. Neither would Hoffmann-Riem, at least not as a judge. He is less known outside legal discussions, although for a brief time he was a senator in Hamburg. When does one become aware of the position of "public intellectual," and what are the factors that lead to it? This heightened visibility of certain constitutional judges didn't exist earlier. For whatever reason, it emerges later on. How did you perceive this?

DG: The status of constitutional judge considerably enhances the attention paid to what one says. It also augments the requests to say something—in lectures, newspaper articles, interviews. This is definitely a temptation. One must handle it with care—while in office, in any case, but equally so if the interest persists after leaving office. I avoid speaking about topics on which I have an opinion but no expertise. I lived through times, however, when even media appearances in one's own area of expertise were not advantageous for one's scholarly reputation. That has changed, though no one wants to be known as merely a TV-professor.

CW: It's still seen as problematic today when it's overly obtrusive. But it's perceived positively in proper doses. In some respects, it's even part of the office of a university professor to inform the public about certain developments or events.

DG: There is even a prize that honors scholarly work for the general public—the Communicator Prize. I can't say exactly when one begins to be regarded as a public intellectual. It apparently has nothing to do with the frequency of media appearances. But it would never come about without media appearances. I first became sensitive to it when the expression was used with

[1] Udo Di Fabio (1954–present), professor of public law at the universities of Münster, Trier, Munich, and Bonn; justice of the Second Senate of the Federal Constitutional Court (1999–2011).

*Dieter Grimm: Advocate of the Constitution.* Dieter Grimm, Oxford University Press (2020). © in the original German edition, Mohr Siebeck GmbH & Co. KG, Tübingen 2017, © this translation, Justin Collings 2020.
DOI: 10.1093/oso/9780198845270.001.0001

increasing frequency to introduce me before lectures or panel discussions. I noticed this with some amazement. But I'm not upset that things came about as they did. In any case, it happened after I left the Constitutional Court. But without the Constitutional Court it might never have happened at all.

CW: Is this also a kind of Americanization?

DG: My impression is that the justices of the US Supreme Court are much more sparing than German constitutional justices when it comes to public appearances, newspaper editorials, and interviews. But they speak willingly in universities. Recently some of them have also written books and hosted discussions about them, but they try to limit the questions to the contents of the book. The justices' public prominence results from their work not being anonymous. Nearly every decision is preceded by oral argument, and the media report on who asked what question or made which comment. They also report on how many years it has been since Justice Thomas[2] asked a question. Unlike in Germany, the published decisions make known who held which view. The justices in the minority, as well as those who agree with the outcome but not with each element of the rationale, feel obligated to share their views in separate opinions. The style, moreover, in which this is done is less dogmatic than in Germany. Justice Scalia was famous throughout the country for his sarcastic, sometimes even hurtful dissents.

OL: Are the universities still sites of societal discourse? Perhaps I have a romanticized image of the past. But in the past weren't more society-wide developments initiated by the universities as well as reflected in them? Perhaps we should ask ourselves where society-wide discussions still take place—evidently, they no longer take place at the universities. Perhaps this is a general problem of society—that discussions that span groups are declining in favor of particularized discussions that rarely reach common ground. Cases before the Constitutional Court then become an important force for societal integration because distortions or deficiencies of representation are counterbalanced through judicial proceedings. Where else in society do we have institutions in which such discussions still take place? The churches and the parties are weakening. The role of intermediary associations like unions has waned. Nor do the universities any longer undertake this societal articulation as they did earlier. Or is that an idealized view of higher education?

[2] Clarence Thomas (1948–present), judge on the US Court of Appeals for the DC Circuit (1990–1991); justice of the US Supreme Court since 1991.

DG: One who succeeded in doing this was Frank Schirrmacher,[3] the editor of the *Frankfurter Allgemeine Zeitung*. It would be interesting to know whether the impetus for the successfully launched discussions came from the universities or whether the topics were his discovery. Constitutional Court decisions can also trigger society-wide discussions. We already spoke in another connection about the crucifix. Headscarves are another example, as is the question of which means of fighting terrorism are permissible and which are not. Von Schirach's much-produced play *Terror* takes up directly the Constitutional Court's judgment on aviation security.[4] But on the question of what role the university plays, I don't trust myself with any overarching judgment. I will, however, mention a couple of debates picked up in society from the universities (or research institutions outside the university). These come to mind off the cuff. The *Historikerstreit* is one example. This was about whether the time was ripe for a historicization of National Socialism. Thirty years ago, society said no. The famous Böckenförde dictum[5] has become a standard motif in all discussions about societal integration. Perhaps these examples are too old for you. In more recent times, one could think of the debates about free will prompted by the insights of brain research. The plagiarism debate could have done the university lasting damage if it had turned out in the chancellor's favor ("After all, I didn't employ a research assistant.").[6] Societal discussion prevented that. Finally: the question of the finality of European integration comes up repeatedly among scholars; politicians avoid it.

OL: In your view have students become less political?

DG: With the exception of 1968, the complaint has always been there.

OL: Then they were too political.

[3] Frank Schirrmacher (1959-2014), journalist; editor of the *Frankfurter Allgemeine Zeitung* (1994–2014).

[4] 115 BVerfGE 118 (2006).

[5] Reference is made to the following, much-cited sentence: "The liberal secular state is sustained by conditions it cannot itself guarantee. That is the great gamble it has made for the sake of liberty." Ernst-Wolfgang Böckenförde, "Die Entstehung des Staates als Vorgang der Säkularisation" in Ernst-Wolfgang Böckenförde, *Recht, Staat, Freiheit* (1991) 92, 112. English translation: (2018) "The Rise of the State as a Process of Secularization" in M. Künkler and T. Stein (eds), Ernst-Wolfgang Böckenförde, *Religion, Law and Democracy. Selected Writings* (Original work published in 1967).

[6] In February 2011, the doctorate of the former minister of defense, Karl-Theodor zu Guttenberg (1971–present) (CSU), was revoked due to plagiarism. The accompanying and ensuing political debate concerned the question whether he could remain in office as minister of defense in spite of the plagiarism scandal. Karl-Theodor zu Guttenberg finally resigned on March 1, 2011. He is now a non-resident "Distinguished Statesmen" at the Center for Strategic and International Studies (CSIS). On the affair see, e.g., Oliver Lepsius and Reinhart Meyer-Kalkus (eds), *Inszenierung als Beruf: Der Fall Guttenberg* (2011); Roland Preuß and Tanjev Schultz, *Guttenbergs Fall: Der Skandal und seine Folgen für Politik und Gesellschaft* (2011).

DG: Then they were too political, yes.

MR: As a former constitutional judge, one not only attracts a lot of public attention, but one surely receives offers to do a lot of things—as a public intellectual and beyond. For example, in addition to your work at the Institute for Advanced Study, you were for several years a member of the administrative board of the Second German Broadcasting network (*Zweites Deutsches Fernsehen*, ZDF).[7] What experiences did you have there and according to what criteria did you choose among the various options?

DG: When I was asked in 2002 to join the ZDF's administrative board, the network had just completed an anguished dispute over the replacement of Dieter Stolte,[8] the ZDF's long-serving director. Wolfgang Clement, who as minister president of North Rhine Westphalia was a member of the administrative board,[9] concluded following this dispute that partisan influence in the ZDF councils needed to be restrained and pronounced himself willing to surrender his seat on the administrative board in favor of an independent expert. I had criticized partisan influence on public broadcasting long before my time in Karlsruhe, and so I gladly seized the opportunity to curb it a little. In any case, I told Clement that I was unwilling to join the informal SPD "circle of friends" on the advisory board or, obviously, the informal CDU circle either. There needed to be clarity on this point since it was common practice for every member of the administrative board to belong to one circle or the other. The circles met for an hour each before the meetings of the administrative board—the CDU circle in the presence of the director, the SPD circle in the presence of the administrative director. There the members of the group would discuss upcoming agenda items. The previous director, Stolte, told me it was a mistake not to belong to a circle because then I wouldn't have access to the information shared in those preliminary meetings. I believed, by contrast, that I couldn't fulfill my role as independent member if I was bound by any ties of partisan loyalty.

[7] Public broadcasting networks like the ZDF are supervised by boards whose members come not only from state and federal governments, but also from different segments of society, thereby ensuring the pluralism that is required by the Federal Constitutional Court. The administrative board of the ZDF supervises the work of its director and decides on leadership personnel and financial matters. It consists of representatives of the state governments, the federal government, and independent members who do not work for the government. In 2014, the Federal Constitutional Court determined that only one-third of the members of these boards may be from federal or state governments or close to the state sphere (136 BVerfGE 9 (2014)).

[8] Dieter Stolte (1934–present), journalist; director of the ZDF (1982–2002).

[9] Wolfgang Clement (1940–present), politician (SPD until 2008); minister president of the state of North Rhine Westphalia (1998–2002); federal minister of labor and the economy (2002–2005).

Clement accepted this, as did the other SPD minister president, Kurt Beck, the chair of the administrative board.[10]

The agenda items during my tenure on the administrative board contained little that was explosive in a partisan sense. The choice of director was over when I arrived. The Brender case[11] lay in the future when I left. There was also no decision for which the outcome depended on my vote. There was really only one deeper dispute in which I was involved: when setting broadcasting fees in 2004, the minister presidents did not follow the recommendation of the Commission for Determining the Financial Needs of Broadcasting Agencies, as the Constitutional Court's 1994 *Broadcasting Fees* judgment[12] required them to do, absent compelling reasons to the contrary. There were no such reasons here; they simply didn't want to raise fees because doing so always stirs discontent among the public. The Association of German Public Broadcasters (*Arbeitsgemeinschaft der öffentlich-rechtlichen Rundfunkanstalten der Bundesrepublik Deutschland*, or ARD) filed a constitutional complaint against the State Fees Treaty of 2004, and the question before the administrative board was whether the ZDF should join the complaint. The director could decide that alone without the approval of the administrative board. But the question came up in the administrative board all the same. I said at the meeting that no one, including me, could predict how the Court would decide, but that if the Court adhered to its first *Broadcasting Fees* judgment, the ARD would win. The State Fees Treaty, as anyone could clearly see, was flatly incompatible with the judgment's requirements. There followed a long, awkward silence, finally broken by the Hessian minister president Koch,[13] who eloquently explained why the minister presidents had nothing to fear. They then proceeded to lose miserably in Karlsruhe.[14]

But this conflict wasn't why, after five years, I lost my place on the administrative board. Clement had given up his seat in the expectation that his gesture would compel the CDU to vacate a minister president seat of their own for a neutral member. The CDU, however, intended nothing of

[10] Kurt Beck (1949–present), politician; minister president of the state of Rhineland-Pfalz (1994–2013); federal chair of the SPD (2006–2008).

[11] Nikolaus Brender (1949–present), journalist; editor-in-chief of the ZDF (2000–2010); the ZDF administrative board denied the renewal of his contract. The conflict gave rise to the Constitutional Court's review of the ZDF's council structure. 136 BVerfGE 9 (2014).

[12] 90 BVerfGE 60 (1994).

[13] Roland Koch (1958–present), politician (CDU); minister president of the State of Hessen (1998–2010).

[14] 119 BVerfGE 181 (2007).

the sort, and so it was clear to me that in the new electoral period an SPD minister president would once more take my place.

In general, though, you are right that the status of a former Constitutional Court judge and a certain public prominence rouse the greed of all sorts of institutions and associations. What I rejected categorically were consultations, amicus briefs, or outright advocacy in connection with cases before the Constitutional Court. But I had no reservations when it came to collaboration in the councils of academic or other scholarly institutions, provided I had a relationship either with the institution or the topic. Just as examples: the curatorship of my old Max Planck Institute in Frankfurt, the jury for the Niklas Luhmann Prize of my former university in Bielefeld, the board of the Foundation for Science and Politics (*Stiftung Wissenschaft und Politik*, or SWP), the academic advisory council of the WZB Berlin Social Science Center, or the Max Planck Institute for Public Goods in Bonn. There is always something to be gained from such activities. One is confronted with avenues and methods of research that redound to the benefit of one's own work.

# XIV.
# From Outsider to the Center of Constitutional Scholarship

CW: Let's trace an arc back once more to the beginning of our interview. The stations of your life are marked by certain places: Kassel, Frankfurt, Paris, Harvard, Bielefeld, Karlsruhe, Yale, and Berlin. The places stand for substance that at the very least they helped to influence. To what degree was your life shaped by these various places? My academic mentor once told me that the style and climate of a faculty are shaped by the place, not by individuals, since the members of the faculty come from all corners of the country and are constantly changing.

DG: Yale could serve as an example for this thesis. That the conversation within the faculty is especially intensive there has something to do, perhaps, with the unattractiveness of New Haven. One is thrown back upon the university. Things would be very different in New York or Boston. Those cities have much to offer beyond the university. But despite its proximity to New York, hardly any Yale colleagues live in Manhattan.

But now to your question: Would I have been a different person if I had studied and started my career in Erlangen, say, instead of Frankfurt? Would I have been a different person if my encounter with America had taken place in Idaho and Texas instead of at Harvard and Yale? Yes, I suppose so. In Erlangen "1968" would presumably have remained something that happened on the news; in Frankfurt it was sometimes a daily challenge. Those who experience America in the form of its famous East Coast universities know, of course, that this isn't the whole of America, and that there are entirely different Americas—the Midwest, for example, or the South. One knows this, but without personal observation the knowledge remains abstract.

If we look at my "*Lehr- und Wanderjahre*" (years of study and travel) in your chain of places up to Harvard, the chain can be read as a progressive broadening of my horizons: from Kassel, a provincial city whose provinciality I recognized only after leaving; to Frankfurt, a German metropolis, occasionally even a flash point; to Paris, a European metropolis and

*Dieter Grimm: Advocate of the Constitution.* Dieter Grimm, Oxford University Press (2020). © in the original German edition, Mohr Siebeck GmbH & Co. KG, Tübingen 2017, © this translation, Justin Collings 2020.
DOI: 10.1093/oso/9780198845270.001.0001

world attraction, a neighbor and yet a foreign country; and finally on to the US, a different continent, which was then much farther away than it is today—seven days, to be exact, the length of a sea voyage from Bremen to New York. And phone calls were so expensive that I spoke with my parents only once, at Christmas. They had to go to the neighbors' because at the time we had no phone. It was all so overwhelming that we wasted the precious minutes in trivialities.

As far as the chain of professional places is concerned, the importance of Bielefeld and Yale might well have become clear in this conversation. Both were places of scholarly broadening and deepening. Since my retirement, I primarily teach comparative constitutional seminars at Humboldt University—something that likely wouldn't have come about without my teaching at Yale. One day I said to myself, "If comparative constitutionalism is so attractive for American students, why not for the Berliners as well?"

MR: Many Berlin students and assistants think the same. To this day, your seminars are in high demand among students, and there is a large circle of regular participants as well. If we follow your occupational chain a little further, what characterizes Karlsruhe and Berlin for you?

DG: Berlin differs from the other places primarily in that my contacts have not been as dominated by study and work but have spread much more broadly—especially into the realms of politics and culture. There are many reasons for this. It has to do, for instance, with the range of people attracted by the Institute for Advanced Study, which for its evening programs (which are not only of a scholarly but often of an artistic nature: every year there are a few fellows from artistic fields—writers, composers, etc.) attracts a varied and interested audience. Other venues for events, which also have a different audience, play a role: the American Academy, the Catholic Academy, the Literary Colloquium, the media and publishing houses. It has to do with the Wednesday Society founded by Gräfin Dönhoff[1] and carried on by Richard von Weizsäcker,[2] with Helmut Schmidt[3] as a regularly participant until shortly before his death. Since 1996, it has been a circle for the regular interchange of ideas among people from politics, business, science, and culture, which initially published its conversations, in accordance with

[1] Marion Gräfin Dönhoff (1909–2002), editor-in-chief and co-producer of the weekly magazine, *Die Zeit*.

[2] Richard von Weizsäcker (1920–2015), politician (CDU); governing mayor of Berlin (1981–1984); federal president (1984–1994).

[3] Helmut Schmidt (1918–2015), politician (SPD); federal minister of defense (1969–1972); federal minister of finance (1972–1974); federal chancellor (1974–1982), editor of the weekly *Die Zeit*.

the wishes of Gräfin Dönhoff.[4] It has to do with the seat of government. Not only did this bring friends and acquaintances from earlier periods to Berlin—Brigitte Zypries, for example, a fellow Kasseler—but one also shouldn't underestimate the importance of spatial proximity for political contacts. Just as, previously, colleagues in Bonn were readily available for information or a conversation, today it is the Berliners. You can affirm that from personal experience, *Herr* Waldhoff; Christoph Möllers could affirm it and so could numerous others, and not only jurists.

CW: And Karlsruhe?

DG: How can I express that Karlsruhe is synonymous with the culmination of my professional life without at the same time denigrating the other stations—especially those that followed Karlsruhe? I don't mean it that way. I've never wished myself away from the university, and if I miss anything, it is the stage of the great lecture hall. I recognize their limited pedagogical value, but also their indispensability. The Court was also a stage—one that was even acted upon in costumes—but it wasn't a place for rhetorical exposition and, in good moments, for the excitement of young people. A judge merely sits in his chair, listens, and asks questions. But I sometimes think that I was especially well suited for that office, or that it suited me, if one can put it that way. The closer I got to the end of my term the sadder I became, though I agree entirely with the rule that limits a term to twelve years. The addition of six months, however, reconciled me to my departure. I feel about the Court the way I feel about Harvard. It is a place of longing, of *Sehnsucht*—but with the difference that one can return to Harvard as a professor but not to the Court as a judge. That's only possible in dreams; and in fact, I dream from time to time that I am sitting there once more, working through papers, discussing cases in the conference room, or taking part in oral arguments. And yet I know, even while the dream lasts, and not just when I awaken, that this simply cannot be.

Karlsruhe was also a space for living—accessible, not hectic, not averse to enjoyment, and blessed with good restaurants, both in the city itself and in its surroundings. In none of the other cities, and from the starting point of no other city, did I do so much walking (*hiking* would be an exaggeration): in the castle grounds, in the Bannwald, in the Turmberg, along the Rhine, in the Black Forest, in the Palatinate, in Alsace—all effortlessly reachable in a brief time. Obviously, my work-related contacts predominated in Karlsruhe, but it wasn't as though I lived in a jurists' bubble. My neighbors

[4] Marion Gräfin Dönhoff (ed.), *Die neue Mittwochsgesellschaft* (vol. 1 1998, vol. 2 1999, vol. 3 2000).

at 24 Bachstraße—Hermann and Sigrid Plambeck, a married couple—saw to that. That brought me together with the Karlsruhe *Bürgertum*, which attended Sloterdijk's[5] lectures and mingled with the Karlsruhe art scene. Horst Antes, for example, was a frequent guest of my neighbors (and was by no means made up of only head and legs).[6] Perhaps *Bürgertum* sounds a bit idyllic. But not a few members of the Red Army Faction emerged from homes in Karlsruhe's *Bürgertum*.

One city is missing from your list, *Herr* Waldhoff, though that isn't your fault. It came up only marginal and belongs more in a personal than in a scholarly biography. And yet, not entirely. The city is Vienna. In almost fifteen years of marriage, I had a dual residence: Frankfurt, later Bielefeld, and Vienna. My wife was an assistant and later a professor on the Vienna law faculty,[7] and our dream of both getting hired at the same university was never fulfilled. We took turns commuting. With Vienna, for me, it was similar to Berlin. I already knew it before I arrived. With the help of a map of Vienna, I had followed the rich cast of characters from Doderer's novels along their constantly intersecting paths, and I was completely familiar with the *Porzellangasse* before I had occasion to frequently pick my wife up there from her ballet lessons.

Vienna offered a sharp contrast to Germany. Vienna hadn't passed unscathed through the Second World War either, but the damage was less noticeable in the city itself. The architectural break with the past that had radically reshaped many German cities (especially Kassel and Frankfurt) hadn't hit Vienna. For me, exploring Vienna was a continual pleasure. I loved the conversations at the Heuriger taverns in Grinzing. Society, too, had been less whirled about than in Germany. For Vienna, 1918 marks a deeper rupture than 1945—from an empire to a tiny state whose capital constantly displays before its denizen's eyes its former stature and present loss. Society's upper and lower orders were much more sharply defined than in Germany. Where one lived, where one socialized, even where one shopped was determined by invisible class boundaries. But self-assessment and reality were often far removed from one another. There was much hypocrisy. Not for nothing, I learned, was Austrian literature much more

[5] Peter Sloterdijk (1947–present), professor of philosophy and aesthetics at the State College of Design in Karlsruhe; rector of this school from 2001 to 2015.

[6] Horst Antes (1936–present), professor of painting at the State Academy of Fine Arts in Karlsruhe. He is famous, among other reasons, for the "Head-Footers," artistic figures comprising only head and legs.

[7] Cf. Chapter IV, fn. 24.

acerbic and malicious than German literature. Thomas Bernhardt was by no means alone in this.

If an appointment at the University of Vienna had been offered, I would surely have accepted it for family reasons, but not with untrammeled joy. Thanks to my wife, I knew the university tolerably well. There, too, a lot of envy and intrigue lurked behind a veil of selected civility. The concern, admittedly, was purely hypothetical. An appointment in Vienna lay beyond what could be plausibly expected. At the time, a public lawyer in Vienna had to be a Kelsenian, and legal science that allowed itself to collaborate with the social sciences was discredited on its face. During this time, I had some very good friends at the University of Vienna—Gerhard Luf, the legal philosopher, foremost among them.[8] But on the whole, I was the opposite of what they were looking for in Vienna for a professorship in public law.

OL: You have dealt with an unusually broad array of topics. If one were to look at the publications list of the average public law scholar today, one would rarely encounter your themes amid such concentration and consistency. This concern with the relations between public law and private law, for instance, including the grounding of constitutional thought in private law. These are approaches for which you have become quite well known—specifically "Grimmian perspectives." I don't know how representative I am in this, but for me these were eye-opening texts, as were your writings about the *Bürgertum* social model. Who besides you wrote about such things?

CW: I would put the point even more sharply, but please don't misunderstand me. From the perspective of public law, you were until 1987 an outsider in the guild of constitutionalists.

DG: So I was.

CW: And since 1987 you've been at the center of interest. In your pre-Karlsruhe phase, your work was intra- and interdisciplinary. After 1987, it was necessarily doctrinal.

DG: What explains this path? The historical interests were there, but likely wouldn't have been so pronounced without the Max Planck Institute (MPI), which fell my way and in which I had to integrate—though without, of course, abandoning my public law ambitions. That found expression thematically, in the relationship between constitution and private law, and methodologically, in the question of the conditions for the emergence and evolution of legal phenomena. This, of course, was of immediate doctrinal use. For doctrinal purposes, too, I ask about the conditions for the

[8] Gerhard Luf (1943–present), professor of legal philosophy at the University of Vienna.

emergence of a norm or institution, about intervening social changes, and the consequences for interpretation in the present. This three-step approach has become almost second nature to me.

But with all the contingencies that prevail in such career paths, there are presumably also some criteria of selection that ensure a certain consistency. In any case, in putting together the volume *Law and the State in Bürgertum Society*,[9] I was astonished at how cohesive it was. It was not a smorgasbord of essays shoehorned together under a mostly meaningless title.

But then came the chair in public law and with it the duty to instruct students how to employ the tools of the trade. Already then, and not just when I joined the Court, did constitutional doctrine move to the fore—but I was interested in a doctrine enriched by the question of meaning. Only that question prevents one from schematically reproducing what has gone before. Thus, the other disciplines—history because of the conditions for emergence and the social sciences because of the conditions for application in the present—remained present. My long stay at the MPI was now paying doctrinal dividends.

I tried, then, to make this knowledge fruitful for the stuff of jurisprudence. The work in which this first took place, and which also won me the attention of public lawyers, was an essay in the *Archiv des öffentlichen Rechts* (AöR).

CW: "Constitutional Function and the Reform of the Basic Law," from 1972.[10]

DG: Here too, chance played a role. I went to see some friends in Göttingen—Helga and Wolfgang Carl.[11] Wolfgang Carl's brother had just passed his state legal exam, and the two took me along to the celebration. Peter Badura, then a young Göttingen professor, was there as well. I fell into conversation with him. The appointment of the Enquete Commission on reforming the Basic Law was then pending.[12] We talked about this, and I mentioned that one shouldn't embark on such an undertaking without a clear view of what a constitution can accomplish and without a knowledge of the conditions for effective reform—points on which political science had something to contribute. "Would you like to write an essay for the AöR about that?" he

[9] Dieter Grimm, *Recht und Staat der bürgerlichen Gesellschaft* (1987).

[10] Dieter Grimm, "Verfassungsfunktion und Grundgesetzreform" (1972) 97 *Archiv des Öffentlichen Rechts* 489; reprinted in Dieter Grimm, *Die Zukunft der Verfassung* (1991) 313; second part: "Notwendigkeit und Chance der Grundgesetzreformen" (1972) 97 *Archiv des öffentlichen Rechts* 508.

[11] Wolfgang Carl (1941–present), professor of philosophy at the University of Göttingen; Helga Carl (1940–present), art historian in Florence.

[12] Cf. *Fragen der Verfassungsreform. Zwischenbericht der Enquete-Kommission des Deutschen Bundestages* (1973); *Beratungen und Empfehlungen zur Verfassungsreform* (2 vols, 1976).

asked. The essay ended up being quite long, so Badura suggested dividing it across two volumes of the AöR.

CW: The article is still very interesting today, and its first part has been reprinted in *The Future of the Constitution*.[13]

DG: The essay begins with the words, "Basic Law reform can only be meaningfully discussed after answering two preliminary questions. The questions are what constitutions can do, and what they should do." I then maintained that the preconditions for a reform discussion established on such a basis were only inadequately met. What was missing was a theory of the constitution. There follow some considerations based on an evaluation of the literature in constitutional law and the social sciences. The second part engaged with the most important topics and proposals for reform and assessed their suitability to meet their stated purpose. Previously, such an intensive engagement with the social science literature and its integration in the context of a legal argument had perhaps taken place only in the aforementioned *Handbook* article. Much later, I had the opportunity to take part in constitutional reforms myself. It was a sobering experience.

CW: You'll have to tell us more about that.

DG: It was in connection with the Federalism Commission, appointed by the Bundestag and the Bundesrat in 2003 to generate proposals for overcoming the long lamented political logjam.[14] It also included a number of experts—constitutional lawyers, political scientists, economists—including me, after a long preliminary conversation with Franz Müntefering,[15] the then chair of the SPD parliamentary group in the Bundestag, and Volker Kröning,[16] the SPD spokesman on the commission then taking shape. The political logjam was the product of differing majorities in the Bundestag and the Bundesrat, which resulted in the government's being able to effect desperately needed reforms only belatedly or in diluted form, and sometimes not at all. CDU and SPD governments suffered equally in this respect. The scope of possible logjams was essentially tied to the extent of the Bundesrat's veto rights,

[13] Dieter Grimm, *Die Zukunft der Verfassung* (1991).

[14] The Federalism Commission was instituted in November 2003 and was supposed to deliver results by December 2004. It had sixteen members from the Bundestag and sixteen members from the Bundesrat. In addition, there were several members without a vote in an advisory capacity, among them several professors. The commission could not agree upon a compromise until December 2004. Only after another federal election, a reform of German federalism was agreed upon in 2006.

[15] Franz Müntefering (1940–present), politician (SPD); federal minister of transportation, construction, and housing (1998–1999); chair of the SPD parliamentary group in the Bundestag (2002–2005); vice chancellor and federal minister of labor and welfare (2005–2007).

[16] Volker Kröning (1945–present), politician (SPD), senator in the government of the state of Bremen in various portfolios (1983–1994); member of the Bundestag (1994–2009).

which had steadily increased over time. The objective, then, had to be reducing veto rights. The states agreed in principle but demanded compensation for every right surrendered. That wasn't easy to find. As a result, the package of reforms expanded more and more and threatened more and more damage to the constitution.

My first disillusionment had to do with the role of experts. When the commission began its work, there was agreement that something must be done but uncertainty about what that could be. During this phase, the experts were listened to. But after a while the politicians thought they now knew enough to take care of the task. They created subcommittees from which the experts were excluded. The experts stayed on as regular members of the commission but were regarded as a nuisance when they pointed out damaging consequences of the politicians' compromises.

I was also disillusioned by the states' lack of awareness that the Federal Republic is a common enterprise among the states and the federation. It was not, as I had expected, the opposition between the CDU and the SPD that shaped the commission's work, but rather the opposition between the federation and the states. The states—at least the large, influential ones—were focused on winning terrain without regard for the whole. As a result, success in the end meant finding any compromise at all. Whether the compromise were a good one didn't seem to matter. Today, the successors of the influential state leaders (Koch, Stoiber,[17] and Teufel[18] most of all; but Steinbrück[19] too, albeit somewhat more moderately) suffer from their forebears' push for expansion, and the first reverse steps have already taken place (Article 91 b GG).

Through this experience, I felt confirmed in my view that the rules for amending the Basic Law are in need of reform themselves. That was already evident with the constitutional amendments connected to Reunification and with the changes to Articles 13 and 16 GG. Accordingly, I had written about it earlier on.[20] But here it became even clearer. Article 79 GG forged no sense of the fundamental difference between amending a constitution and amending legislation. Instead, the very same actors do both, and they

[17] Edmund Stoiber (1941–present), politician (CSU); minister president of the state of Bavaria (1993–2007).

[18] Erwin Teufel (1939–present), politician (CDU); minister president of the state of Baden-Württemberg (1991–2005).

[19] Peer Steinbrück (1947–present), politician (SPD); minister president of the state of North Rhine Westphalia (2002–2005); federal finance minister (2005–2009).

[20] See the pieces, previously published in newspapers, collected in Dieter Grimm, *Die Verfassung und die Politik* (2001) 58, 82, 126.

do so with the same procedure. The only difference is that constitutional amendments require a two-thirds majority. But, at least in times of grand coalition governments, two-thirds majorities have long been the norm in the politics of the Federal Republic, as well as with everything that gets decided in the mediation committee of the Bundestag and Bundesrat. We need to incorporate "breakers" into the routine function, as many constitutions of other European states already do. I devoted my 2007 farewell lecture at Humboldt University to the necessity of amending the rules for constitutional amendments.[21]

OL: Doesn't that contradict your view that constitutional amendments are a legitimate means of correcting constitutional jurisprudence? How can the two positions be reconciled? Should jurisprudentially triggered constitutional amendments follow the provisions of Article 79 and amendments motivated by political or operational considerations follow a delaying procedure?

DG: The incorporation of breakers, as I have called them, has the purpose of highlighting the difference between constitutional amendments and amendments to legislation. It should prevent parliamentary parties from amending the constitution all by themselves and giving free reign to their tendency to hedge. This has frequently led to functionally incompatible inflations of the constitution. The proposal is not addressed to constitutional amendments that react to trends in case law. I also didn't mean to recommend differentiated amendment procedures. The procedure doesn't change in accordance with the causes for and the motives of the amendment pursued.

CW: Let's go back once more to your AöR essay. It is one of the very few essays in Germany that have dealt with the functions of a constitution. Things are different in Switzerland, thanks to perennial constitutional reforms. I have occasionally grappled with the issue and, on the German side, it was effectively to you that one could turn. In particular, the related question about the limits of what constitutions can accomplish is understood as a Grimmian issue. In this connection, I'd like to take up a second thing that has always amazed me—your 1969 essay on "Law and Politics."[22] I recently

[21] Unpublished, but the topic was taken up in a speech before the German Bundestag honoring the publication of the proceedings of the Parliamentary Council. Deutscher Bundestag (ed.), *Wie wir mit dem Werk des Parlamentarischen Rats umgehen—oder: Wie viele Änderungen verträgt das Grundgesetz?* (2010).

[22] Dieter Grimm, "Recht und Politik" (1969) *Juristische Schulung* 501.

reread the essay for a publication of my own,[23] and in doing so was struck by the fact that the expression "constitution as framework" might well have appeared there for the first time and not in Böckenförde's writing on the "Uniqueness of Constitutional Law." In my view it is an absolutely central, pathbreaking essay, which irritatingly appeared in the *Juristische Schuling*, an educational periodical, and wasn't reprinted in the volumes of your collected essays.

DG: This essay also has a particular explanation. As noted earlier, I got to know Otwin Massing through the Frankfurt *Cusanus* group, and through him some of the left-leaning Frankfurt political scientists. These decided to produce a critical introduction to their discipline and offered me a chapter on "Law and Politics." But they didn't like the product that I submitted. In their view, it was phenomenological, not critical; it didn't conceive of law as a symbolic form. My manuscript was rejected.

OL: No superstructure . . .

DG: At the time that really hurt me. But then I made my way to Beethoven Square and the office of Herrmann Weber[24] of the Frankfurt branch of C.H. Beck. He accepted the manuscript—not, as I had hoped, for the *Neue Juristische Wochenschrift*, but for the *Juristische Schulung*.

CW: I know of no article in Germany that develops the problem with such clarity.

DG: Legal scholars took note of it. Ten years later, many people who met me at my first conference of constitutional law scholars said, "Ah, Grimm—Law and Politics. Is that you?" I took up the topic once more in the Festschrift for Ernst Benda.[25] It appears in that form as the introductory essay to the collection *The Constitution and Politics*.[26]

OL: The mainstream view is rather that law and politics are distinct and that law controls politics. But you correlate law and politics. There are always repercussions. Politicians make law, and law naturally influences politics. Law provides the framework for politics. For you this is a dynamic relationship, whereas German constitutional scholarship strove to separate the two spheres. You advocate a different perspective on the relationship between law and politics—a perspective that perhaps reflects an American

[23] Christian Waldhoff, *Der positive und der negative Verfassungsvorbehalt. Überlegungen zu einer Regelungstheorie im Grenzbereich von Verfassungsdogmatik und Verfassungstheorie* (2016).

[24] Hermann Weber (1936–present), active since 1965 in various functions with the C.H. Beck publishing house; editor of the *Neue Juristische Wochenschrift* (1974–2001).

[25] Dieter Grimm, "Politik und Recht" in *Festschrift für Ernst Benda* (1995) 91.

[26] Dieter Grimm, *Die Verfassung und die Politik. Einsprüche in Störfällen* (2001) 13.

influence, but which also simply takes stock, for once, of democratic realities and doesn't try to reduce law to a purely supervisory dimension and doesn't understand politics as a "dirty business." That strikes me as an original perspective—rather that of an outsider within the framework of German constitutional scholarship.

CW: That's just what I mean. There was no article like that before . . .

OL: . . . because this supervisory perspective, which comprises part of the basic socialization of our discipline, leads to the swift rejection of political argumentation as "unscientific."

DG: In this case I had no fear of ruffling feathers. Whether my perspective was mainstream wasn't a relevant consideration.

MR: The Basic Law is twelve years younger than you. From various perspectives, you watched it "grow up" and took part in its development—first as a politically interested student; then, most of all, as a scholar and constitutional judge; and finally as a public intellectual. In connection with the broadcasting freedom, you have already said that you are a "friend of the constitution."[27] What does that mean for you? Is this attachment to the Basic Law also a biographical attachment?

DG: The Marbach Literary Archive recently hosted an exhibit on the topic "The Original." I had to write an entry on the original of the Basic Law. To that end, I asked if I could see it. It was retrieved for me from the vaults of the Reichstag building. With white gloves I was allowed to handle it and leaf through it. The thoughts that then came to me are perhaps the best reflection of my relationship with the Basic Law.[28] I can't repeat them here, but I will say this much: The Basic Law is the constitution under which the history of the Federal Republic has unfolded in a relatively felicitous way. How large a part the Basic Law played in that is hard to tell. Perhaps we constitutionalists exaggerate its role. Perhaps historians underestimate it when they afford it hardly any role in their histories of the Federal Republic. In any event, I've always been conscious of the relative importance of the constitutional text and the immense importance of the context in which a constitution operates, as well as of the independent significance of constitutional interpretation in the face of shifting circumstances.

According, I've felt it necessary to defend the Weimar constitution against the charge that it was a bad constitution. I've often asked myself

[27] Cf. Chapter VI, p. 80.

[28] Dieter Grimm, "Das Grundgesetz" in Deutsches Literaturarchiv (ed.), *Der Wert des Originals* (2014) 148 *Marbacher Magazin* 133–36.

how the Weimar constitution would have fared under the circumstances of the Federal Republic—and how the Basic Law would have fared under the circumstances of the Weimar Republic. Such "what if" questions cannot be reliably answered. But they do serve to prevent overhasty conclusions, both positive and negative. Indeed, I could recount many things that don't redound to the Basic Law's advantage—in particular, many things about its numerous amendments. But despite all of that, it is the constitution under which I could lead a freer life than my parents and grandparents. It is the constitution in whose realization I could, in various capacities, take part. In that respect, it is also "my" constitution—using the possessive pronoun in the sense that, apart from all its defects, I can identify myself with it.

CW: Beyond the Basic Law itself, the constitution as a category is the great theme of your life: as an object of scholarly reflection, as the measuring standard of your occupation as a judge, and as a phenomenon for which the public must constantly be sensitized anew. To begin with, you classified the rise of modern constitutions in Germany from the very beginning in comparison with the constitutional states of the West. For me, your distinction between the Western model of "constituting rule" in opposition to the German model of merely "modifying rule" was an experience in my legal education that opened up the world of constitutional history. Next, the great doctrinal themes between the university and the Court were associations and parties (under the watchword "neocorporatism"), freedom of speech and broadcasting, personality protection, and the impact of fundamental rights on private law. We've spoken about all of this in detail. In more recent years—and especially quite lately—you've often been concerned with preserving what has already been achieved, since various erosions of this success story, if they haven't set in already, might yet be imminent. How do you view the future of the constitution today?

DG: Because I regard the constitution as one of the great achievements of civilization—though I realize that for a long time it was more promise than reality—I have always been sensitive to things that endanger it. After all, one wouldn't write about the "future of the constitution" if one thought that future were secure. Early on, the challenge posed to the constitutional state by the transition to a party state and a welfare state stood in the foreground. Then the erosion through internationalization and globalization demanded attention. It is clear that, after the rise of a supranational public authority, the constitution can no longer play the same role it did during times when public authority was synonymous with the authority of the state. It's important to me that this not be understood as a lament. The developments that led to the erosion are structurally conditioned and are therefore to be accepted as a given and not bemoaned as a misfortune. In light of this situation, the things that make the constitution an achievement must be preserved wherever possible. Whether this happens in the form of a constitution or in some other form is of secondary importance. I presume that in international or even globalized standards something new will emerge that will, for a time, carry the name of "constitution." I have always insisted on the distinction between the legal foundations of the state on the one hand and of political entities beyond the state on the other, so that the similarity of names doesn't disguise the fact that international orders can be characterized as "constitutional" only by sacrificing much of what makes up a constitution at the national level. Accordingly, I have tried to introduce the legalization of public authority as an overarching concept, beneath which the constitution represents an historically contingent subcase rather than the end point of a development. The legalization of public authority is the benchmark. The transitory forms follow shifting conditions. The constitution is a particularly ambitious form. The goal should be to save as much of it as possible at the supranational level.

OL, CW, MR: *Herr* Grimm, we warmly thank you for this conversation.

# Index of Names

*For the benefit of digital users, indexed terms that span two pages (e.g., 52–53) may, on occasion, appear on only one of those pages.*